【一段回望重拾的历史 一个寻找回来的英雄】

Recollecting on an episode in history
Remembering a returned national hero

珍藏方大曾

Treasuring Fang Dazeng

战地记者的光影故事 A War Correspondent's Stories

冯雪松 著 By Feng Xuesong

First Edition 2018

Written by Feng Xuesong
Translated by Yao Wenhao
Designed by He Yuting

ISBN 978-7-5104-6590-1

Published by
NEW WORLD PRESS
24 Baiwanzhuang Street, Beijing 100037, China

Distributed by
NEW WORLD PRESS
24 Baiwanzhuang Street, Beijing 100037, China
Tel: 86-10-68995968
Fax: 86-10-68998705
Website: www.nwp.com.cn
E-mail: nwpcd@sina.com

Printed in the People's Republic of China

寄给母亲的照片（原底片收藏于中国国家博物馆）

A photo mailed from Xiao Fang (Fang Dazeng) to his mother (original film maintained in the National Museum of China)

方大曾有关卢沟桥事变和抗日军事活动的一大批新闻照片，是对伟大的全民抗战的忠实纪录。它体现了抗日军民抵御外侮敌忾同仇的民族精神，鼓舞了士气和斗志，也保存了许多拍自第一现场的珍贵画面，具有重要的历史文献价值。我们为历史上有过如此杰出的新闻摄影记者感到骄傲。他将永远活在我们的心里。

方大曾与范长江双峰并峙，二水分流，一个长于摄影，一个长于文字，是中国新闻史上的双峰，可以并存于世，并存于史，并存于书。

方汉奇

中国新闻史学会创会会长

中国人民大学荣誉一级教授

The large batch of news photographs taken by Fang Dazeng about the Lugou Bridge Incident and the anti-Japanese front faithfully record the great nationwide Anti-Japanese War. They exhibit the Chinese national spirit of safeguarding national dignity against Japanese aggression through concerted effort. They are also a record of many valuable scenes on their original sites, serving as important historical documents. We are proud of this eminent journalist in history, who shall continue to live forever in our hearts.

Fang Dazeng and Fan Changjiang are two peaks towering next to each other. Their talents are comparable and complementary. One excels at photography and the other excels at writing. They are two peaks in Chinese journalistic history who are both well worth being remembered by the people, history, and literature.

Fang Hanqi
First President of the Chinese Association of the History of Journalism and Mass Communication (CAHJMC) & Professor of Renmin University of China

目录

Contents

引言

天边划过一颗星

方大曾去哪里了？他在今天还留下什么痕迹？20年来，随着纪录片《寻找方大曾》、专著《方大曾：消失与重现》《方大曾：遗落与重拾》和文集《解读方大曾》的相继问世，他的生命轨迹如同暗房显影般渐渐清晰，鲜活形象开始走进当代公众的视野。多年来，我一直搜寻着有关他失踪的答案，但是直到今天，还没有确切的结果，而人们对他的认识，已经由摄影师到战地记者再到国际反法西斯战士，其事迹不断丰满立体，影响由国内到境外，跨洋过海声名远播，这是我在决定寻找之初没有想到的。

中国新闻史学界泰斗方汉奇先生说，方大曾是一颗给世界带来耀亮的彗星，他迅疾地划过星空，而后消失，给人们留下一声长久的叹息，好在经过长时间的寻找，被湮没了80多年的杰出新闻工作者和摄影记者小方又回来了。

上世纪30年代中期，方大曾以小方为笔名活跃于中国新闻界与摄影界，他是中外新闻学社的重要成员，与范长江、徐盈等人同负盛名。他关注民生和时局，以笔和相机为武器，投身爱国救亡运动，深入底层民众生活并全方位报道了“绥远抗战”。卢沟桥事变爆发后，他第一时间赶赴前线，拍摄了大量来自战地的珍贵照片，《我们为自卫而抗战》《为国捐躯》《抗战图存》等报道引发强烈社会反响，被中外媒体广泛使用，鼓舞了士气和斗志。他在长篇通讯《卢沟桥抗战记》中预言“伟大的卢沟桥也许将成为伟大的民族解放战争的发祥地了”。1937年9月18日，方大曾从河北蠡县发出了《平汉线北段的变化》一文，从此杳无音信。

62年后，1999年秋天的某一个下午，我在夹杂于报纸间的一页传真上，第一次看到了方大曾这个陌生的名字，从那一刻起，这位失踪于抗日前线，

Foreword

A Star Streaking Across the Horizon

Where did Fang Dazeng go? What trace of him can be found today? Over the past 20 years, documentaries such as *In Search of Fang Dazeng*, monographic publications like *Fang Dazeng: Disappearance and Reappearance* and *Fang Dazeng: Lost and Found*, and anthologies like *Interpreting Fang Dazeng*, have shed more light on, and clarified, his life – like a photograph being developed in a darkroom. His fresh image has started to enter the vision of the contemporary public. For many years, I have searched for the key to the mystery of his disappearance. However, I still have no precise answer. Fang Dazeng's identity in people's eyes has changed from a photographer to a war correspondent to an international anti-Fascist warrior. His stories have become increasingly three-dimensional, with his impact expanding and reputation spreading both at home and abroad. This reaches beyond the expectations I had when I began my journey in search of Fang Dazeng.

Mr. Fang Hanqi, a titan in the field of Chinese journalism history, said that Fang Dazeng was a comet that brought the world shining brilliance. He swiftly streaked across the starry sky and disappeared, with later generations mourning such a big loss. After over eight decades of obscurity, this eminent journalist and press photographer, Xiao Fang, has returned.

In the mid-1930s, using the pen name Xiao Fang, Fang Dazeng was active in journalism and photography in China. He was an important member of the Chinese-Foreign Journalism Society, as well-known as figures like Fan Changjiang and Xu Ying. He cared about people's livelihood and the latest social affairs. He used his pen and camera as weapons and devoted himself to the patriotic campaign of resisting Japanese aggression and salvaging China from subjugation. He went deep into the midst of the common people and comprehensively reported the Suiyuan Campaign. After the outbreak of the Lugou Bridge Incident, he immediately arrived at the front and took many valuable photos on the battlefield. Xiao Fang's reports, including *We Fight against Japanese Aggression for Self-Defense*, *Sacrifice for Country*, and *Fight against Japanese Aggression to Salvage China from Subjugation* generated a great sensation in society and was extensively adopted by Chinese and Western media. These reports boosted the Chinese people's morale and

被范长江先生念念不忘、屡次提到的年轻人引起了我的好奇。

在中国摄影出版社陈申先生的帮助下，我见到了时年 85 岁的方大曾的胞妹方澄敏，至今我仍然无法忘记老人无助的表情和面颊上的两行泪水。木盒中哥哥留下的 837 张底片，数十年历经劫难，被她整齐地排列着。阳光下，一张张黑白底片向我展开了 60 多年前已经消失了的车站码头、苦力、车夫和牧羊人的画面，还有战争前线的震撼场面，我不敢相信这些珍贵的照片出自一个 25 岁的青年之手。

尽管他在当时已经闻名长城内外，但是彗星一般的耀亮和迅失，使他在《中国摄影史》中，不仅没有独立的篇章，也没有完整的生平，关于他的描述加起来不足 100 字，而在《中国新闻史》中更是难觅其踪。

作为纪录片工作者，我在长时间的寻找中，通过史料发掘和实地寻访，努力去还原一个真实的、热爱和平与自由的生命，这个年轻人用生活做背景，用生命做胶片，为我们真实纪录了当年国难当头的中国大地。如果说，我最初的寻找完全是出于对人物的兴趣和探求未知的欲望，那么在过程中，随着了解的深入，已不知不觉变成了对于一种高尚精神的认同和追随。

纪录片《寻找方大曾》2000 年在中国中央电视台播出近 20 年来，方大曾是我放不下的心事，这份情感，如同酿酒，时间越久越陈越醇，我渐渐成了他的“家人”，对于亲人的找寻，难道还需要有什么世俗的动机吗?

令人欣慰的是，在好心人的帮助下，《方大曾：消失与重现》和《方大曾：遗落与重拾》相继出版后，即获得了来自文学界、学术界和新闻界人士的至高赞誉。著名军事史专家周小宁评价：“（两部作品）不仅对于深化细化中国新闻事业史人物研究、中国战地新闻摄影史研究和中国抗日战争史研究具有重要学术价值，填补了学术空白，而且对于弘扬伟大的抗战精神，弘扬中华民族同仇敌忾共御外侮的民族精神，伸张正义和牺牲奉献精神，具有极为宝贵的社会价值。”

strengthened their will to fight. In the long report *Lugou Bridge Battle against Japanese Aggression*, he predicted that "The great Lugou Bridge may be the birthplace of our great war for national liberation!" On September 18, 1937, Fang Dazeng sent the report *Changes in the Northern Section of the Beiping-Hankou Railway* from Li County, Hebei Province: He has not been heard ever since.

Sixty-two years later, on an afternoon in the autumn of 1999, hidden in a fax between the pages of a newspaper, I saw a strange name, Fang Dazeng, for the first time. Since that moment, this young man, who went missing on the battlefield against Japanese aggression and who has been borne in mind and mentioned many times by Fan Changjiang, has aroused my attention.

With assistance from Mr. Chen Shen of the China Photographic Publishing House, I met Fang Chengmin, Fang Dazeng's 85-year-old younger sister. I still cannot forget her helpless expression and the tears on her face. The 837 negatives left by her brother in a wooden box had endured decades of vicissitudes and were well arranged by her. In the sunlight, these black and white negatives presented to me the stations, wharfs, laborers, carters, and shepherds that had disappeared, along with the shocking battlefield front scenes from over 60 years before. I could not believe that these precious photos were taken by a 25-year-old young man.

Although so well known throughout China, Xiao Fang appeared and disappeared like a comet. As a result, in the *Chinese History of Photography*, there was no independent chapter for, or complete biography of, him. There were less than 100 total words describing him. It was even harder to find a trace of information about him in the *Chinese History of Journalism*.

As a documentary maker, through long-term study of historical materials and field research, I worked diligently to present a real peace and freedom loving man. This man took real life as background and his own life as film to record the real China in national crisis. I studied Xiao Fang out of a deepening interest, understanding, and curiosity that developed during the process. This endeavor was naturally driven by my recognition of, and longing for, a kind of noble spirit.

The documentary *In Search of Fang Dazeng* was aired on CCTV in 2000. For 20 years, Fang Dazeng has been on my mind. Like fermented wine, the longer this affection ferments, the mellower it becomes. Gradually, I somehow became his "family." Should there be any worldly motivation to search for one's relatives?

I am delighted that, with help from good-hearted people, after *Fang Dazeng: Disappearance and Reappearance* and *Fang Dazeng: Lost and Found* were successively published, they immediately gained high praise from literary circles, academics, and the industry. Zhou Xiaoning, a famous military historian, said: "They are of great academic significance for an in-depth, detailed study of the figures in the Chinese history of journalism, battlefield press photography,

小方的生命轮廓是破碎的，遗存的作品是散碎的，再加上我的业余时间是零碎的，这三重碎片摆在面前，连缀方大曾的生命样貌，重现其精神华彩的这一梦想是困难的。

从小方家人留下的遗物遗照入手，进一步对他的朋友圈、师友圈、战友圈进行梳理，读者眼前的这本《珍藏方大曾》无疑是多年寻找和研究的最新成果，责任编辑李莎莎给这本书加了“战地记者的光影故事”的副标题，则更加突出了文本的性质和内在含义。

中国新闻史学会副会长、中国人民大学教授王润泽说：“以前传教士拍摄的中国人是麻木的、愚昧的，眼睛是死的，方大曾拍的中国人是有感情的，眼睛是明亮的，我们的小孩是阳光的，充满笑容的，我们中国人的心灵不是麻木的，我们是积极向上的。”这本书中汇集的400多幅图，以得之不易的小方作品、私人照片和文献为主，相互交织推进时间轴线，用图传的形式呈现，每一幅都是精心挑选的，基调是阳光的，主题是昂扬向上的。合卷回想，我们会惊奇地发现，观察小方25岁的生命中的行与思，与这一基调高度契合，与主题充分一致。

2017年5月，我在纽约州立大学做了两场寻找方大曾的讲座，孔子学院美方院长Guiherme Albieri在致辞时表示，方大曾和冯雪松是不同时代的两位英雄。方大曾不顾安危第一个抵达卢沟桥用镜头记录下历史，其勇气令人钦佩，其作品具有深远的意义。而如果没有冯雪松，我们便不知道方大曾的故事，冯雪松踏上漫长的寻找之旅，把方大曾的伟大事迹讲述给后人听，让人们了解到这位英雄所做的贡献。

无疑，方大曾是中国的，也是世界的，他关注民生，不畏艰难困苦，忠实地记录时代，触及我们的内心，震撼我们的灵魂。小方是一位不受时代局限、不受年龄段影响、没有国界的英雄，他所呈现的魅力和价值是所有行业和职业人的终极品质。

寻找方大曾是一次关乎历史追问的行动，也是由媒体人通过影像表达进行的一次关于历史责任的书写，对我而言，更是一次家国情怀的洗礼和

and the War of Resistance against Japanese Aggression. They have filled the academic gap and are socially significant in promoting the great spirit of fighting against Japanese aggression, the national spirit of fighting against foreign aggression, and the spirit of justice, self-sacrifice and devotion."

The outline of Xiao Fang's life is fragmented, as are the works he left behind. In addition, my spare time is fragmented. With these fragments facing me, it is so very difficult to realize my dream of restoring the real life and spirit of Fang Dazeng.

I started with those things and photos kept by Xiao Fang's family and further studied his friends, teachers, and comrades-in-arms. This book, *Treasuring Fang Dazeng*, is undoubtedly my latest finding after years of searching for, and researching, Fang Dazeng. Li Shasha, the editor-in-charge, added the subheading "A War Correspondent's Stories," which further explains and highlights the stylistic features and implications of this book.

Mr. Wang Runze, Vice President of the Chinese Association for History of Journalism and Mass Communication and a professor of Renmin University of China, commented that "The Chinese people photographed by missionaries before looked numb and dumb with spiritless eyes. However, the Chinese people photographed by Fang Dazeng were vivid and alive with bright eyes. The Chinese children were shining and smiling. The soul of Chinese people was positive, not negative." The over 400 pictures collected in this book were painstakingly retrieved works of Xiao Fang, also including his private photos and related literature, which collectively weave a timeline of his life. This is a pictorial biography. All the pictures have been carefully selected, with a bright keynote and a positive theme. When you close the book and reflect on the content, you will be surprised to realize that the journeys and thoughts of Xiao Fang during his 25-year life are highly in line with such a keynote and theme.

In May 2017, I presented two lectures on searching for Fang Dazeng at the State University of New York (SUNY). Guiherme Albieri, American Dean of SUNY's Confucius Institute, delivered a speech to point out that Fang Dazeng and Feng Xuesong are both heroes in their times. Fang Dazeng was the first to arrive at the Lugou Bridge to record the real history, regardless of the danger. His bravery is admirable and his works profound and influential. However, without Feng Xuesong, people would never know Fang's stories. Feng traveled a long way in search of Fang and narrated the great stories of Fang to later generations so they can learn about contributions made by this hero.

Undoubtedly, Fang Dazeng belongs to China and the world. Caring about people's livelihood, he braved all the difficulties to faithfully record history, touching our hearts and moving our souls. Xiao Fang is a hero who has gone beyond the limits of time, age, and nationality. His charm and value exhibit the ultimate virtues of all professionals in all trades.

Searching for Fang Dazeng is a campaign to

追问初心的自省。

方大曾不应该被历史和时代遗忘，至少我们要用自己的行动，挽回那缕若隐若现的荣光，让他永留人间，使正义、良知、家国情怀长久流淌在人类精神的主动脉。

方大曾不应该被民族和后辈遗忘，至少我们要用自己的努力，拨开那些若有若无的尘埃，让他泽被来者，使他的肯担当、勇敢、有崇高理想的精神品质永远行走在世界共融的主航道。

珍藏方大曾，也是珍藏我们自己的宝贵记忆，因为他代表着青春、高尚和牺牲。我想，只有后辈坚持在寻行的路上，小方的精神才能永不消失，天边彗星的光芒，才能永留人间。

无论你身在何处，只要被方大曾的故事所感动，我们就是同路人。

本书中的照片大部分历经劫难，由于匆匆离开，小方没有来得及留下标识和说明。岁月的流淌，渐渐模糊了城乡景观和人物面庞。在纪录片拍摄初期，面对的是底片编号中断、庞杂无序、不知道该从哪里入手的情形，于是先用最笨的办法，把能找到的他写的几篇通讯所涉内容与图片大致对位，后再细分。这样，十几年来，随着寻找的深入，图片所涉内容地点大体清晰。撰写图说时，结合家人回忆，对于确切的信息，力求精准，未知和模糊部分留待细考。至今，还有一些照片不能确定时间和地点。但希来日，追寻途中的我们，会有更多更新的发现、更详更实的成果，不断矫正，不断前行，使方大曾的生命轮廓更加清晰饱满蕴藏丰富。

冯雪松

unveil the truth of history. It is also an opportunity to give expression to the historical responsibility of media professionals through pictures and videos. For me personally, it is an opportunity to bathe in patriotism and a self-reflecting journey to seek my pure heart.

Fang Dazeng should not be forgotten in history or time. We should do something to retrieve that gleaming glory, make him forever remembered in this world, and keep justice, conscience, and patriotism permanently flowing through the main artery of human spirit.

Fang Dazeng should not be forgotten by the Chinese nation or later generations. We should work hard to remove the dust of history, have his spirit enlighten later generations, and keep the sense of responsibility, bravery, and lofty ideals forever carried forward toward world harmony.

Treasuring Fang Dazeng is also treasuring our own precious memories because he represents youth, dignity, and the spirit of self-sacrifice. I believe that only if later generations constantly follow his steps will Xiao Fang's spirit live on and the brilliance of this comet forever be with us.

No matter where you are, if you are touched by Fang Dazeng's stories, we are fellow travelers.

Most photos in this book have experienced and survived calamities. Since Xiao Fang left in such a hurry, he had not yet labeled and described them by himself. The flowing time gradually blurred the look of cities and towns and the faces of people. When I started to make the documentary, I felt at a loss to deal with the disorganized photos which were discontinuous and massive in number, so I had to adopt the most primitive method to match up generally several of his news reports available with the photos for further categorization. Then, in the past over ten years, with constant effort, I have basically learned where these photos were taken. When I wrote the descriptions for the photos, I referred to the recollection of Fang's family, endeavoring to present the concrete information precisely while leaving the unknown and ambiguous parts for future research. Up to now, I am still unsure of when and where some photos were taken. So, I hope that in the future, as Fang Dazeng's followers, we can have more and newer findings, gain more detailed and concrete results, and further trace the sources and move forward constantly, so as to draw a more vivid, detailed and accurate picture of Fang's life.

Feng Xuesong

方大曾的光影记录
Photos by Fang Dazeng

小方拍摄的煤矿工人
The coal miners photographed by Xiao Fang.

方大曾镜头里的前线指挥官
Commander at the front photographed by Fang Dazeng.

船工照片的底部还能隐约看到小方画上去的剪裁线
Clipping lines drawn by Xiao Fang still seem visible on this photo of the boatman.

矿工
Coal miners.

小方冀东之行经过的塘沽车站

Tanggu Station, photographed by Xiao Fang during his journey to Eastern Hebei.

小方绥远之行的第一站

First stop on Xiao Fang's journey to Suiyuan.

绥远之行途中所见

One of the lama temples Xiao Fang passed during his journey.

守卫城门

Guarding the city gate.

方大曾的新闻作品
News Reports by Fang Dazeng

小方拍摄的《北平学生大露营》，发表在上海《国民周刊》

Beiping Students Camping by Xiao Fang. Published in the *Chinese People Weekly* (Shanghai).

小方在《国民周刊》（1937 年第 1 卷第 5 期）发表的《国内时事动态》

Current Domestic Affairs by Xiao Fang. Published in the *Chinese People Weekly* (No. 5, Vol. 1, 1937)

发表于 1937 年上海《申报》的 3 组摄影报道之《雄视察北的大碉堡》

A Large Fortress Overlooking Northern Chahar, one of three reports by Xiao Fang published in *Shun Pao* (Shanghai) in 1937.

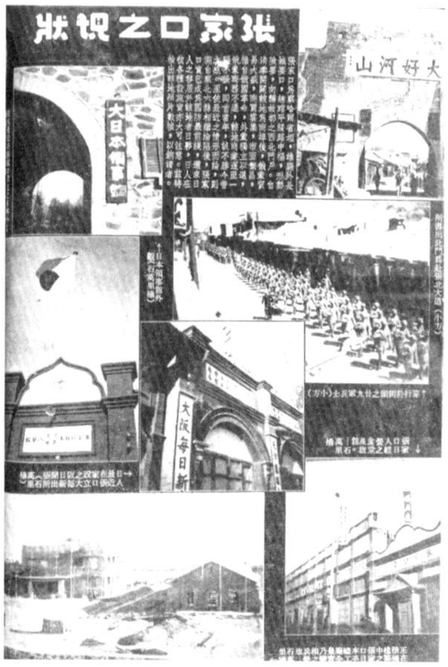

发表于 1937 年上海《申报》的 3 组摄影报道之《张家口之况状》

Situation in Zhangjiakou, one of three reports by Xiao Fang published in *Shun Pao* (Shanghai) in 1937.

小方的通讯报道《敌人觊觎下的绥远》

Suiyuan Coveted by Enemy, a news report by Xiao Fang.

绥远之行后小方发表在《美术生活》杂志的 3 组之《绥远阅兵典礼》

Military Review Ceremony, one of three reports by Xiao Fang published in *Fine Arts Life* magazine after his journey to Suiyuan.

发表在《申报》的《卢沟桥事件发生后之北平》

Beiping after the Lugou Bridge Incident, published in *Shun Pao*.

小方最后的报道之《我们为自卫而抗战》

We Fight against Japanese Aggression for Self-Defense, Xiao Fang's last report.

晉北我軍血戰大捷
敵精銳部隊全覆滅
平型關戰線空前大勝利
平漢平綏戰局自此一轉
血戰居庸關

发表于上海《大公报》的战地通讯《血战居庸关》

Heroic Battle at Juyong Pass, a news report published in *Ta Kung Pao* (Shanghai).

從娘子關到雁門關
（一）
小方
（一）進入娘子關
（二）太原的一日

连载于 1937 年 9 月 17、18 日上海《大公报》的小方通讯《从娘子关到雁门关》

From Niangzi Pass to Yanmen Pass, by Xiao Fang. Serialized in *Ta Kung Pao* (Shanghai), September 17-18, 1937.

第一章 少年方德曾

Chapter One: Fang Dazeng's Youth

现在摄影艺术一天天发达，进步，摄影人才也能在艺术上占了重要地位，得社会的赞许，于是研究摄影的团体就渐渐地多起来了。但是我们看看，少年摄影团体的组织，还是很少，以至我们虽是很好这种艺术，而终是不得其门而入，这是何等的苦恼呢！所以我们有组织少年摄影团体的必要。做少年摄影界的先进队，何等的伟大！何等的有趣呀！少年们！小朋友们！快来报名！踊跃！努力！

——方德曾《少年影社征求社员宣言》

Photographic art is making progress every day. Talented photographers play an important role in art, winning social recognition. As a result, there are increasing associations studying photography. However, there is still a lack of youth photography clubs. Our photos are good artistic works, but can hardly be accepted into large circles of society. So, we need to establish youth photography clubs. What a great mission, and how interesting, to be a pioneer in the youth photography community! Young friends! Dear friends! Come to us! Come on! Come on!

Youth Photography Club Call for Members, by Fang Dezeng

20 世纪 30 年代中期，方大曾是中国摄影界、新闻界一个响亮的名字。他 1912 年 7 月 13 日生于北京，原名方德曾，笔名小方，毕业于中法大学经济系，是当时活跃在长城内外的知名记者，与范长江、徐盈等人同负盛名。

方大曾的父亲方振东（又名方祖宝）曾在译学馆学习法语，后到外交部工作，母亲方朱理是一个开明的家庭主妇，会些中医，经常给头痛脑热的邻居们开药方。他们一家住在东单协和胡同的一座四合院内，家境优裕。祖辈原居无锡，后进京做官，至小方已经五代。

父亲的达观，母亲的善良，对于小方的个人成长而言，无疑是大有裨益的，正直、明理、与人为善，从小就成为他为人处事的准则。

从出生到成长过程，方大曾所处的时代，正是中国和世界最为动荡的时期。工业化进程的迅猛发展，对原有的农业文明秩序冲击最大，加之不断战争，促使人类的价值观从简单到多元。世界格局悄然发生着变化，现代化所带来的力度和速度前所未有，在大起大落中，卑鄙和高尚，富有和贫穷，高贵与卑微，仿佛一夜之间就可以颠倒，毫无征兆的变数无时不在，人们生活在欣喜中，也生活在恐惧中。

对于新鲜事物，方大曾总是乐于尝试。“拍照片”是让他最为着迷的，为了满足他的这一爱好，母亲用了七块大洋为儿子买了一个相机。这是一个不菲的价格，在当时，一块大洋就可以解决三口之家半个月的口粮，十块大洋就可以开一个小餐馆。

1929 年，方大曾 17 岁，他在北平的《世界画报》上发表《爱好摄影的小朋友们注意——少年影社征求社员宣言》，宣称“现在摄影艺术一天天的发达，进步，摄影人才也能在艺术上占了重要地位……所以我们有组织少年摄影团体的必要。做少年摄影界的先进队，何等的伟大！何等的有趣呀！少年们！小朋友们，快来报名！踊跃！努力！少年影社以研究摄影艺术为宗旨，凡有摄影器，对于摄影发生兴趣者，不论有无经验，年在十六岁以内者，均得自由加入本社为社员。少年影社通讯处：北平外交部街协和胡同 7 号方德曾”。据史料记载，这是中国北方第一个少年摄影社团。

In the mid-1930s, Fang Dazeng was well-known in Chinese photography and press circles. He was born on July 13, 1912. His original name was Fang Dezeng, and his pen name was Xiao Fang. He graduated from the Department of Economics at the Lyon Sino-French Institute. He was a popular journalist, active throughout China; as reputed as figures like Fan Changjiang and Xu Ying.

Fang Zhendong (also named Fang Zubao), father of Fang Dazeng, studied French at the Translation School and later worked for the Ministry of Foreign Affairs. Fang Zhuli, mother of Fang Dazeng, was an open-minded housewife. She knew the basics of traditional Chinese medicine (TCM) and gave prescriptions to her neighbors with minor illnesses. Their family lived in a quadrangular courtyard in Xiehe Hutong (lane), in the Dongdan area of Beijing, enjoying an affluent life. Fang Dazeng's ancestor used to live in Wuxi and later became an official in Beijing, the capital. Xiao Fang was of the fifth generation.

The optimism of his father and kindness of his mother were undoubtedly quite beneficial to Xiao Fang's growth. Integrity, reason, and friendliness was his code of conduct from childhood.

Fang Dazeng grew up during a time when China and the world were in the greatest chaos. Rapid industrialization exerted the greatest impact on the order of the previous agricultural civilization. In addition, unceasing wars changed human values from simple to diverse. Given this changing world pattern and unprecedentedly influential and rapid modernization, concepts of up and down, humble and noble, rich and poor, dignitary and lowly could reverse overnight. Life was full of contingencies. People lived in joy and horror.

Faced with so many new things, Fang Dazeng always liked to try. Taking photos is what fascinated him most. To support her son's hobby, Fang's mother spent seven silver coins to buy him a camera. This was a high price at the time as one silver coin could provide food to support a three-member family for half a month and ten silver coins could open a restaurant.

In 1929, when Fang Dazeng was 17 years old, he published "Young Photography Fans, Attention Please: Youth Photography Club Call for Members" in *World Pictorial Magazine*. In the article, he stated:

"Photographic art is making progress every day. Talented photographers play an important role in art, winning social recognition. As a result, there are increasing associations studying photography. However, there is still a lack of youth photography clubs. Our photos are good artistic works, but can hardly be accepted into large circles of society. So, we need to establish youth photography clubs. What a great mission, and how interesting, to be a pioneer in the youth photography community!

当年9月，北平第一次公开摄影展览会在中山公园和青年会相继展出时，方大曾作为青年代表，也选了多幅作品参展，受到了社会的广泛好评。荫昌之子、摄影家荫铁阁曾撰文评介说：“方德曾之《寒夜》亦具西风，所取色调，尤能增其冷静”（北平《世界画报》205期 1929年9月29日出版）。接着，他拍摄的《寒夜》《青年会童子军团野外庆祝会》《北郊之大钟寺》等作品，在《世界画报》陆续发表。此时的方大曾，已经在中国北方的摄影圈中崭露头角。

本章图片多选自方大曾家人所珍藏的《私人照相簿》，时间大体在20世纪20年代至30年代初，大部分照片系首次公开。

Young friends! Dear friends! Come to us! Come on! Come on! The fundamental goal of our Youth Photography Club is to study photographic art. As long as you have a camera and are interested in photography, with or without experience, and are below age 16, you can join us. Address: No. 7 Xiehe Hutong, Ministry of Foreign Affairs Street, Beiping. Fang Dezeng."

According to historical records, this is the first youth photography club in northern China.

In September of 1929, the 1st Beiping Open Photography Exhibition was held at Zhongshan Park by the Chinese Young Men's Christian Association (YMCA). Fang Dazeng, as a youth representative, selected some of his works to be exhibited, which were widely welcomed by society. Yin Tiege, son of Yin Chang and also a photographer, once wrote an article in which he said: "*Cold Night*, by Fang Dezeng, features a western style. The color he uses especially adds to the photo's tranquility" (Published by *World Pictorial Magazine*, Vol. 205, September 29, 1929, Beiping). Later, *Cold Night*, *YMCA Scout Field Celebration*, *Big Bell Temple* in *Northern Suburbs*, and many other works by Xiao Fang were published in *World Pictorial Magazine*. At this time, Fang Dazeng had already become a figure in the photographic circles of northern China.

The photos in this chapter are mostly from the *Private Photo Album* kept by Fang Dazeng's family, taken between the 1920s to the early 1930s. Most of them are published for the very first time.

北京东单协和胡同，清末时称为“蝎虎胡同”。当年的 7 号院后来改为 10 号院，是方大曾的家，他的青少年时代大部分是在这里度过的（冯雪松摄于 2013 年）

Xiehe Hutong (lane) in the Dongdan area of Beijing. The No. 10 house, formerly called No. 7 house, used to be Fang Dazeng's. He spent most of his youth here (photos by Feng Xuesong, 2013).

方大曾的父亲方振东，又名方祖宝，译学馆法文专业毕业，在外交部管理档案及总务工作，政府南迁后，前往天津谋职

Fang Zhendong, father of Fang Dazeng, also named Fang Zubao, graduated from the Translation School and majored in French. He once worked for the Ministry of Foreign Affairs, in charge of archive management and general affairs. After the government moved south, he went to work in Tianjin.

母亲方朱理，北京人，家庭主妇，会中医

Fang Zhuli, mother of Fang Dazeng, was a local Beijing resident. She knew the basics of traditional Chinese medicine (TCM).

小方儿童时代影存（目前发现他最早的自拍照）

Xiao Fang during childhood (the earliest known photo of him taken by Fang Dazeng).

在东单附近的诊疗所前留影

A photo taken in front of a clinic near Dongdan.

从小爱旅行，妹妹方澄敏对此印象深刻

From childhood, Fang loved traveling. Fang Chengmin, his younger sister, remembered this very clearly.

与同学郊游中的小方（前），底片上有他画的剪裁线

Xiao Fang (front) on a class outing. On the negative, there are clip lines drawn by him.

早期留影（左一小方、左三妹妹方澄敏）

A photo from Xiao Fang's early years (first left: Xiao Fang; third left: Fang Chengmin, his younger sister).

北京西山环谷园，初中时期，小方就读于附近寄宿制的温泉中学。这所学校由李石曾等人设立，与中法大学一脉相承（1926 年）

A photo taken at Huangu Park in Beijing in 1926. Xiao Fang once studied at the nearby Wenquan Middle School. This school was built by Li Shizeng and others in 1923, who later founded the Lyon Sino-French Institute.

站在学校门前，准备启程去露营的小方（右一）
Xiao Fang (first right) standing in front of the school gate, ready for camping.

80 多年过去，北京市第四十七中学院内的温泉中学旧址至今保存完好，现为敬德书院（冯雪松摄于 2016 年）

The well-preserved site of the Wenquan Middle School inside the Beijing No. 47 Middle School today. Currently, it is the Jingde Academy (photo by Feng Xuesong, 2016).

北京，小方拍摄朋友们在八大处野餐
Picnic at Badachu Park in Beijing, taken by Xiao Fang.

小方（右四）与友人在北京十三陵

Xiao Fang (fourth right) and his friends at the Ming Tombs in Beijing.

父亲工作地点的门卫，方大曾少年时期的人物摄影（20 世纪 20 年代）

A doorman on duty at the work place of Xiao Fang's father. This is a figure photo by young Fang Dazeng (in the 1920s).

少年方大曾摄影习作

Works by Fang Dazeng while he was learning photography.

除了景物和人物，小方还以抓拍的方式练习纪实拍摄

Besides photographing scenery and figures, Xiao Fang also practiced documentary photography by capturing images.

攀登的少年，择高处立，向宽处行（20 世纪 20 年代）

A young man climbing, standing high, and exploring further (in the 1920s).

小方旅行纪念（未剪裁）
A photo taken during travel (unclipped).

郊游间歇的小方（左一）
Xiao Fang (first left) taking a break during an outing.

方德曾高中就读的北京一中（1928—1930）

The Beijing No. 1 Middle School where Fang Dezeng once studied (1928-1930).

小方（左二）高中时期留影

A photo of Xiao Fang (second left) in high school.

北京郊区（1929 年）
In a suburb of Beijing (1929).

天津，海河边（原底片受潮损坏）
By the Hai River, Tianjin (the original film was damaged).

愛好攝影的小朋友們注意

少年影社徵求社員宣言

現在攝影藝術一天天的發達，進步，攝影人才也能在藝術上佔了重要的地位，得社會的贊許，於是研究攝影的團體就漸漸的多起來了。但是我們看看，少年攝影團體的組織，還是很少，以至我們雖是很好這種藝術，而終是不得其門而入，這是何等的苦惱呢！所以我們有組織少年攝影團體的必要。做少年攝影界的先鋒隊，何等的偉大！何等的有趣呀！少年們！小朋友們！快來報名！踴躍！努力！

少年影社，以研究攝影藝術為宗旨，凡有攝影器，對於攝影發生興趣者，不論有無經驗，年在十六歲以內者，均得自由加入本社為社員

少年影社通訊處　外交部街協和胡同七號方德曾。

小方在《世界画报》1929 年第 201 期刊登征友广告

The advertisement for Youth Photography Club membership posted by Xiao Fang in Vol. 201 of *World Pictorial Magazine*, 1929.

母亲眼中，胆子大、好奇心强、爱冒险的孩子

A bold, curious, and adventurous boy in his mother's eyes.

小方的摄影启蒙者蒋汉澄，协和医院任职，后成为中国医学摄影的奠基人

Jiang Hancheng, Xiao Fang's first photography teacher, working at the Union Hospital. Mr. Jiang later became the founder of medical photography in China.

十八年九月二十九日　第二百零五期

世界畫報

每星期日出版一張零售大洋四分長期訂閱半年大洋一元外埠加郵費二角五分凡係直接訂閱世界日報者按期附送

本報徵求實事照片美術攝影中西名畫游藝裝束學校生活等照片一經登載酬金從豐凡名貴照片於製版後立即寄還

北平第一次公開攝影展覽會記　（蔭識閣）

北平的攝影風氣，極盛一時，攝影家亦多所發明，可惜沒法介紹，致使一般對攝影感有興趣的人，未能盡窺全豹，好友蔣君漢澄，施君畚厂等三數攝影同志，有見於此，遂相約發起北平第一次公開攝影展覽會，假中山公園展覽四日，後復借青年會展覽二日，以茲觀摩，參加者有二十餘人，作品多至二百五十餘件　誠北平數年來之盛會也。

現在把我個人觀察的介紹數幅，處前王後，尚希原諒可也

趙澄之「煤金」一幅甚能得光之變化，明與暗均含有偉大的意義，色調尤為濃厚，施畚厂之「媽媽」係取反光，色調清爽，光線明亮，取景及姿勢，皆具秀氣。蔣漢澄之「三角」復雜中能見條理為Mechanical Photograph之佳作。魏守忠之「泥濘」頗具泰西作風，光調濃厚，足見魄力。金哲浩之「曉舟」景色絕妙，觀之起人雄心，而一角船捆，亦屬罕見，宗惟賡之「斜」攝法新奇，雖僅楊樹數株而不覺枯燥　伍保基之「夕領林腰」取景雄偉，光線尤為明朗，此誠風景中之上作。吳宗濟之「線上」攝法新奇，章法正齊，近代攝取人物之新法也。鄂鶴紀之「荒涼」取景單簡不俗，頗有畫意。索仁甫之「閃」明暗得宜，亦為會中傑作。楊朗之之「弱不禁風」處處透明，別具見地。谷靖塵之「日炎」色調濃厚，尤顯建築之偉大。方德曾之「寒夜」亦具西風，所取色調，尤能增其冷靜。張之達之「烟」頗具沈靜之意。又如李堯生之「吹簫」。許智之「泙」。尾巴先生之「小鬼」。秦元華之「樹影」又如金浩如，金默園，關紫荊諸君，傑作甚多，限于篇幅，未能盡述，良深遺憾也。

再此首次展覽之結果，同人發起組織華北攝影研究社，已於九月十七日在公園董事會正式成立，但社址尚未選定，暫以東單火神廟五號為通訊處，並以此次展覽籌備匆促，有未及加入者，同人議決雙十節移津展覽三日，地點正在接洽中，並望同志踴躍參加也。

師大高材生吳敬仁（左）與張挽華兩女士合影

（上圖）寒夜……方德曾作　（下圖）大掃除……金開義作

《世界画报》1929 年第 205 期刊登小方参加北平第一次公开摄影展览会作品《寒夜》（左下）

World Pictorial Magazine (Vol. 205, 1929) published *Cold Night*, a work of Xiao Fang exhibited during the 1st Beiping Open Photography Exhibition (lower left).

小方（右一）和友人齐伦（右二）等在颐和园

At the Summer Palace, Beijing (first right: Xiao Fang; second right: Qi Lun).

小方（站立者）与小伙伴在十三陵

Xiao Fang (standing) and his friends at the Ming Tombs.

小方（右一）与少年影社成员合影
Xiao Fang (first right) and other Youth Photography Club members.

小方镜头中的朋友们

Xiao Fang's friends.

进入大学前的暑期旅行（1930 年）
A summer vacation before starting college (1930).

第二章 **大学**

Chapter Two: College Days

过了塘沽以后，乘客渐渐稀少了，由于我身旁背着的照相机引起了押车警的好奇，于是我们就谈起话来，我乐得乘着这机会向他问了些冀东的近况，才知道冀东并不是如一般人所想象的那样神秘与恐怖，对于旅行者是很方便而自由的。后来，由于此行的经历，我也觉得冀东伪组织虽然已成立了一年之久，但它的统治是散漫的，工作是混乱的，基础是摇动的，社会是荒淫的……这且待我一段一段写出来。这次冀东的旅行，共经五日，而大部分时间是在唐山，滦县及昌黎。本想也到山海关去一趟的，但是在中途遇着大风雪因未带寒衣，只得折回。

——方大曾《冀东一瞥》

After passing Tanggu, the number of passengers became less and less. Because the camera I carried attracted the security man, we started to talk. I was so delighted for this chance to ask him about the news in eastern Hebei. I learned that eastern Hebei was not as mysterious and horrible as people imagined. Visitors could actually enjoy convenience and freedom. Later, I also learned from this trip that although the puppet government in eastern Hebei had been in place for nearly a year, it was slack, disorderly, unstable, and dissolute. I noted examples, one-by-one. This trip to eastern Hebei lasted five days, with most of my time spent in Tangshan, Luan County, and Changli. I originally planned to also visit the Shanhai Pass. However, I encountered a blizzard halfway into the trip and had no thick clothing, so I had to return.

A Glance at Eastern Hebei by Fang Dazeng

大学期间，小方在协和胡同家中留影
Fang at his house in Xiehe Hutong, during his college days.

1930 年，刚满 18 岁的方大曾考入中法大学经济系，这期间，他与诗人方殷一起编辑《少年先锋》杂志，从写稿、印刷到分发，几乎都是他们两个人完成的。1935 年，从中法大学毕业后，他前往天津基督教青年会工作，任少年部职员。他发表作品时常常以方德曾或小方署名，这时拍照的主要内容是风光、人物和学生运动。

方大曾时常离家外出旅行。天津、北京的周边，河北、山西和内蒙古一带，是他的主要拍摄地，他带着折叠式的相机，记录走过的乡村和城市。他的许多照片上，今天仍清晰地保留着为冲洗和放大画上去的剪裁线，这些画面给我们带来了早已消失了的码头和工厂，布满缆绳的船帆，荒凉的土地，还有旧时代的生活和风尚。从他拍摄的下层民众脸上的表情来看，他们之间有着足够的信任和平等。

小方不拍美人照，他与劳动者结下了不解之缘。他到黄河岸边，煤矿的井

In 1930, just after he turned 18 years old, Fang Dazeng was admitted by the Department of Economics of the Lyon Sino-French Institute. During his college days, he and poet Fang Yin worked together as joint editors-in-chief of *Youth Pioneer* magazine. From writing to printing and distribution, they did the entire job. In 1935, after he graduated from college, Xiao Fang worked as a staff member for the Youth Department of the Chinese Young Men's Christian Association (YMCA) in Tianjin. When he published reports, he often signed as Fang Dezeng, or using his pen name of Xiao Fang. The main content of his photos during this period included scenery, figures, and student activities.

Fang Dazeng often left home to travel. The surrounding areas of Tianjin, Beijing, and Hebei, along with Shanxi and Inner Mongolia were the main sites where he took photos. He took a folding camera to photograph the villages and cities he visited. In many photos, clip lines for photo development and magnification are still clearly visible. These photos include the wharfs and factories that had disappeared long before, sail boats covered with mooring ropes, wastelands, and traditional life and customs. From the expressions on the faces of the masses in his photos, we see they enjoyed mutual trust and equality with Fang, the photographer.

Xiao Fang did not take photos of beautiful women. Instead, he focused on laborers. He ventured far down the bank of the Yellow River and deep into coal mines. He conducted field research to present first-hand material to readers. "He took photos of the poor masses in China, the boatmen on the torrents, and miners under the ground. He showed great care and sympathy for their real living conditions," said Mr. Wu Qun, an authoritative scholar of Chinese photography history.

Writer Yu Hua said: "On seeing Fang Dazeng's works, I was immediately fascinated, which proved again that reality can have a greater impact than the so-called art. I can imagine that in that age of chaos, Fang Dazeng constantly pressed his shutter – he did not need to design any presentation of the pictures in the frames. On one hand, this shows how talented he was as a photographer. On the other, this proves that reality is beyond art. Actually, many things that disappeared have not actually disappeared. When we see his works today, do we feel intimacy? In his works, we see expressions of numbness and joy that are often seen today. This is how that 'disappeared world'

下，经过实地调查，把第一手材料介绍给读者。研究中国摄影史的权威人士吴群说："他把镜头对准中国的劳苦大众，位于激流中和地底下的船工矿工，对他们的实际生活境况，表示极大的关怀与同情。"

作家余华在接受笔者采访时说："一看方大曾的作品，瞬间的感觉把我给抓住了。这似乎再次证明了，现实可能比我们认为的艺术更加有力。我可以想象，方大曾是在那么一个动乱的年代，他的快门不断地按动；进入取景框的那个时代的画面是不需要构思的，一方面体现他作为一名摄影师的才华，另一方面说明现实高于艺术。其实很多消失的东西并没有消失。我们今天看到他的作品后，怎么那么地亲切？（他的作品中）有我们这个时代所熟悉的麻木，也有我们这个时代所熟悉的欢乐和表情，这就是我们如何对待那个消失的世界，其实，那个世界没有消失，它无非是以今天的方式存在着。"

读大学时，方大曾已经在北平的摄影圈颇有名气，经常参加各种展览，开始在报刊上发表摄影作品。方澄敏回忆，上大学后，哥哥就不再向家里要钱了，他用稿费支付生活用度，买胶卷、药水，自己冲洗照片，放大机是他用纸盒做的。他不仅是个摄影家，还是旅行家，周边的寺庙都去过。那时候没那么好的路，多半是步行，有时候骑自行车。"每次都拍好多照片回来，一开始不会洗时，在外面洗，后来钻研会了，就自己洗。他的照片洗得还是不错的，从小号到大号的，都是慢慢积累下来的，这么多年了，颜色不变。而且还热衷参加各种学生活动。"

九·一八事变后，华北之大，已容不下一张书桌，方大曾像所有的热血青年一样，义无反顾地汇入了时代洪流。他参加了"反帝大同盟"的机关报《反帝新闻》的编辑工作。在好友方殷眼里，他是一个"英俊青年"，"人品纯正，热情。精力充沛。……好像总是在走路，奔忙，不知疲倦"。相机无疑是他最便捷的武器。30年代的热血青年都有着或多或少的进步倾向，方大曾也同样如此，他的革命道路"从不满现实、阅读进步书刊到参加党的外围组织的一些秘密活动"。

方澄敏在回忆文章中写那时候的哥哥，常常只带一把雨伞、一条毛毯、一个背包、一架相机就离开家了，活跃于平津及晋、察、冀、绥一带。

每次旅行回来，方大曾总是抓紧写稿和洗印照片。他在自家院子里用木头制作了一个暗房，供冲洗和放大胶片使用，有时候妹妹方澄敏也跑过来，帮着定影，打打下手。

has never actually disappeared, but remains alive in its current form."

During his college days, Fang Dazeng was well known in Beijing photography circles. He often attended exhibitions and started to publish photos in newspapers. As Fang Chengmin recalled, after beginning college, her older brother stopped asking the family for money. He used money earned through photography to cover his living expenses and buy film and photograph development materials. He made a magnifier with a paper box. Xiao Fang was not just a photographer, he was a traveler. He had been to all the surrounding temples, even though, at that time, there was no well-built road in the area. In most cases, he walked, and sometimes rode a bicycle. Fang Chengmin commented: "Whenever he returned home, he would bring back so many photos that he took. At first, he did not know how to develop film, so he had someone else do it. Later, he learned to develop film and became very skilled at it. More and more photos, small and large, were accumulated. Over all these years, the colors in these photos have not changed at all. He was also an active participant in all kinds of student movements."

After the September 18th Incident, no one in northern China was in the mood to stay in school. Like other zealous youth, Fang Dazeng devoted himself, without hesitation, to this historical torrent and worked as an editor for *Anti-Imperialist News*, the official newspaper of the China Anti-Imperialist League. In the words of his friend, Fang Yin, he was a "handsome young man who was righteous, passionate, and full of energy... always on the move; busy working, never tired." His camera was undoubtedly his weapon. In the 1930s, those zealous youth were more or less progressive, as was Fang Dazeng. His revolutionary path evolved from feeling dissatisfied with reality to reading progressive books and joining underground activities of the peripheral organization of the Communist Party of China (CPC).

In an article, Fang Chengmin wrote that her brother often left home with only an umbrella, a blanket, a backpack, and a camera. She also recalled that he remained active in the Beijing, Tianjin, Shanxi, Chahar, Hebei, and Suiyuan areas.

Every time he returned from traveling, Fang Dazeng wrote reports and developed film. In the courtyard of his house, he built a makeshift darkroom to develop and magnify film. Sometimes, his younger sister, Fang Chengmin, would run over to help as his assistant.

In Fang Dazeng's works, there is no sign of playboy hobbies such as playing with birds or enjoying dramas. He took his camera and visited ancient temples, the countryside, fields, and markets near Beijing. His pictures included the Great Wall, vendors doing business, poor ladies making a living by sewing, porters wearing ragged clothes, and white flour carriers feeding on black chaff. As a youth, Xiao Fang began to learn about society with his camera and footsteps. What impressed me deeply was his caring for the people and their living conditions, a virtue shared by all great achievers.

"There is no trace of manipulation or decoration. The expressions of people in the photos are so natural, with scenery and figures

在方大曾留下的作品中，几乎没有“玩鸟唱戏”之类的癖好，他带着相机，行走于北京城周边的寺庙古刹、乡村田野、商埠市集。在他的镜头中，有肃穆的长城、讨生意的小贩、蜷缩在墙角下的缝穷者、破衣烂衫的码头工人，还有吃黑面扛白面的苦力。少年小方，就是用相机和脚步开始认识社会的，而他给我留下深刻印象的是，对于人和生存环境的关心，这一点，正是每一个能成就大业者所具备的。

“没有任何摆布和雕琢的痕迹，被摄者喜怒哀乐神态自然，画面情景交融。”范长江新闻奖获得者徐京星评价，“在那个胶片照相机为绝对稀有物的年代，拿着相机的他似乎像空气，无所不在，又让被拍摄者视而不见，可见方大曾先生深入生活的功夫和心境。”

30 年代中期的北平，对于青年学生来说，是民主和自由的城，各种思潮此起彼伏，新鲜事物不断涌现。东城因为离外国使馆区最近，所以洋东西多集中在这里，连南纸铺也变成了洋纸行，面包房、鲜花店、电影院一应俱全。还设有跳舞厅，而在其他地方是找不到的。中法大学正是处在这个洋味充斥的地方，学生时尚教师洋派。

在方大曾的私人照片中，有一张在山间赤身挥手的自拍照，方澄敏说，那是哥哥看完电影《人猿泰山》后，模仿着泰山的造型拍摄的。这部电影由米高梅公司出品，片长 101 分钟，1932 年 3 月 25 日在美国上映，轰动一时，不久后进入中国的影院，主演是约翰尼 · 韦斯穆勒，他曾在游泳比赛中 67 次打破世界纪录。模仿泰山的造型，无疑是被电影的情节、异域的风光和韦斯穆勒的力量所震撼，在小方的成长履历中，新奇、阳光和正义是不变的主题。

在近期资料查找过程中，有一个小方不为人知的被捕经历浮出水面。在北京市档案馆目录数据库，有关中法大学的 500 份卷宗里，一份 1932 年 1 月 19 日北平市警察局内二区的案卷引人注意，内容是“解送中法大学王良骥、方德曾等十三人游行被捕案”。事由记录大意为“当日下午，青年学生集会后赴市党部抗日请愿，沿街高呼‘打倒国民党’等口号，并捣毁数面牌匾，奉令将肇事学生揪获送局，计男女生十三名。”

案卷内有小方亲笔书写的事情经过，全文如下：

方德曾，江苏无锡人，中法大学学生，年十九岁，住协和胡同三号。

在南京被捕的同学蔡华义，是中法大学的学生，他前两天被放回北平。他

well blended," Xu Jingxing, a Fan Changjiang Journalism Award winner, said. He further commented: "In that era, when film and cameras were very rare, this cameraman was like air – he was everywhere, yet invisible to those he photographed. This is where we see the superb skills and mental state of Fang Dazeng in delving into life."

Beiping (Beijing), in the mid-1930s, was a city of democracy and freedom for young students, with the emergence of various ideological trends and novelties. Since Dongcheng District was nearest to the foreign embassies, many foreign activities occurred there. Even the old stationary shops were turned into western-style stationary stores. There were bakeries, flower shops, and screening rooms. There were even ballrooms, which could not be found in other places. The Lyon Sino-French Institute was located in this area filled with exoticism, fashionable students, and progressive teachers.

Among the private photos of Fang Dazeng, there was a photo of him, undressed, waving his hand on a mountain. Fang Chengmin said he was imitating Tarzan after watching the film *Tarzan the Ape Man*. This film was produced by MGM, with a running time of 101 minutes. It was first played in America on March 25, 1932 and immediately created a great sensation. Soon, it entered cinemas in China. The main character was played by Johnny Weissmuller, who had 67 times broken the world record for swimming. Xiao Fang imitated the posture of Tarzan, undoubtedly because he was fascinated by the film's plot, exotic scenery, and by Weissmuller's power. Novelty, brightness, and justice was a permanent theme in the growth of Xiao Fang.

When I recently reviewed the literature, I found that Xiao Fang was once arrested. From the 500 files about the Lyon Sino-French Institute in the catalog of the Beijing Municipal Archives, there was one regarding the Inner 2nd District Branch of the Beijing Municipal Police Station, recorded on January 19, 1932. The catalog read: "Case of Escorting Arrested Wang Liangji, Fang Dezeng, and 11 other Lyon Sino-French Institute Students Attending Parade." The general description of the case says: "On that afternoon, after the young students assembled, they went to petition the municipal KMT office regarding the fight against Japanese aggression. These students paraded on the street, shouting slogans such as 'Down with the Kuomintang' and smashing several plaques. As ordered, we arrested these 13 male and female, trouble-making students and escorted them to the police station."

In the file, Xiao Fang described the entire experience, writing:

Fang Dezeng, Wuxi ancestral origin (Jiangsu Province), a Lyon Sino-French Institute student, 19 years old, currently lives at No. 3 Xiehe Hutong.

Cai Huayi is a Lyon Sino-French Institute student who was arrested in Nanjing. He was just freed and returned to Beiping days ago. He's a close friend of mine. Today, he told me there would be a meeting to reward the faculty of law, and he invited me to go. The faculty of law was very close to us. Originally, I had no plan to go, but, by happenstance, my family asked me to go to Xicheng District to do something. After I completed that business, I stopped by the meeting on my way back. When I arrived, it was already 4 o'clock and everyone had gone out to parade. I followed them.

是我的小朋友，今天他告诉我，在法学院有一个慰劳他们的大会，约我去看看。本来法学院离我们很远，我是(想)不去的，正好因为家里叫我到西城有一点事，我的事办完之后，就顺便到法学院去了。到时已然四点钟，正是他们要出发游行，我就尾随着跟去了。我因为将病好，什么口号也没有叫。等他们到市党部去请愿，我也跟着去看热闹。后来，他们把大门关上，好些个人就将市党部的牌子打下来了，打了之后就都跑了。我也不知道为什么要跑，所以我等在门口，看看究竟是怎么回事再说。哪知道，不一会儿大门开开，一大堆警察追了出来，怕得我往西就跑，因为将病好，脚还不很得力，被三四个人给捕了去。一到市党部里，看见还有我们的同学王良骥也在那里，他叫我不要怕，我问他看见有我们学校的同学没有？他说他也没有看见。我真后悔不应该来，义勇军的军帽也丢了，我们每天还要练操呢！

方德曾民国二十一年一月十九日

显然，这份《事情的经过》是打了“埋伏”的，“避重就轻”地把一个精心策划有意为之的行动，描述成了一个临时起意无辜被捕的偶然事件，足见小方的沉稳和机智。一句“我问他看见有我们学校的同学没有？”把他的心思表露无遗。少年老成，巧妙迂回，对抗日义勇军的身份“轻描淡写”，如此“经过”居然瞒过了警局。不久，他们被告诫一番后，未再深究，被北平抗日团体保释出来。由此看来，小方走上救亡道路并不是偶然的。

为此，他被学校降了一年级。1935年6月，方大曾与夏农苔、曹承宪、黄淑清、孙以坚等经济学系的9名同学从中法大学毕业。夏农苔和曹承宪要出国深造，继续求学，其他同学各有规划，而小方要到父亲做事的天津去谋职。

本章图片选自方大曾大学期间旅行、习作、交往等内容，镜头中的小方和师友风华正茂，对未来充满憧憬，拍摄时间约为1930年至1935年。

Because I have just recovered from an illness, I did not shout any slogans. When they went to the municipal KMT office to petition, I went along as an onlooker.

Later, after the gate was closed, many of them smashed the plaque and ran away. I had no idea why they ran, so I waited at the gate to see what was going on. To my surprise, the gate opened and many policemen ran out. I was very scared and ran west. Because I just recovered from an illness, I could not run fast. I was captured by three or four police officers. When I arrived at the police station, I saw Wang Liangji, my classmate, who told me everything was fine. I asked him whether he had seen any other students from our school. He said no. I very much regret coming here today, as I lost my Volunteer Army cap that I needed for my drill tomorrow morning!

Fang Dezeng,

January 19th, 21st year of the Republic of China

Obviously, this description was tactfully manipulated. Xiao Fang described a well-planned and purposeful activity as an impulsive, innocent incident. We see that Xiao Fang was very calm and intelligent. The line "I asked him whether he had seen any other students from our school" sounds very innocent. Despite his youth, Xiao Fang exhibited sophistication and intelligence in describing the event and casually mentioning his association with the Volunteer Army against Japanese aggression. After being admonished, the students were soon bailed out by an anti-Japanese organization in Beiping. Thus, we see that Xiao Fang intentionally chose a path of resisting Japanese aggression and salvaging China from subjugation.

Because of this incident, the school punished Xiao Fang by making him repeat a year. In June of 1935, Fang Dazeng, Xia Nongtai, Cao Chengxian, Huang Shuqing, Sun Yijian, and 4 other students from the Department of Economics graduated from the Lyon Sino-French Institute. Xia Nongtai and Cao Chengxian were continuing their studies abroad while the rest had their own career plans. Xiao Fang was to find a job in Tianjin, where his father worked.

The photos in this chapter are selected from those taken by Fang Dazeng during traveling, practicing photography and socializing. Xiao Fang and his teachers and friends in the photos look young and vigorous, full of expectations for the future. These photos were taken between 1930 and 1935.

东黄城根北街甲 20 号，原中法大学旧址，现为北京市文物保护单位（冯雪松摄于 2016 年）

Old site of the Lyon Sino-French Institute, currently a cultural relic protection site. No. A-20, Donghuangchenggen North Street (photo by Feng Xuesong, 2016).

中法大学教室的基本格局未变（冯瑞濠摄于 2016 年）

A basically unchanged classroom of the Lyon Sino-French Institute (photo by Feng Ruihao, 2016).

1930年秋，方大曾（后立者）考入中法大学文学院经济学系

In the autumn of 1930, Fang Dazeng (standing behind) was admitted by the Department of Economics to the Lyon Sino-French Institute.

中法大学校徽，象征自由、平等、博爱

The emblem of the Lyon Sino-French Institute, representing liberty, equality, and fraternity.

九·一八事变后的小方，参加“反帝大同盟”，编写《反帝新闻》

After the September 18th Incident, Fang Dazeng joined the China Anti-Imperialist League and worked as an editor for *Anti-Imperialist News*.

主编《少年先锋》杂志时的小方（中）和方殷（右二）等人合影（1932 年）

A group photograph of Xiao Fang (middle), Fang Yin (second right), and others when Xiao Fang was co-editor-in-chief of *Youth Pioneer* magazine (1932).

《资本论》最早中文译者之一、大学老师王慎明（左）对方大曾的成长进步影响很大

Wang Shenming (left), a college instructor and one of the earliest Chinese translators of *Das Kapital*, greatly impacted Fang Dazeng's growth and progress.

中法大学女子排球队，小方记录照片的光圈、速度等笔迹留在底片右侧

The women's volleyball team at the Lyon Sino-French Institute, with Xiao Fang's notes about aperture, speed, etc. on the right side of this negative.

在中法大学教书时期的张友渔

Zhang Youyu, when teaching at the Lyon Sino-French Institute.

范文澜先生经常把进步思想带入中法大学的课堂

Fan Wenlan often introduced progressive thought into classrooms at the Lyon Sino-French Institute.

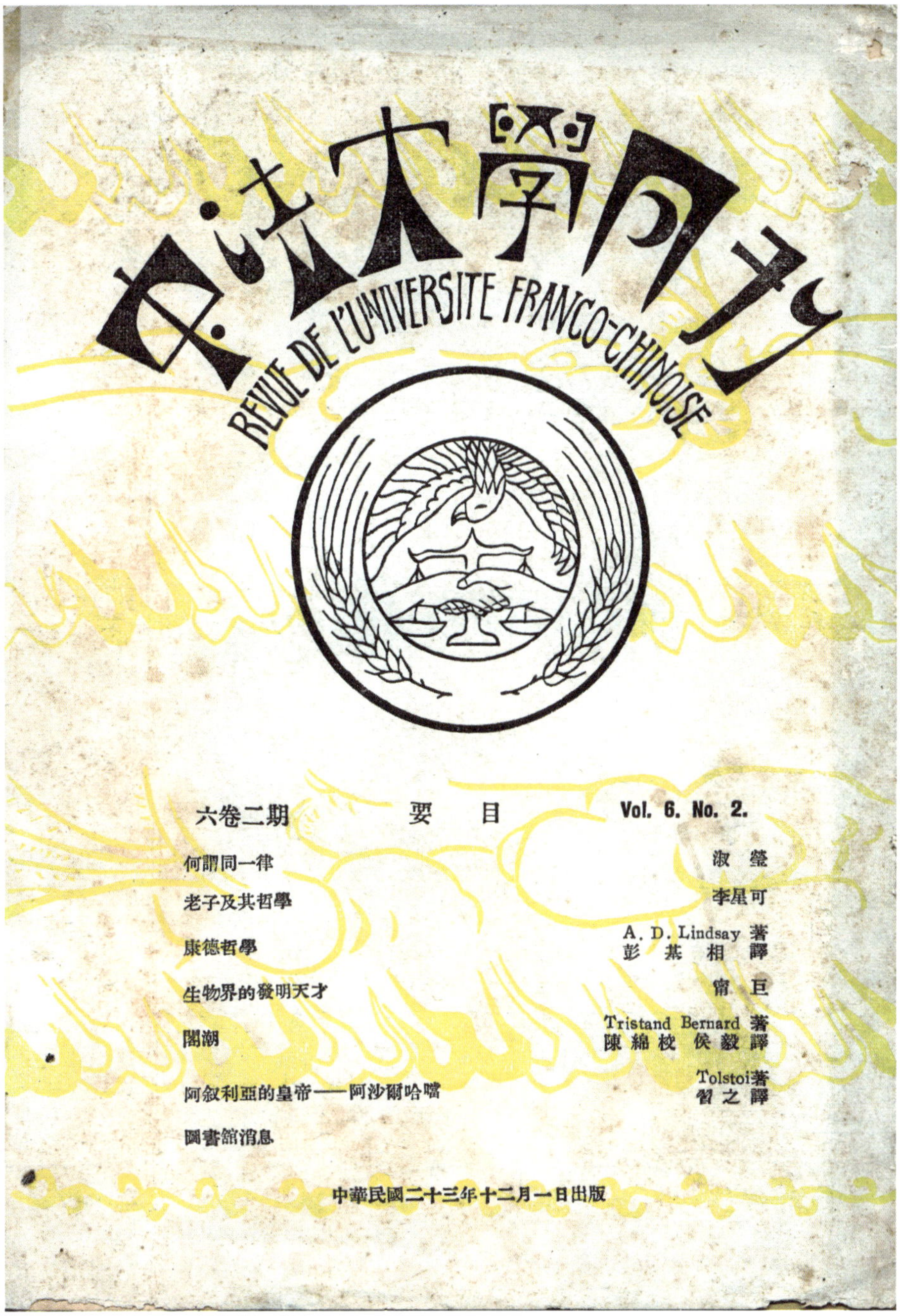
中法大學月刊

REVUE DE L'UNIVERSITE FRANCO-CHINOISE

六卷二期　要目　Vol. 6. No. 2.

何謂同一律	淑瑩
老子及其哲學	李星可
康德哲學	A. D. Lindsay 著 彭基相 譯
生物界的發明天才	甯巨
閣潮	Tristand Bernard 著 陳綿校 侯毅譯
阿叙利亞的皇帝——阿沙爾哈噹	Tolstoi著 習之譯
圖書館消息	

中華民國二十三年十二月一日出版

《中法大学月刊》是学生们认识世界的一扇窗

The *Lyon Sino-French Institute Monthly* was a vehicle for students to learn about the world.

私立中法大學文學院（服爾德學院）學生 以姓氏筆劃繁簡為序

姓名	別號	性別	年歲	籍貫	科系及年級	通信處	電話
王崇恩		男	二五	河北宛平	經濟學系四年級	大中公寓	
王皖瑩		男	二六	江蘇泰縣	法國文學系四年級	北大西齋	
王聯曾		男	二五	山東濟寧	法國文學系四年級	西安門酒醋局八號	
王金綬		男	二六	河北定縣	經濟學系四年級	雙輦胡同二十三號	
王季文		男	二五	雲南昆明	法國文學系三年級	京兆公寓	
王嘉瑞		男	二二	河北宛平	本科一年級	西單大栅欄二十五號	
方德曾		男	二二	江蘇無錫	經濟學系三年級	協和胡同七號	
文雝模		男	二四	江西萍鄉	本科一年級	西城前撒袋胡同一號	
朱淑貞		女	二三	安徽合肥	法國文學系三年級	大栅欄興隆街廿二號	
朱尚英		男	二一	四川江津	本科一年級	西單新皮庫胡同十八號	

王方文朱

四三

48

1934 年中法大学花名册，方德曾名列其中（北京市档案馆提供）

The 1934 roster of the Lyon Sino-French Institute, with Fang Dezeng's name included (provided by the Beijing Municipal Archives).

大学期间，小方经常参加学生爱国运动
During college, Xiao Fang often joined student patriotic movements.

在中法大学伏尔泰学院阅览室

In the reading room of the Voltaire School of the Lyon Sino-French Institute.

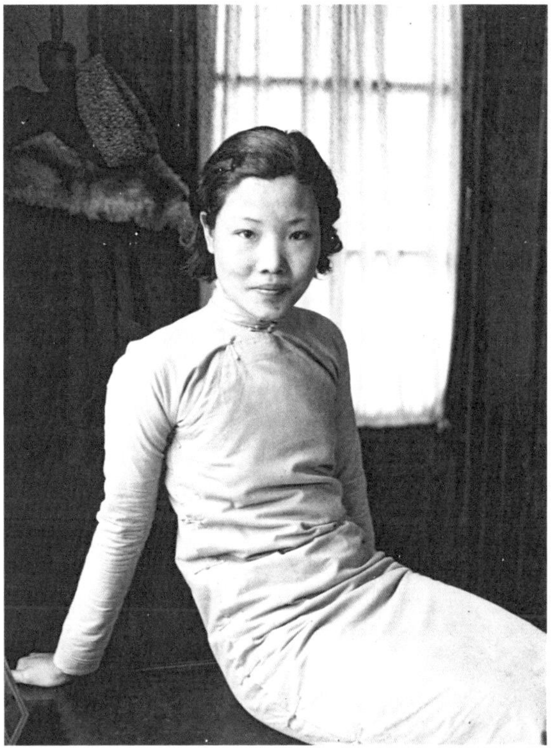

小方拍摄的师友中有些人已经无从知道他们的名姓

These teachers and students, whose names are unknown, were people Xiao Fang often photographed.

小方拍摄的师友中有些人已经无从知道他们的名姓

These teachers and students, whose names are unknown, were people Xiao Fang often photographed.

光与影，大学时期的自拍照（1931 年）
Light and shade. A photo of Xiao Fang during college (photo taken by Fang Dazeng, 1931).

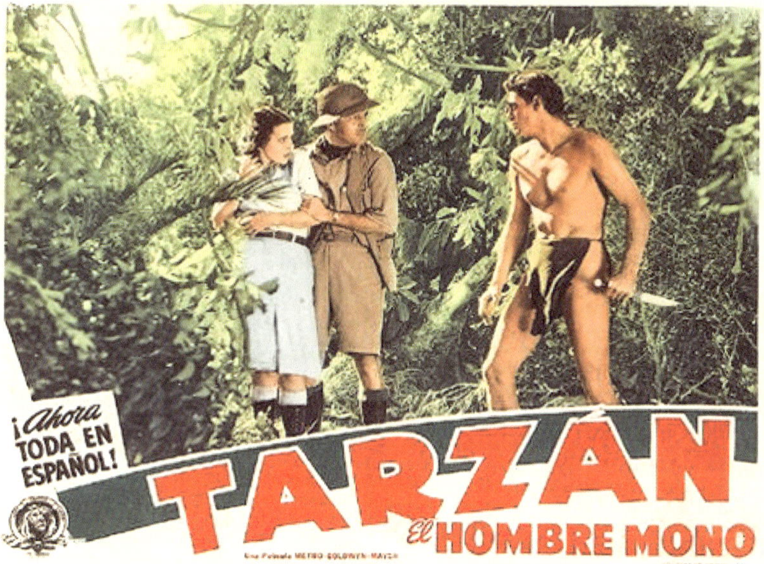

1932 年电影《人猿泰山》在中国上映，主演韦斯穆勒孔武有力，使小方对于正义和力量更加向往

The film *Tarzan the Ape Man* was played in China in 1932. The main character, played by Weissmuller, appeared strong and energetic, which made Xiao Fang long for justice and power even more.

小方在北京西山附近模仿韦斯穆勒的造型自拍照

Xiao Fang imitating Weissmuller's posture (Western Mountain, Beijing, photos taken by Fang Dazeng).

小方与姐夫张孝通（方淑敏丈夫、沈钧儒夫人张象徵的侄子）

Xiao Fang and his brother-in-law Zhang Xiaotong (husband of Fang Shumin, nephew of Zhang Xianghui, who was Shen Junru's wife).

京西千灵山，留有小方的足迹（1931 年 7 月 7 日）

Xiao Fang visited the Qianling Mountain west of Beijing (July 7, 1931).

与同学的北京香山之旅

A trip to Fragrant Hills in Beijing with a classmate.

小方（右中）与进步同学组织读书会，并亲自编写学习研究社会科学理论的讨论提纲，内分哲学、政治经济学和社会主义三个部分（1933 年春）

Xiao Fang (third right) and his progressive classmates formed a reading club. They drafted outlines of discussions to study social science theories, including three sections: philosophy, political economics, and socialism (spring, 1933).

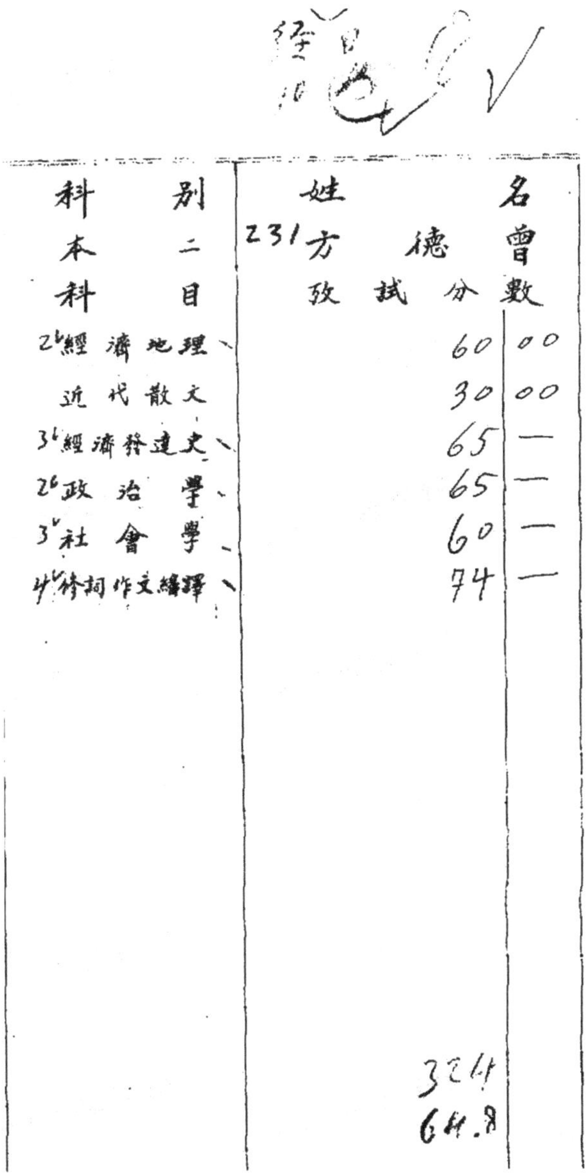

科別	姓名	
本二	231 方德曾	
科目	考試分數	
2 經濟地理	60	00
近代散文	30	00
3 經濟發達史	65	—
2 政治學	65	—
3 社會學	60	—
4 修詞作文編譯	74	—
	324	
	64.8	

大学时期的成绩单（北京市档案馆提供）

Xiao Fang's college transcript (provided by the Beijing Municipal Archives).

小方和同学夏农苔（中）、曹承宪（右一）等在门头沟（原图未剪裁）

Xiao Fang and his classmates, including Xia Nongtai (middle) and Cao Chengxian (first right) in Mentougou (unclipped).

小方（高坐者）与爱国进步教师往来密切

Xiao Fang (sitting above) and patriotic teachers.

未名湖畔博雅塔前留影

A photo by the Weiming Lake and the Boya Pagoda.

清华大学、燕京大学等高校是方大曾常去的地方，图为他拍摄的清华大学西校门

Fang Dazeng often went to universities, including Tsinghua and Yenching universities. This was a photo of his of the western gate of Tsinghua University.

小方在三一八烈士公墓前。同学高云晖忆述："方德曾是共青团的活跃分子，他时常向我输送一些《红色中华》、英文《苏联建设》画报及海参崴、巴黎出版的一些革命书刊，还给我介绍东安市场的丹桂商场一家旧书店的老板，从那里可以秘密买到翻印的一些党内书刊，如《中国大革命史》《肃反》等。"

Xiao Fang in front of the March 18th Martyrs' Cemetery. As recalled by his classmate, Gao Yunhui: "Fang Dezeng was an active Communist Youth League member. He introduced me to the *Red China* newspaper, the English pictorial magazine, *USSR in Construction*, and revolutionary books published in Vladivostok and Paris. He also introduced me to an old bookstore owner in the Dangui Store at the Dong'an Market, where I could secretly buy reprinted books of the CPC, such as *History of the Great Chinese Revolution*, *Elimination of Counterrevolutionaries*."

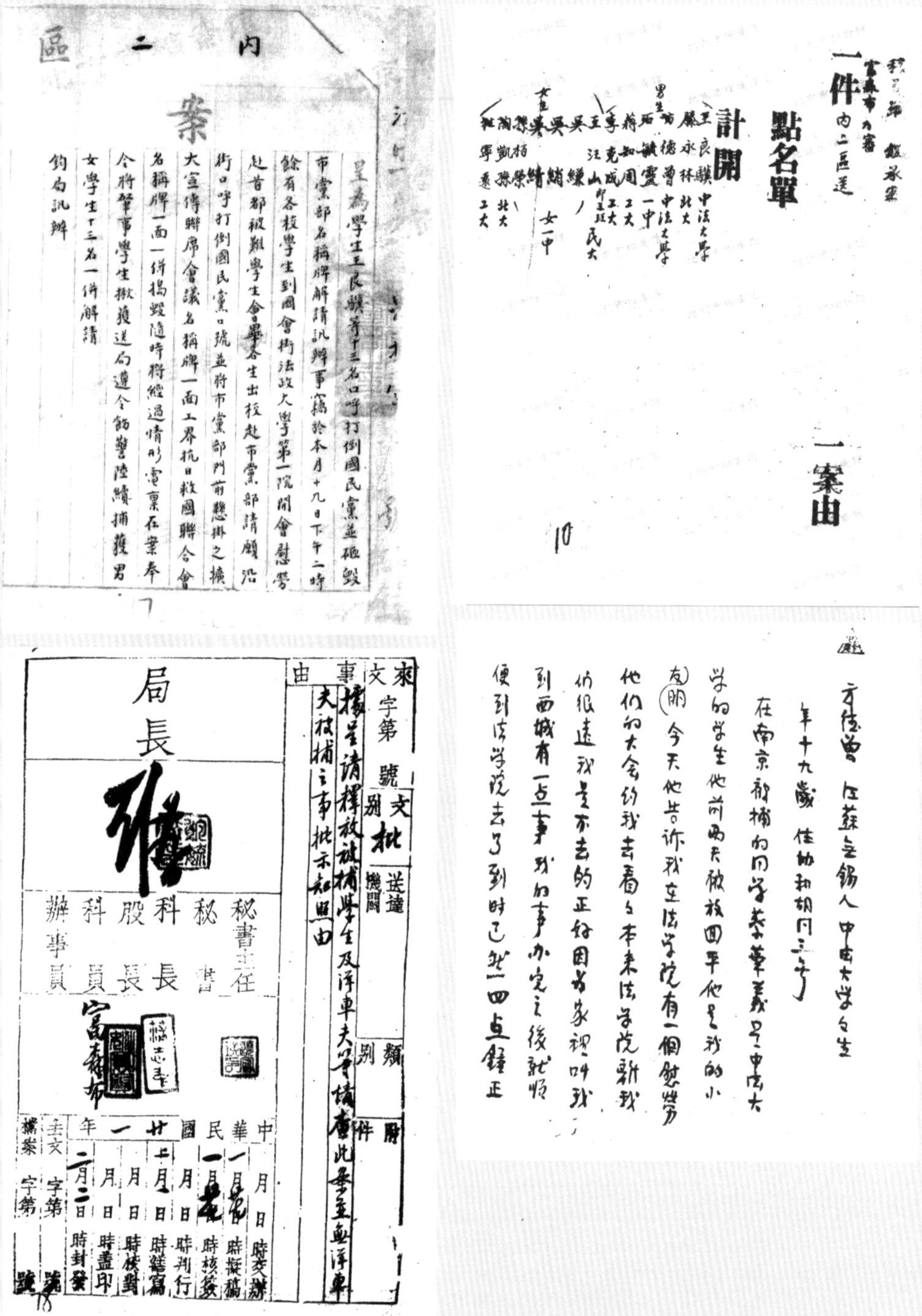

內二區

案

呈為學生王良驥等十三名口呼打倒國民黨並砸毀市黨部名稱牌解請訊辦事竊於本月十九日下午二時餘有各校學生到國會街法政大學第一院開會慰勞赴首都被難學生會畢各生出校赴市黨部請願沿街口呼打倒國民黨口號並將市黨部門前懸掛之擴大宣傳聯席會議名稱牌一面工界抗日救國聯合會名稱牌一面一併揭毀隨時將經過情形電稟在案奉令將肇事學生撤獲送局遵令飭警陸續捕獲男女學生十三名一併解請

鈞局訊辦

點名單

計開

案由

局長

秘書主任

方大曾 江蘇無錫人 中法大學學生 年十九歲 住協和胡同三號

在南京被捕的同学李華義是中法大学的学生 他前两天被放回平 他是我的小朋友 今天他告诉我在法学院有一個慰劳他們的大会 約我去看看 本來法学院离我的很遠 我是不去的 正好因為家里叫我到西城有一点事 我的事办完之後就顺便到法学院去了 到时已經一四点鐘正

1932 年 1 月 19 日，小方因参加抗日请愿游行与其他 12 人被捕，其案卷现存北京档案馆。他从未向亲友提起过这一经历，数天后，被北平抗日团体保释，学校给予其“降级一年”处分

On January 19, 1932, Xiao Fang and 12 other students were arrested because they attended a parade and petitioned for the fight against Japanese aggression. The file for this case is currently collected by the Beijing Municipal Archives. Xiao Fang never mentioned this experience to his family and friends. Days later, he was bailed out by an anti-Japanese organization in Beijing. The school forced him to repeat a year as punishment.

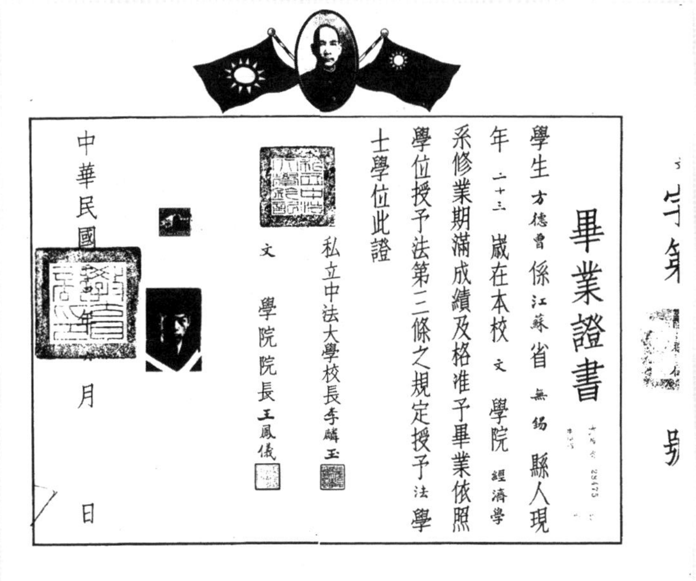

畢業證書

學生方德曾係江蘇省無錫縣人現年二十三歲在本校文學院經濟學系修業期滿成績及格准予畢業依照學位授予法第三條之規定授予法學士學位此證

私立中法大學校長李麟玉

文學院院長王鳳儀

中華民國　年　月　日

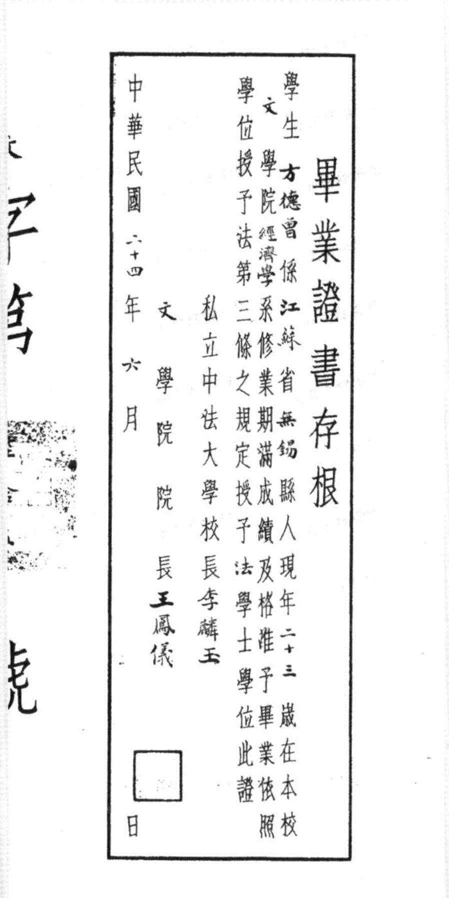

畢業證書存根

學生方德曾係江蘇省無錫縣人現年二十三歲在本校文學院經濟學系修業期滿成績及格准予畢業依照學位授予法第三條之規定授予法學士學位此證

私立中法大學校長李麟玉

文學院院長王鳳儀

中華民國二十四年六月　日

方大曾中法大学毕业证及存根（1935年6月）

Fang Dazeng's Lyon Sino-French Institute graduation diploma and its office copy (June, 1935).

1935 年 6 月，大学毕业前夕，即将步入社会的小方

Xiao Fang, prior to college graduation, about to work (June, 1935).

第三章 **天津时光**

Chapter Three: Life in Tianjin

走私的经营者，在这地带建筑了好多大小不同的席篷，当作临时的货栈，也都竖起各自的商旗，戴河口有一个“旭株公司”英文音为“Asahi”，所以他的商旗上就写着一个大大的“A”字。私货来时就将旗升起，搬卸完毕后即降下来。像这种的席篷，现在还继续建造新的，以便容纳更大量的“需要”。席篷的体积，较大的长约二百尺，宽约三十尺，高约二十五尺。但货物上了岸不一定要往篷里搬，大多还是放置在露天地方，因为很快就可以装好大车运到北戴河车站去了，除非有特别情形，货物是不需要在这里停留的。北戴河，留守营，昌黎，滦县等车站，都有“运输会社”或“转运代理店”一类的机关，这种机关，和北宁路各火车站上的日本宪兵驻守所一样，飘扬着“光荣的”太阳旗，做着这“文明”的事业。

——方大曾《天津通讯 走私在海滨》

Smugglers built many mat sheds of different sizes here in Tianjin as temporary warehouses and set up their own business flags. At the estuary of the Dai River, there was a company named Asahi with a big “A” on its flag. When smuggled goods arrived, the flag was raised. After the goods were unloaded, the flag was lowered. They are building more sheds like this to cater to greater “needs.” Larger sheds were around 66.66 meters long, 10 meters wide, and 8 meters deep. However, once unloaded, goods would not necessarily be carried into the sheds. Most were placed in the open air because they would soon be loaded and transported to Beidaihe Station. Unless there was a special situation, goods would not be held here. In the Beidaihe, Liushouying, Changli, and Luan County stations, there were offices called transportation firms or transshipment agencies. These agencies, like Japanese military police stations, were doing “civilized” undertakings, with the “glorious” Flag of Rising Sun fluttering.

Report from Tianjin: Smuggling on the Beach, by Fang Dazeng

方大曾1935年大学毕业后来到天津。当时，《大公报》《益世报》等在全国范围内影响很大，著名记者范长江就在天津《大公报》供职。

因为彼此相熟，北平基督教青年会少年部主任高尚仁把小方推荐给从前的同事杨肖彭，任天津基督教青年会少年部职员。

不久，小方与吴寄寒和燕京大学新闻系毕业的周勉之等进步的青年知识分子，在海河之滨成立了“中外新闻学社”，其宗旨是通过研究新闻和新闻写作，向国内外传播抵御外侮及学生运动的图文报道。由于关注时局，贴近民生，短短的时间内，新闻学社发布的消息和图片被上海、北平、天津等地的报刊大量采用，迅速在国内外新闻界产生了较大的影响。

有资料显示，中外新闻学社是在中国共产党的指示下成立的。当时，方大曾是中外新闻学社唯一的摄影记者，在他尘封的作品中，能看到80多年前天津的海河、海轮、万国桥和各行各业的劳动者，还有关于“海河浮尸”等热点报道。

在小方留下的文字里，没有发现他对于照相器材的使用心得，也没有发现他关于拍照的经验体会。他似乎更为关注被拍摄的内容，而不是设备的好坏和构图的美观。他喜欢简单和直接，不喜欢复杂和婉转。平视是方大曾关注社会和民生的视角。他有很多人像作品，都是一些没有留下名姓的人，但我们今天能看出这些人的瞬间表情，从神态中能看出摄影者和他们之间隐含着彼此的尊重和交流。

对于摄影的态度，小方曾经在文章中，把绥远跟河北的老百姓做过比较，绥远的百姓喜欢和他们的牲畜一起合影，河北的呢，一见相机就远远地跑开，生怕把他们的“运气”照走了。尽管如此，方大曾还是想尽办法接近他们，尤其是面对底层的劳动者。这些经验来自于他和家门口老宋等车夫们的交流，来自于他对于在生死线上的采煤工的了解，更来自于他东奔西走一路得来的见识。

站在风景区的山头上，或者是海岸上，往西南望去，总可见到几只火轮浮

After graduation from college in 1935, Fang Dazeng went to Tianjin. At that time, newspapers such as the *Ta Kung Pao* and *Yishi Daily* were very influential nationwide. During this period, Fan Changjiang, a famous journalist, worked for the *Ta Kung Pao* in Tianjin.

Because they knew each other well, Gao Shangren, Director of the Youth Department at the Chinese Young Men's Christian Association (YMCA) in Beiping, recommended Xiao Fang to Yang Xiaopeng, one of his previous colleagues, to work for the Youth Department of YMCA in Tianjin.

Before long, Xiao Fang, Wu Jihan, Zhou Mianzhi (who graduated from Yenching University with a journalism major), and other progressive young intellectuals founded the Chinese-Foreign Journalism Society on the beach of the Hai River. Their mission was to spread, both at home and abroad, photos and reports about the fight against foreign aggression and about student movements through the study of journalism and news writing. Because of their close attention to current affairs and its relation to people's livelihood, within a short period, a lot of news and pictures released by the Journalism Society were adopted by newspapers in Shanghai, Beiping, and Tianjin. They quickly made a great impact in journalism circles worldwide.

Data indicates that the Chinese-Foreign Journalism Society was founded under instructions of the Communist Party of China. At that time, Fang Dazeng was the only press photographer in the Society. In his dust-laden works, we still see, over 80 years later, the Hai River, seagoing vessels, Wanguo Bridge, and laborers from all trades in Tianjin. We also see reports on hot issues, such as "floating corpses on the Hai River."

Among the words left behind by Xiao Fang, there is no mention of his experience using photographic apparatus or composing photos. He seemed to care more about content than he did equipment or composition. He preferred simplicity and straightforwardness over complexity and ambiguity. From a horizontal perspective, Fang looked into society and people's livelihood. He took many photographs of people, most of whose names are unknown, but today, these photos show their expressions at that captured moment in time. From their expressions, we see the underlying respect and communication between these people and their photographer.

As for people's attitude toward photography, in one article, Xiao Fang compared the commoners in Suiyuan and Hebei. Commoners in Suiyuan would joyfully take photos with their livestock. However, those in Hebei would flee upon seeing a camera, worrying photos would "steal their luck." Even so, Fang Dazeng tried his

在遥遥的海面上，那就是走私的景况。方大曾在通讯《走私在海滨》中写道，出了风景区，往西走过一条小溪，有个村庄叫河东寨，“河东寨”想必就是指戴河之东的意思。这是“参观”走私的一个起点，从此往西去，那里有无数的“奇观”供你鉴赏，其实这与其说是走私倒不如说是自由贸易了。别看这里没有那些现代化的码头设备，但这却干着“超现代”的勾当。小方用照片和文字向公众揭露日本侵略者搜刮中国的野心。在小方的作品里找不到一点儿虚浮的痕迹，他的作品几乎都是以纪实的方式完成的，可是来自镜框的感觉又使人觉得这些作品的构图是精心设计的，这里将快门按下时的瞬间感觉与构图时的胸有成竹合二为一。

本章图片选自方大曾天津工作期间的拍摄成果，这一时期他更加关注底层命运和社会现实，拍摄时间约为 1935 年夏至 1936 年春。

best to get close to them, especially laborers at the bottom of society. These experiences came from his conversations with carters, his knowledge about miners on the verge of death, and, more importantly, his travels.

Standing on a hill, or on the coast, while looking southwest, one could always spot several cargo ships floating on the boundless sea. They were, in fact, smuggler ships. In his report *Smuggling on the Beach*, Fang Dazeng wrote that west of the scenic spot and across a stream, there was a village called Hedong (literally, river east). Hedong must refer to the area east of the Dai River. This was a starting point to "pay a visit" to the smuggling areas and activities. Moving westward from here, you could encounter numerous "wonders." Seemingly, people were conducting free trade rather than smuggling. Even without modernized wharf facilities, people here were conducting illicit business beyond the times. Xiao Fang used his photos and words to disclose the Japanese invaders' ambition to plunder China. In his works, there was no trace of falsehood or fickleness. Almost all his works were documented. Yet, these works, framed by a lens, seemed carefully designed in composition. Fang Dazeng was highly skilled at capturing the perfect instant to take a photograph with a thoroughly planned composition in mind.

The photos in this chapter are selected from those taken by Fang Dazeng when he worked in Tianjin. During this period, he paid more attention to the life of the underclass and the real look of the society. These photos were taken between the summer of 1935 and the spring of 1936.

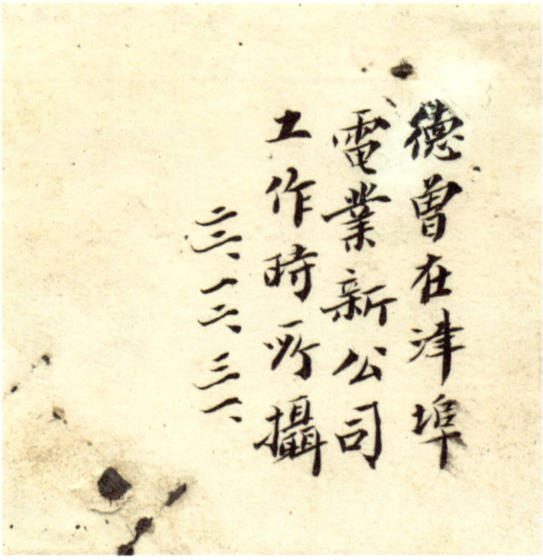

小方在天津的最早留影，照片背面有父亲方振东的字迹（原件）

The earliest photo of Xiao Fang in Tianjin, with his father Fang Zhendong's words on the back (original).

因父亲工作变动，从少年起小方就经常往来海河两岸

Because of the changes in his father's career, as a teenager, Xiao Fang often traveled between the two banks of the Hai River.

天津基督教青年会旧址，小方毕业后的第一个工作地点，现为少年宫（资料图）

The old site of the Chinese Young Men's Christian Association (YMCA) in Tianjin. This is the first workplace of Xiao Fang after graduation, currently used as the Tianjin Children's Palace (archive photo).

青年会室内篮球馆现已成为少年宫的排练场（冯雪松摄于 2016 年）

The basketball court of the YMCA has been converted to a rehearsal room for the Children's Palace (photo by Feng Xuesong, 2016).

青年会大堂、旧地面、楼梯和小方工作过的少年部（孙楠摄于 2016 年）

The YMCA main hall, with the old floor, stairs, and Office of the Youth Department where Xiao Fang once worked (photos by Sun Nan, 2016).

本會幹事及職員

總幹事 陳錫三
會員部 王子英（主任） 王錫昌 王雲波
智育部 王正路（主任） 岳世楚
少年部 楊肖彭（主任） 方大曾 陳鴻保
體育部 毛駿民（主任） 錢靈甫
事務科 鍾嗣庭（主任） 吳世昌
文牘科 桂逢伯（主任） 莫家鼐
會計科 邵杏題（主任）

天津基督教青年会花名册，方大曾任少年部职员

Roster of the YMCA in Tianjin, with Fang Dazeng as Secretary of the Youth Department.

初到天津工作的小方（左二）与友人（1935 年秋）

Xiao Fang (second left), who had just started work in Tianjin, with his friends (autumn, 1935).

小方镜头中的天津万国桥

The Wanguo Bridge in Tianjin photographed by Xiao Fang.

如今的天津万国桥（孙楠摄于 2016 年）

The present Wanguo Bridge in Tianjin (photo by Sun Nan, 2016).

天津市立图书馆（1935 年冬）
Tianjin Municipal Library (winter, 1935).

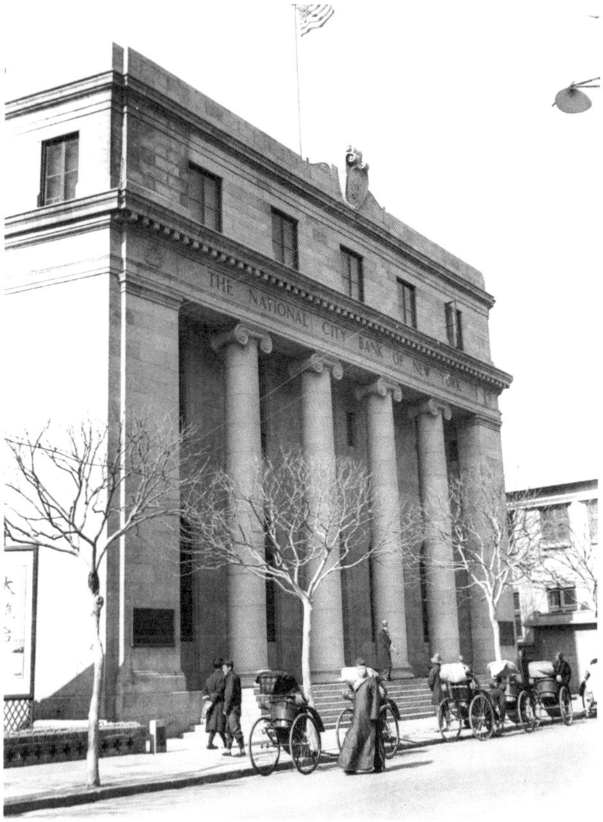

花旗银行
The Tianjin branch of the National City Bank of New York.

中原百货

Central Plains Department Store.

海河码头
A wharf by the Hai River.

劝业场

Tianjin Quanye Mall.

天津街头

Street in Tianjin.

岸边接驳

Barges by the bank.

小方（左一）与吴寄寒（右三）等人成立中外新闻学社

Xiao Fang (first left) and Wu Jihan (third right) co-founded, with others, the Chinese-Foreign Journalism Society.

中外新闻学社所在大厦入口（小方摄于 1936 年）

Entrance of the building where the Chinese-Foreign Journalism Society was located (by Xiao Fang, 1936).

同一位置，80 年后实地寻访（冯雪松摄于 2016 年）

The same location 80 years later (photo by Feng Xuesong, 2016).

海河纤夫

Boat trackers by the Hai River.

齐步向前（1937 年 6 月 24 日北平第一届摄影联合展览会，小方的参展作品 ）

Striding Forward (a work of Xiao Fang at the 1st Beiping Open Photography Exhibition, June 24, 1937).

棉花转运

Transshipment of cotton.

穿过浅滩

Wading across the shoal.

忙碌的码头

Busy wharf.

彼岸遥望

Looking into the distance from the other side of the river.

谋生在海河边上

Making a living on the bank of the Hai River.

吃黑面的人扛白面（1937 年 6 月 24 日北平第一届摄影联合展览会，小方的参展作品）

White Flour Carriers Feeding on Black Chaff (a work of Xiao Fang at the 1st Beiping Open Photography Exhibition, June 24, 1937).

《吃黑面的人扛白面》原图，上有小方画的剪裁线

Original photo of *White Flour Carriers Feeding on Black Chaff* (with clip lines drawn by Xiao Fang).

天津，万国桥，丰收的棉（1935 年冬）
A good cotton harvest (Wanguo Bridge, Tianjin, winter of 1935).

缝穷者（载于《玫瑰画报》，1936 年）

A poor old lady makes a living by sewing (published in *Rose Pictorial Magazine*, 1936).

扛白面的人

White flour carriers.

中外新闻学社所在的原新华信托大厦，天津工作期间，小方的摄影和通讯作品经常由此发出（资料图）

The Xinhua Trust Building, where the Chinese-Foreign Journalism Society was located. When Xiao Fang worked in Tianjin, his photos and news reports were often published from here. (archive photo)

无忧虑的日子

Carefree life.

淘气（1937年6月24日北平第一届摄影联合展览会，小方的参展作品）

Naughty Kids (a work of Xiao Fang at the 1st Beiping Open Photography Exhibition, June 24, 1937).

北戴河，走私货栈（1935 年）
A smuggler's mat shed in Beidaihe (1935).

起航

Setting sail.

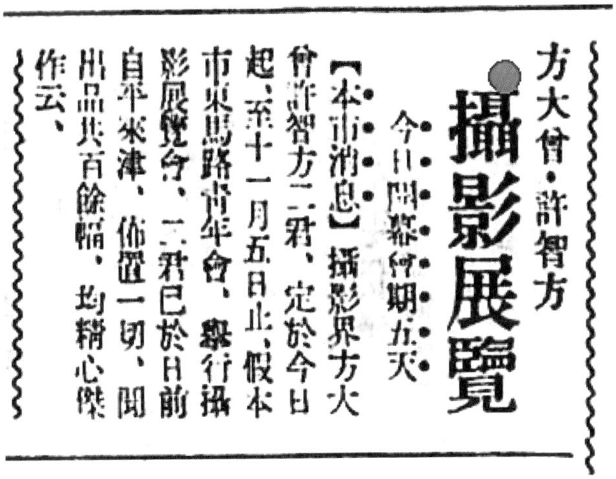

方大曾・許智方

攝影展覽

今日開幕會期五天

【本市消息】攝影界方大曾許智方二君、定於今日起、至十一月五日止、假本市東馬路青年會、舉行攝影展覽會、二君已於日前自平來津、佈置一切、聞出品共百餘幅、均精心傑作云、

11月4日 (中華民國二十五年即丙子年九月二十一日) 第7364號　14 / 14

方大曾、許智方

聯合影展觀賞記

○水皮○

、方君的作品之主題，是描寫現實的生活與勞工的活動，雖然題材方面也許被高貴的人目爲醜惡，但經過他的鏡頭的渲染，便成爲美麗的畫面，例如「頂天立地的英雄漢」，「中國勞動者的命運」，「飢渴所迫」，「吃黑麵的人抗白麵」以及農家的生活寫實等幅，都是他的力作，使人看了要引起人的同情或是興奮，每張畫面中心意識都極尖銳的表現出來，他是一個喜歡探險的青年，有着沉毅的意志和熱烈的情緒，爲了滿足他冒險，放棄了發掘出優的位置，而冒着西北風去作報道等的徒步旅行，除了用文字紀述外，更用照相機攝取各地的風光和社會現象。「介利塔的壯

，亦一個分明的印象，就是方許二君的作風有着顯然的分野，但決不是描寫程度上或時間上的差別，而是說他們代表兩種相對而且並存的思想與意識，按美學的觀點來解釋，許君的作品是表現着「秀麗」，「典雅」的柔性美，方君的作品，却是表現着「雄壯」，「勁健」的剛性美，按着他們的生活地位而言，恰又合於「駿馬秋風冀北，杏花春雨江南」兩句古詩裏所象徵的兩種美的類型。

他認爲攝影是現階段的新聞事業中最好的報導工具或抗爭的武器，所以他的視野展開，轉向勞苦大衆的生活，去發掘廣大材料的資源，他在門頭溝煤礦中攝的「光」，作者

1936 年 11 月，天津《益世报》刊登方大曾、许智方摄影展讯和展评，文中称小方“有着沉毅的意志和热烈的情绪”

In November of 1936, *Yishi Daily* (Tianjin) published news of, and commentary on, Fang Dazeng and Xu Zhifang's joint photography exhibition, saying Xiao Fang had a "stern will and strong enthusiasm."

大公报社旧址，小方曾来此联系发稿。多年后，范长江回忆，曾在编辑部见到过他的名片（孙楠摄于 2016 年）

The old site of the *Ta Kung Pao* office. Xiao Fang once came here to inquire about publication. Years later, as recalled by Fan Changjiang, he saw Xiao Fang's business card in the editorial office (photo by Sun Nan, 2016).

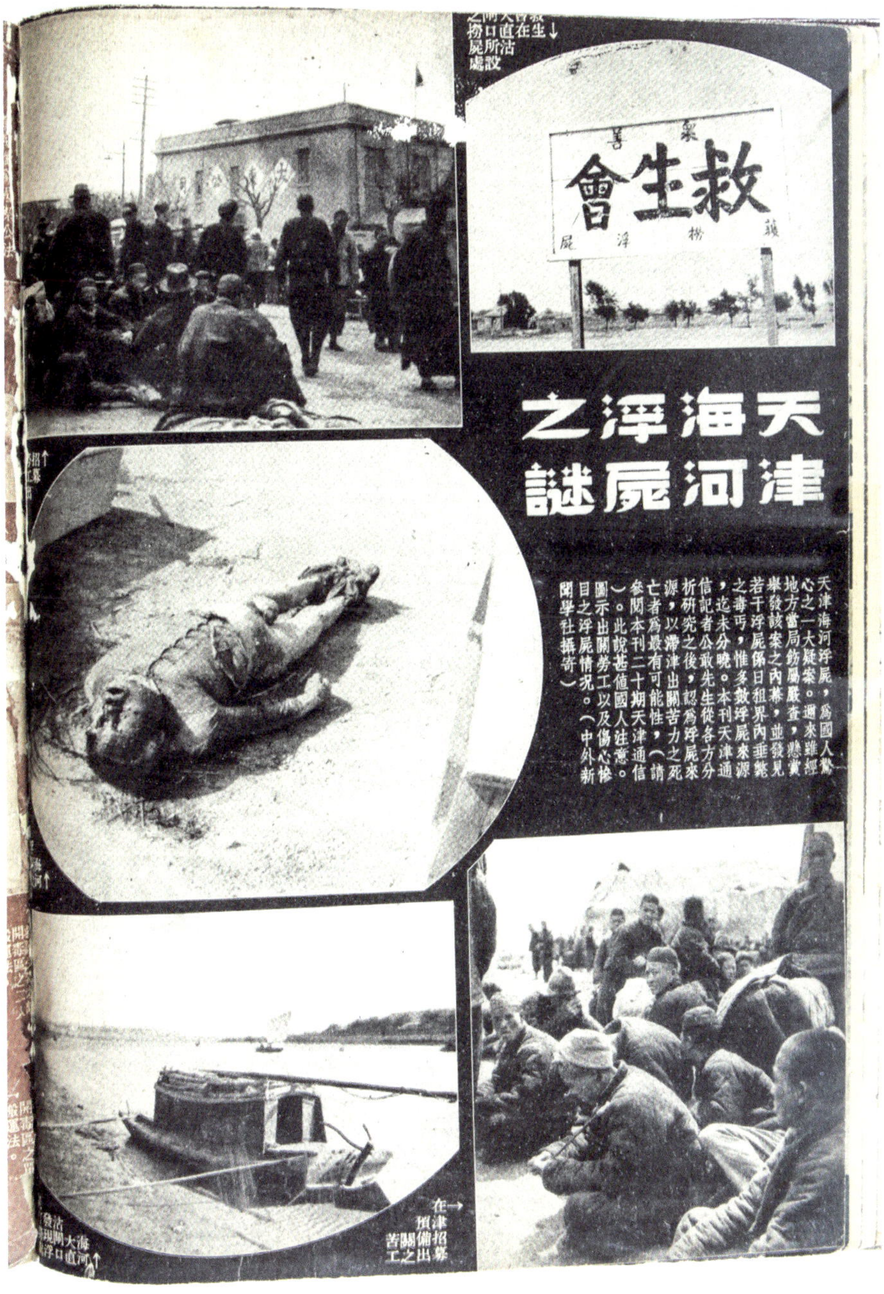
天津海河浮屍之謎

天津海河浮屍，爲國人驚心之一大疑案。邇來雖經地方當局飭屬嚴查，懸賞舉發該案之內幕，並發見若干浮屍係日租界內垂斃之毒丐，惟多數浮屍來源，迄未分曉。本刊天津通信記者公敢先生從各方分析研究之後，認爲浮屍來源，以滯津出關苦力之死亡者爲最有可能性，（請參閱本刊二十期天津通信）。此說甚值國人注意。圖示出關勞工以及傷心慘目之浮屍情況。（中外新聞學社攝寄）

方大曾发表在上海《申报》第 2 卷第 22 期的《天津海河浮尸之谜》

Secret of Floating Corpses on the Hai River in Tianjin, by Xiao Fang (*Shun Pao*, Shanghai, No. 22, Vol. 2).

天津，新兴工厂
New factory in Tianjin.

北戴河之滨
Beach in Beidaihe.

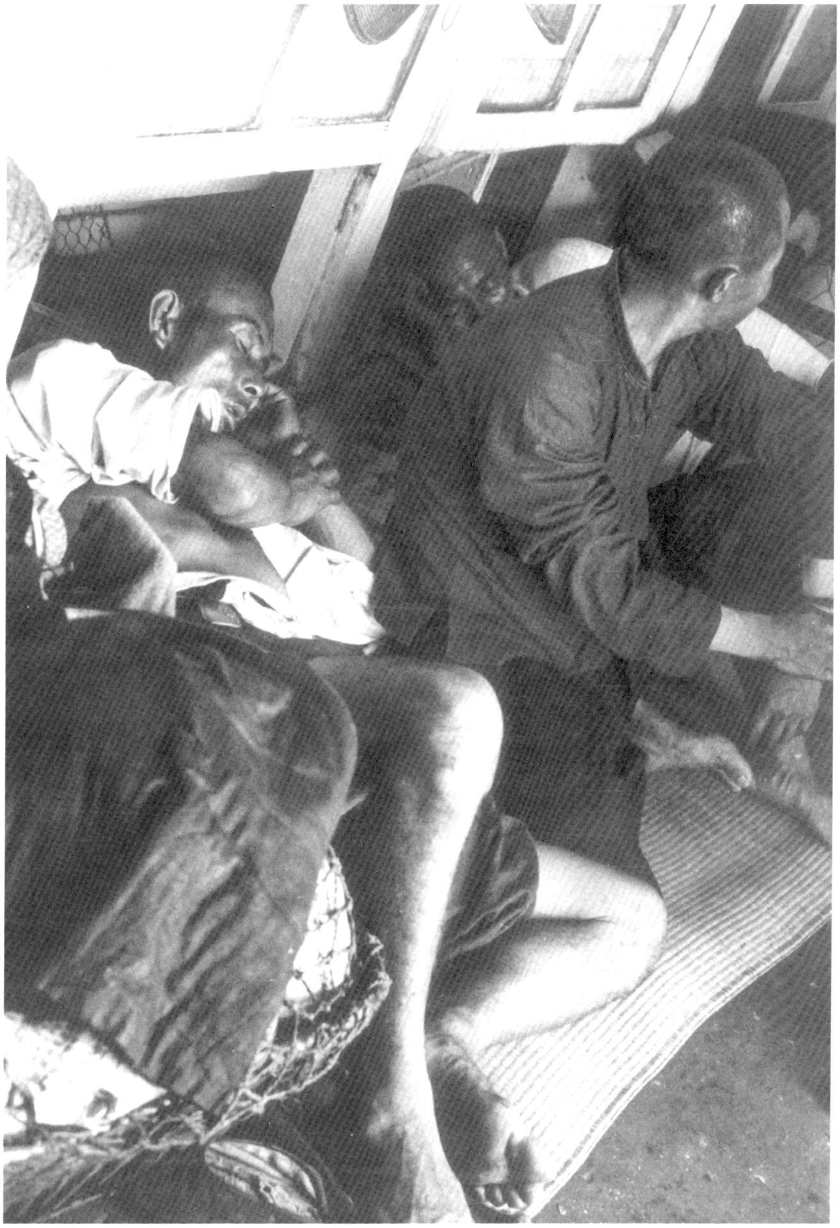

晌午，简单的休息
A casual nap at noon.

早晨，待发的船

A ship that will depart in the morning.

码头，劳动间歇，片刻的沉思

A brief period of contemplation by a wharf laborer during a break.

天津的夜晚（1936 年春）

Night in Tianjin (spring, 1936).

第四章 行走与记录

Chapter Four: Traveling and Recording

记者过南口时，曾遇见两个青年农人，身上背着与记者同样简单的行李，迎面走来向我打听门头沟的去向。问他们详情，则云来自怀来县，因本县无法为生，所以去门头沟煤矿谋一个“背煤”的活儿。从怀来到南口是一百华里，他们已走了一整天。被农村经济破产逼走了的这两位可爱的青年，不知这当夜将宿于何处，更不能预料他们将来的命运！记者在察境内几段徒步的旅程上，遇到这种情形很多，农民们都是异口同声地说不能聊生。又有一次，在新保安附近，和两个扒草根的小孩谈话，知道他们因为粮食不足，只得捡些草根充饥，这种草根，名为“苦菜”。恐怕城市的人从未听见过吧。此外，随时随地遇到的老年乞丐，亦不在少数。察哈尔的农村，也正是中国农村的一个代表，破产情形的缩影，年青的逃向都市去找工作，年幼的勉强在农村挣扎着，年老的则只有等着饿死。

——方大曾《察哈尔视察记》

When I passed Nankou, I met two young peasants carrying simple luggage like mine. They walked up to me and asked how to get to Mentougou. After we talked, I found out they were from Huailai County. Because they could not sustain their life there, they went to work as coal carriers in the Mentougou Coal Mine. It was 50km from Huailai to Nankou. They had walked an entire day. I didn't know where these two young men, driven from home by poverty, could rest that night or what their future would be! I traveled on foot to inspect this area and encountered many people like them. The peasants all said their life could not be harder. One day, I talked to two children who were digging grass roots near Xinbaoan. Due to lack of food, they had to live off such grass roots, known as "bitter herbs." I was afraid no one in the city had ever heard of this. I saw old beggars everywhere, so many! Villages in Chahar were the best examples of Chinese villages, epitomes of bankrupt economies. In these villages, the young were fleeing to cities for jobs, the small struggling to survive, and the old waiting to starve to death.

Inspection of Chahar, by Fang Dazeng

在北平青年会工作期间，小方成为少年部干事

When he worked at the Chinese Young Men's Christian Association (YMCA) in Beiping, Xiao Fang was Secretary of the Youth Department.

1936 年年初，小方从天津回到北平，任基督教青年会少年部干事。部门主任是相识多年的高尚仁，对他的才华非常欣赏，会员和孩子们都喜欢他，彼此关系非常融洽。"大家都听他的，所以就聘他当了干事"，当时，少年部会员多达 900 人。

在少年部的楼厅内悬挂着"四愿八句"愿词：道德高尚、思想清洁、学习进步、知识发达、精神活泼、身体健康、广交朋友、服务社会。其宗旨是发扬德、智、体、群"四育"精神，培养学生健全人格，丰富课余生活。少年部还成立了"四育养成团"，将会员中自愿参加的学生，按年龄分成若干团组，每团 10 到 20 个人不等，聘请品学兼优的人做领袖。小方曾担任过成绩突出的"光明"A、B 两个团的领袖，在遗留的私人照片中，就有一张他带领光明团的学生在小汤山活动时的留影，照片背后，还有他写的团员名字的笔迹。除了组织团员们参加郊游和球赛等活动，小方还与他们讨论有关品德方面的问题，比如行为举止、言谈修养、尊敬父母等等，他不只是传授知识的教员，还是无私无畏的榜样和引领人生正途的向导。

1936 年 6、7 月间，小方受《生活星期刊》等杂志之约，前往山西、河北、内蒙古（原晋察绥地区）采访，拍摄了许多底层民众的生活劳动状态，并发表数篇旅行通讯。

本章照片选自 1935 年至 1936 年方大曾的几次旅行采访，期间，他一边拍照一边撰写通讯，收获颇多。

Early in 1936, Xiao Fang returned from Tianjin to Beiping and served as Secretary of the Youth Department at the Chinese Young Men's Christian Association (YMCA). The director of his department was Gao Shangren, who had known Xiao Fang for years. Gao thought highly of Xiao Fang's talent, and the members and children loved him. Xiao Fang and Gao enjoyed a very close relationship. "Everyone listens to him, so he's elected Secretary," Gao said. At that time, there were about 900 members in the Youth Department.

Hanging on the balcony of the Youth Department was the motto "Maintaining integrity, purifying thought, making progress, enriching knowledge, remaining innovative, keeping fit, making friends, and serving society." The aim of the Youth Department was to promote student morality, intelligence, physical health, and team spirit (known as the four merits) for overall development and an enriched extracurricular life. The Youth Department set up the Four-Merit Groups. Among YMCA members, students could voluntarily join the groups, categorized by age. Each group had 10-20 members and a supervisor who excelled at both conduct and learning. Xiao Fang once worked as supervisor of the "Light" Groups A and B, making excellent achievements. There is a private photo of him and students of the Light Group when he led them on Xiaotang Mountain. On the back of the photo, there were students' names written by Xiao Fang. In addition to organizing members to participate in outings and ball games, Xiao Fang also discussed morality with them, such as codes of conduct, speaking art, and filial piety. He was not only a teacher imparting knowledge, but also a fearless role model and an insightful, upright guide to these students.

During June and July of 1936, Xiao Fang was invited by magazines, including *Life Weekly*, to visit Shanxi, Hebei, and Inner Mongolia (former Shanxi-Chahar-Suiyuan Region) to conduct interviews. While there, he took photos of the life and work of many common people and published several travel reports.

The photos in this chapter are selected from those taken by Fang Dazeng during his trips to do interviews between 1935 and 1936. During this period, he took photos and wrote news, with a great number of fruits yielded.

1936年春，颐和园，小方转任北平基督教青年会少年部干事，手持福伦达相机

In the spring of 1936, at the Summer Palace, Xiao Fang worked as Secretary of the Youth Department of the Chinese Young Men's Christian Association (YMCA) in Beiping, with a Voigtlander camera in hand.

福伦达相机，20 世纪 30 年代德国产，与小方使用的同款（冯雪松摄于 2016 年）

A Voigtlander camera, made in Germany in the 1930s, same as Xiao Fang's camera (photo by Feng Xuesong, 2016).

八达岭，长城脚下的小贩

Vendors below the Badaling Great Wall.

北京，玉泉山，玉峰塔
The Jade Peak Pagoda on Yuquan Mountain, Beijing.

河北，平绥路上（1936 年 6 月）
The Beiping-Suiyuan Railway, Hebei Province (June, 1936).

劳力的午休

Noon break for the laborers.

青龙桥车站，詹天佑像

Zhan Tianyou’s statue at Qinglongqiao Station.

《平绥路沿线》原载《生活星期刊》第一卷第 26 号，1936 年 11 月 28 日出版

Photo series entitled Along the Beiping-Suiyuan Railway, originally published in Life Weekly, No. 26, Vol. 1, November 28, 1936.

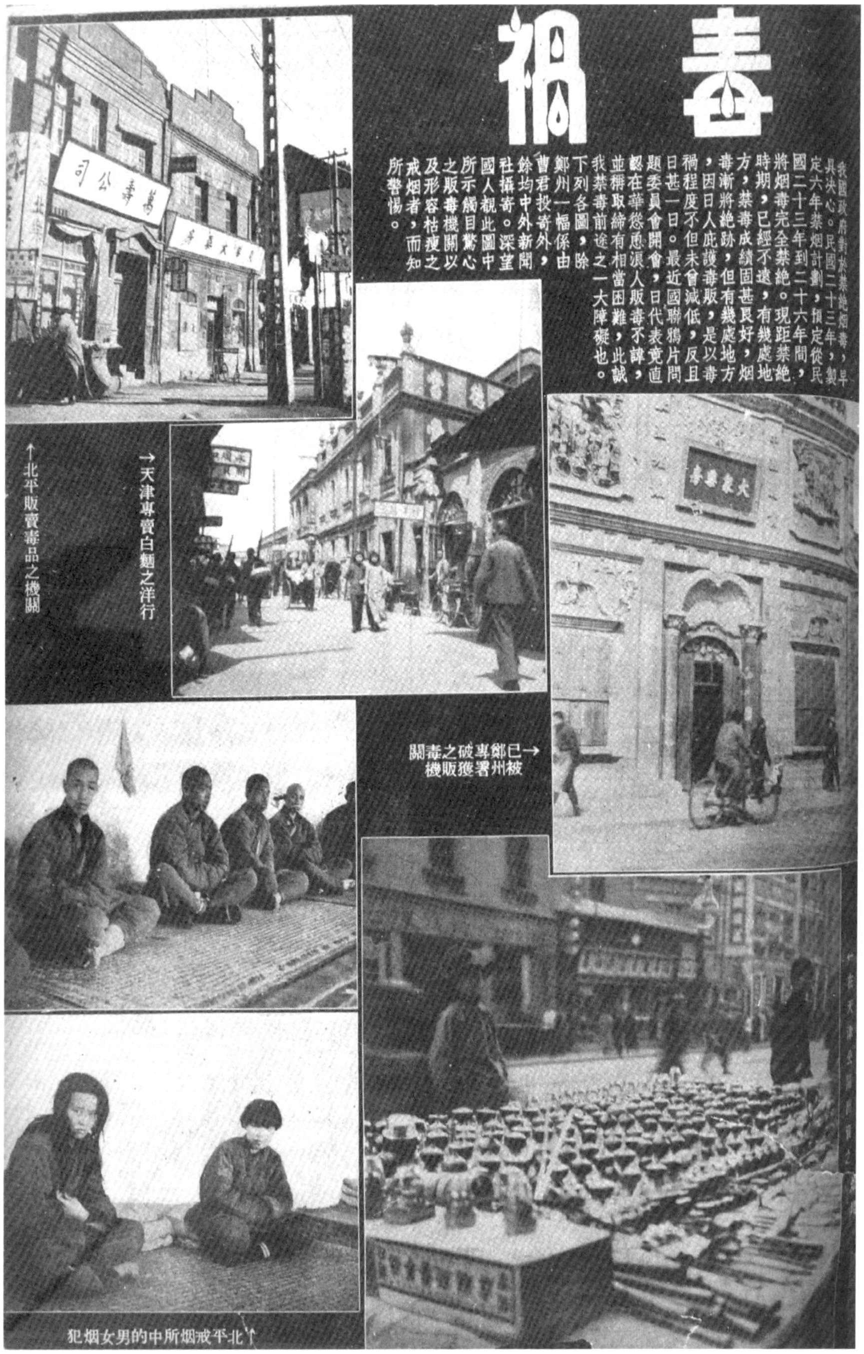

毒禍

我國政府對於禁絕烟毒，早具決心。民國二十三年，製定六年禁烟計劃，預定從民國二十三年到二十六年間，將烟毒完全禁絕。現距禁絕時期，已經不遠。有幾處地方，禁毒成績甚良好，烟毒漸將絕跡，但有幾處地方，因日人庇護毒販，是以毒禍程度不但未曾減低，反且日甚一日。最近國聯鴉片問題委員會開會，日代表竟直認在華慫恿浪人販毒不諱，並稱取締有相當困難，此誠我禁毒前途之一大障礙也。下列各圖，除鄭州一幅係由曹君投寄外，餘均中外新聞社攝寄。深望國人觀此圖中所示觸目驚心之販毒機關以及形容枯瘦之戒烟者，而知所警惕。

↑北平販賣毒品之機關

→天津專賣白麵之洋行

→已被鄭州專署破獲之販毒機關

↑北平戒烟所中的男女烟犯

《申报》周刊第 23 期发表的《毒祸》组照

Photo series entitled *Drug Plague*, published in *Shun Pao* Weekly (No. 23).

綏遠的鴉片問題

（旅行通信）

方大曾

記者最近在平綏路上作了五個星期的旅行，沿途考察所得，尤以綏遠的鴉片情形，使我感覺很大的興奮，同時也是非常痛心。這裏，且就該省鴉片之產、運、銷的概況及官方對禁煙的實情與人民受毒的苦狀等，與以簡略的記述，俾社會對這嚴重的問題，多一層了解。

綏遠省是允許人民種植鴉片的，每年七月間，往西北去的人，一入綏境，就可見到鐵路兩旁盛開着的罌粟花，其形狀，很像是春和月裏的芍藥，煙花開過之後，再過兩個星期的光景，就要實行收穫了。鴉片的收穫工作就是刺漿，即以利刃把煙苞割開，將苞裏的煙漿取出，然後再晒乾，就爲成品的煙土了。

狀似芍藥的罌粟花

今年的情形稍有不同，因爲省當局的禁煙計劃，是先從鐵路沿線作起，所以第一步先令沿鐵路線附近五里內禁絕種煙，以後再年年的推廣下去，直到「綏遠無煙」的理想之實現。不過，實際上，在綏東一帶，未出鐵路一里多地，還是煙花遍地；而在綏西，則一如往昔，火車仍就穿行於罌粟花的花園裏！

綏遠全省每年能產多少鴉片，恕我未能調查其確數，然而由省府發表的公報中，知道上年度「煙畝罰欵」項下的收入即有七十三萬元。

「煙畝罰欵」即是煙田的錢糧，普通，一畝煙地須納「罰欵」由十元至十六元之譜，這是按其土地的肥瘠程度爲根據的，此項「罰欵」還有一條「特惠」辦法，即如遇收成不佳的年成，還可酌量遞減，這也多少帶有奬勵的性質。到了煙熟時期，官方就派丈量人員來查核，而丈量人員是否有受賄虛報的事情，自然也很難說了，所以在這七十三萬的「罰欵」數下，多少還有一部分私吞的尚未計入。

以上係「產」稅而言，至於「銷」的方面，官方所得的稅欵，自然更加可驚，至少也要四五倍於「產」稅收入之上，所以，綏遠的財政，全靠鴉片來支持。

在民國十三年時，綏遠曾經實行過一次嚴勵的禁煙，然而一方面由於人民嗜煙者太多，一方面因爲綏遠的煙土本是該省主要的「出口特產」，所以結果弄得大家還要從甘寧一帶去購煙，以致人民手中的現欵都落到別省的「煙畝罰欵」項下了，而本省的財富外流，省庫的收入拮据，以致綏遠的「元氣」大損，從此，歷屆的執政者都不敢再去妄試禁煙了！

綏遠主要的農產物爲麻子與油麥，麻子一項還是出口之大宗，在綏東一帶——豐鎮平地泉等處，有十幾家運輸糧棧，專門經營麻子往海外出口。然而，這種麻田，每畝錢糧只不過六七分錢，而收成亦只值三元左右。反之，如種鴉片，每畝平均可收一百五十兩煙漿，晒乾後，可得五十兩煙土，每兩地價——即在當地售與煙販之價，可合到一元左右，雖然種煙的工本及「罰欵」都很大，這在農家亦是很合得來，况且煙地從種到收，只要一百天的短時間，資金流轉之速，也給與種植者以莫大的利益，所以良田都種了毒品，劣田才去種糧食。

到處皆是的小烟館

鴉片在綏遠可以稱得起大衆化了，富人家之吸食，自不用說，就連苦力們也有很多的癮君子。我這次的旅途中，每在極窮陋的小店裏，也可遇到那些連鞋都穿不起的同胞們，也二三其聚的圍着煙燈而爲「煙畝罰欵」盡着義務。綏遠的勞動本就很低賤，苦力勞動一日的工資只有兩三角錢，幸而他們吃的莜麵是很

旅行通讯《绥远的鸦片问题》原载《申报》（每周增刊）1936 年第 41 期

Opium Problem in Suiyuan, a travel report originally published in *Shun Pao* (weekly supplement, No. 41, 1936).

河北，平绥线旅途

Trip along the Beiping-Suiyuan Railway, Hebei Province.

唐山，火车站，日本太阳旗高悬（1936年春）

The Japanese Flag of the Rising Sun hung high at a railway station in Tangshan (spring, 1936).

山西，粮食

Grain (in Shanxi Province).

山西，小方在口泉矿区采访（1936 年 6 月）
Xiao Fang conducting interviews at the Kouquan Coal Mine in Shanxi Province (June, 1936).

纯靠人力运输的传统步窑

Traditional, manual method of carrying coal on foot.

口泉矿，碎煤筛选

Coal beneficiation at the Kouquan Coal Mine.

入窑前

Before entering the coal pit.

父子碎煤工

Father and son coal crushers.

母女碎煤工

Mother and daughter coal crushers.

没有欢乐的童年

Childhood with no joy.

山西，矿井上下的黑白时光

Black and white time, in and out of the coal pit in Shanxi Province.

山西，良田遍开罂粟花

Poppies in the field in Shanxi.

山西，田间休息

A break in the field in Shanxi.

山西，扬场

Threshing in Shanxi.

河北，乡村即景

Village scenery in Hebei Province.

车马小店

Shabby roadside inns.

灌溉

Irrigating.

小河流水洗衣忙

Washing clothes in the flowing river.

山西客栈

An inn in Shanxi.

过河

Wading.

生命线

Lifeblood

行走太行

Traveling in the Taihang Mountains.

参加学生集会

Participating in a student gathering.

遍地风流

A place of sensuality.

冀东一瞥

A glance at eastern Hebei.

德和永批發貨店
貨店

長春旅社
長春旅社
長春旅社

開豐洋行
開豐洋行

河北山西等地的商铺

Stores in Hebei, Shanxi, and other places.

北平，日本妓女

Japanese prostitutes in Beiping (Beijing).

北平，庙会上的长者
An elder at a temple fair in Beiping.

讨价还价
Bargaining.

北平，城外市集
A bazaar outside Beiping.

绥远，卖毡鞋的小贩（1937 年 1 月）
Vendors selling felt shoes in Suiyuan (January, 1937).

張垣一瞥

小芳

本篇之作者實地遊歷張垣後的紀述，對于張垣各方面都有簡明敘述。當此華北危機日迫的時候，我們看了這篇文章，會有無限的感慨。

張家口是察哈爾的省會，故名張垣，本來是中國內地與俄及外蒙古的通商大埠，如今，已成了邊境要塞了。

××……張垣的形勢……××

張家口的形勢，是三面環山的，只有南面是一片開廣的原野？從車站到商埠裏，要經過清河橋，過了這座美麗的綠色鐵橋，就是下堡地方。原來張家口本有兩個城垣，一在北面山坡上，名爲上堡，所以在北面的地方，亦通稱爲上堡，南邊則爲下堡，上下堡，由一條繁盛的大街連通起來。上堡建於明萬歷四十一年，下堡建於明宣德四年，當初也是爲了鎮敵而設的

××……許多鴉片莊……××

在這一條最繁盛長街上，有許多叫明其妙的商店，有的寫「某某某發貨莊」「零整批發」、「批發貨莊」、…這些都是專營鴉片的行頭我覺得全世界裏，佈置得最簡陋最單調的商店，當要屬于這些發貨莊了那些發貨莊裏面簡直甚麼也沒有，只是一個櫃台，和四面皆白的牆壁，再配上兩三個店員，這種商店，在張垣有五六十家之多，察省境內本不產烟，然而對烟的消費與專業的經營則很盛飯館裡都預備煙燈，並且有女招待作陪，據說清查五月份的收入就有三十萬元之多呢！

××……麻將不算賭……××

麻將牌，也到處都可聽到並且見到，這是絕對公開的，記者以此事詰之公安局的職員，據云國民政府的新憲法上說明，四人以下，不算「聚賭」，聽他的話，使我很慚愧，並且也深感自己常識不足了！

××……要人的公園……××

察哈爾大飯店與太平公園，位於清河西岸是最近才建築的，主要的用處，是招待外賓和本國的要人。建築的經費，由中央給了十萬，同時又由張垣的房捐上加徵三月。得二十萬，共合用了三十萬建設費不是很可觀的嗎？然公園裡亭子已有一座被風括倒，大飯店的房屋，說是用洋鐵架，實際則爲磚築。

××……兩座「鎮物」……××

站在空廣一點的地方，可以見到山頭上的幾座美麗的小亭子和東西兩大土墩，土墩的形狀，頗似砲台，這事當年「五二六」抗日事變結束後，哲元氏到張垣時所築的，他當時一面嚴厲的清除「危險青年」，一面說是建築砲台準備抗敵，哪知祇有這兩座土墩！而這兩座土墩的建築，只是那時一位精通「地理」省府的秘書的主張，說是爲了張家口的風水關係。不得不建了這兩座「鎮物」在國家來說，可以保存領土的不再爲人侵犯，對個人說可以保他坐鎮西北，果然，現在張垣安隱，　先生的權位也是日益　高！

××……賜兒娘娘廟……××

賜兒山上娘娘廟，爲張垣名勝，有平坦的汽車路，可直達半山間。老遠的即可見到山楷上題著「普因普果」，這是新近才寫上的娘娘廟已重修一新，寺內有冰水二洞，相隔僅數尺，一爲冰一爲水，正是形容世態之炎涼，自民國十九年後，冰洞已損，不復結冰，水洞現仍存。

××……廟宇甲各埠……××

這裡本來到處都是廟宇。寺院之多，眞可甲於各埠了。　主席在任時。又在北上麓下，建設了一處關岳武廟。大概這也是爲了保衛國民的意思。這兒的統治勢力，正在向一個神道設教路途邁進中，不信請看這些新的建設事業吧！

原载《大众知识》1936 年第 5 期和《生活日报》等报刊的旅行通讯和摄影报道

Travel and photo reports published in *Popular Knowledge* (Vol. 5, 1936) and *Life Daily*.

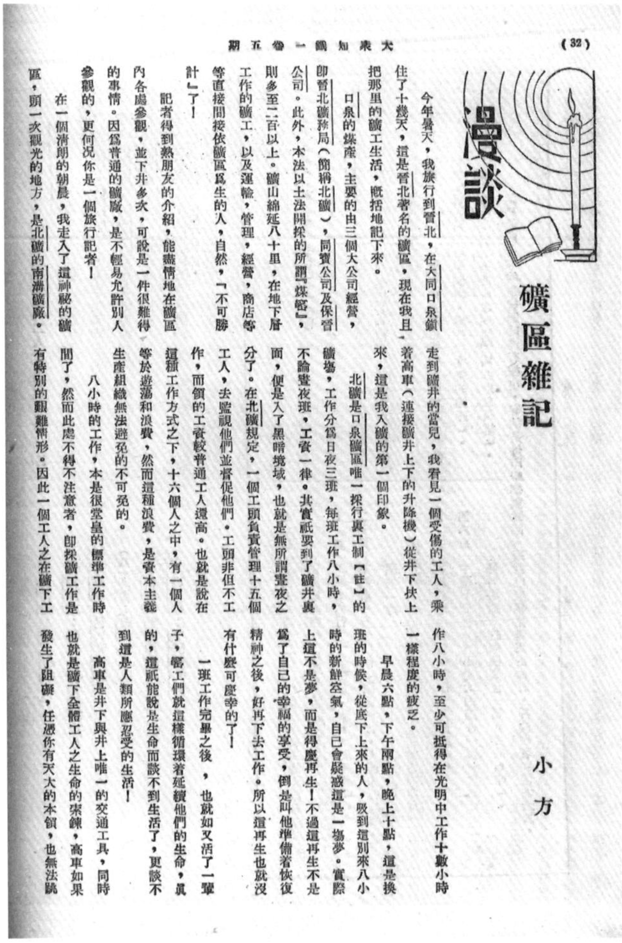

(32)　　大衆知識一卷五期

漫談

礦區雜記

小方

今年暑天，我旅行到晉北，在大同口泉鎭住了十幾天，這是晉北著名的礦區，現在我且把那里的礦工生活，概括地記下來。

口泉的煤產，主要的由三個大公司經營，卽晉北礦務局（簡稱北礦），同寶公司及保晉公司。此外，本法以土法開採的所謂『煤窰』，則多至二百以上。礦山綿延八十里，在地下層工作的礦工，以及運輸，管理，經營，商店等等直接間接依礦區爲生的人，自然，「不可勝計」了！

記者得到熱朋友的介紹，能盡情地在礦區內各處參觀，並下井多次，可說是一件很難得的事情。因爲普通的礦廠，是不輕易允許別人參觀的，更何況你是一個旅行記者！

在一個淸朗的朝晨，我走入了這神祕的礦區，頭一次觀光的地方，是北礦的南滿礦廠。走到礦井的當兒，我看見一個受傷的工人，乘着高車（連接礦井上下的升降機）從井下扶上來，這是我入礦的第一個印象。

北礦是口泉礦區唯一採行眞工制【註】的礦場，工作分爲日夜三班，每班工作八小時，不論晝夜班，工資一律。其實祇要到了礦井裏面，便是入了黑暗境域，也就是無所謂晝夜之分了。在北礦規定，一個工頭負責管理十五個工人，去監視他們並督促他們。工頭非但不工作，而領的工資較普通工人還高。也就是說在這種工作方式之下，十六個人之中，有一個人等於遊蕩和浪費，然而這種浪費，是資本主義生產組織無法避免的不可免的。

八小時的工作，本是很堂皇的標準工作時間了，然而此處不得不注意者，卽採礦工作是有特別的艱難情形。因此一個工人之在礦下工作八小時，至少可抵得在光明中工作十數小時一樣程度的疲乏。

早晨六點，下午兩點，晚上十點，這是換班的時候，從底下上來的人，吸到這別來八小時的新鮮空氣，自已會疑惑這是一場夢。實際上這不是夢，而是得慶再生！不過這再生不是爲了自已的幸福的享受，倒是叫他準備着恢復精神之後，好再下去工作。所以這再生也就沒有什麼可慶幸的了！

一班工作完畢之後，也就如又活了一輩子，礦工們就這樣循環着延續他們的生命，眞的，這祇能說是生命而談不到生活了，更談不到這是人類所應忍受的生活！

高車是井下與井上唯一的交通工具，同時也就是礦下全體工人之生命的桊鍊，高車如果發生了阻礙，任憑你有天大的本領，也無法跳

從張垣至大同

小芳

六月四日晨離張垣沿鐵路西南行出南桊園。回顧遠山近水，天容襯著一塊塊濃的白雲，不是身臨其境，眞不知大好山河之可愛。

徐步三十里，至孔家莊，繼搭火車至柴溝堡，時已黃昏，當夜卽宿於站旁一個客棧中。靠近車站的客棧，房價往往要比城裏面的小店貴上三四倍，其實設備之簡陋，都是半斤八兩。窯外是滿院的馬糞，屋裏則是土炕上舖著破蓆，夜間下火車的人，進不了城，于是才不得已多花幾個錢住在城外這臭的店錢，單間七角，夥炕二角，均有價目表貼于上，然而經過短時間講價後，記者得以一角五分而睡夥炕，晚間，夥計們就把烟燈拿出來，客人說不客氣的噴起雲霧，一個抽完一個接，想像著他們在那一轉瞬間，生活是多麼的逍遙自在！

圍着火爐吃西瓜

柴溝堡爲察邊一大鎭，城東郊有一片美麗的草原。溪水縱橫，風景幽雅。女孩婦人們，沿著流水在洗衣服。因爲北天寒的關係，田地裡還正在播種。男孩們，赤裸裸身子在恬靜的小河裡撈魚，這一帶的氣候很怪，穿棉不熱，赤身不冷；所以俗語說得好：「早穿皮，午穿紗，圍著火爐吃西瓜。」

堡子街頭，盡是些打鐵的工匠：製造的都是農具，還有一家拍賣行，這舖子實在令人疑心，在這窮　僻鎭的地方，怎麼會有模登的拍賣行呢？並且行裏面非但沒有貨物，而且連夥計也找不到。經過多方的打聽，才知道這舖子開了不久，東家不是中國人，內容是作烈性料子（白面）的營業，暗中還負某種政治上的活動！

五日中午，乘火車離柴溝堡，九十里至天鎭，這段路的中間，卽是晉察交界處，晉省本有路不拾遺，夜不閉戶之風，自此次赤禍之後，經過嚴厲的清　之結果，山西省已成爲「好人國」了。

公道爲立省之本

察省以「八德」治民，山西則以「公道」爲立省之本，全省均有「主張公道團」之組織，閻主任自任總團長，縣有縣團部，區有區團部，正如當年的黨部和現在南京政府所提倡的新生活運動的組織相仿佛入團者，均係職業界人，是爲「好人」。總團長印發有主張公道團概說等之宣傳小　分發各好人去誦讀研究，各團部均有指導幹事，每週分別拜訪各好人考好人信條及團章團規等；答不對的限一星期後再試！不識字者，令其找能識字者代爲講解，使他們對于團章，有深切的了解而已！

學生倒也還自由

天鎭車站上，憲警檢查特嚴，唯對于學生裝束者倒並無多大留難只要名片一張卽可放行，這與平津各地之特別注意學生，是迥然不同。原因是此次共產黨到了山西，替它作內應的以本地不安份的農民爲多，學生份子除省垣外幾乎沒有。被逮捕的共黨間諜又多是本省人，于是他們的嫌疑較學生更爲重大了。後來記者到大同時，聽著這樣一件案子：某夜，四個警察在一家小店裏檢查出兩個有嫌疑的農民，於是留兩個人在那裡看守，另兩個出去打電話報告公安局，等打電話的回來時，兩位看守的巡警已死在血泊裡，當夜全城戒備搜查，也沒有將兇手查獲，直到如今，尙未破案，還是前一個多月的事情。自從這事件發生以後，警察對于農裝旅客的檢查，是又小心又響怕，在他們行步中，幾乎連一個包茶葉也要打開看看的。

好人地界的春聯

好人地界自然也有其特的風光，天鎭站旁的一家客店門前，新貼的這樣一幅春聯：「來往過客生意多，預防共黨保鄉土」。橫批則爲「主張公道」，從這幅門聯裏也許就能了解山西的全面了。此外如同「主張在公道，生意保興隆」等類的語句，更是到處可見。

天鎭是晉省一個小縣治，縣城離車站還有七里路在城裏的一家小　裡，與記者同坑者，有十幾位青年農人，他們是「應差」來縣城的，原來縣城西門外有一道河，縣裡下令各鄉派義務工人每鄉出十五人來縣修治河工共有二百多人被派，這就謂之「應差」「應差」非但不給工資，而且食宿均須自備一幹就得兩三個月才完事，農民們日常所的捐稅，不知道都用到什麼地方去了，遇著眞正的建設工作，則仍須以「應差」來徵發義務勞動，大概這種毫不給酬的剝削，也可美其名爲「人民服役運動」吧？此種超經濟的統治關係，亦爲半封建之中國政治所特有的現象之一。（未完）

原载《大众知识》1936 年第 5 期和《生活日报》等报刊的旅行通讯和摄影报道

Travel and photo reports published in *Popular Knowledge* (Vol. 5, 1936) and *Life Daily*.

郊外集会
Outskirt gathering.

北平，一二·九运动（1935 年）
December 9th Patriotic Parade (Beiping, 1935).

围观

Onlookers.

山西，行走中的小方背影（1936 年 6 月）

Xiao Fang walking in Shanxi Province (June, 1936).

第五章 **黑与白**

Chapter Five: Black and White

童工在矿下工作，除了管送镐针者之外，还有就是管理风门的工作。各煤巷如蜘蛛网一样散布在一个平面上，都有一定的空气流通路线，各置风门来节制和调动。这些风门的旁边常有一个十二三岁的孩子在那里孤独而冷静地把守着，如同一个警察的岗位。因为这些地方都是不经过煤车的，也很少有人走过，所以阴暗，森冷得很，不知道这些可爱的孩子们是不是会害怕呢？

——方大曾《矿区杂记》

When child laborers worked in coal mines, they were responsible for delivering pickaxes to miners and managing ventilation doors. Coal roadways scattered on one surface like a cobweb, with air flow passageways controlled and activated by many ventilation doors. Next to each door, there would be a 12- or 13-year-old child standing guard, lonely and cold, like a policeman. With no coal wagon and few people passing by, these places were deadly dim and chilly. I wondered whether these children were scared.

Anecdotes in Coal Mine Area, by Fang Dazeng

方大曾留下的照片中，有一部分是他到河北、山西的煤矿，甚至深入井下拍摄的。在那里，从不被人关注的矿工们，成了他镜头里的主角，他们的命运和境遇震惊了这个来自大都市的青年。

在一个清朗的早晨，小方走进了南沟矿厂，在井口，看见一个受伤的工人，乘着连接升降机，从井下被扶上来，这是他到矿区采访的第一个印象。

在同时拍摄的照片中，小方还记录了许多煤矿工人的生活情形：条件简陋的井下采煤工作面、衣衫褴褛的采煤工、捡柴做饭的煤矿工人，一幅幅照片令人触目惊心，心酸落泪。这些珍贵的影像，如果不是作者俯下身子，放低身段，走入矿工生存状态的隐秘角落，是不可能拍摄到的。尤其是下到采煤作业面，危险系数很高，没有获得高度的认可，是不会有人愿意引领你下去的。他力求最及时地出现在最佳的拍摄位置，尽可能靠近所拍摄的对象，从尽可能多的角度进行拍摄，在最关键的瞬间按动快门，他与镜头中的人物间确立了真诚的信任与理解。实地观察了种种现象后，小方在《晋北煤业现状》中做出判断：“提到了晋北煤业，也正是反映着我们中华民族的前途，我们必得改善大众的生活，努力建设事业，不然就等候着灭亡了。”

方大曾何时开始使用“小方”这个笔名的，已经无从考证，从他发表的通讯和照片来看，1935 年到 1937 年，使用最为频繁。那一时期，他的照片经常刊载于上海的《生活周刊》《良友画报》《现代画报》，英文《中国呼声》周刊，美国的 *Life*，英国的 *Illustrated London News*，法国的 *Nouveau Observateur* 等。署名小方的珍贵照片，是今天人们了解抗战初期的重要影像。

当时的艺术评论家秋尘格外看重方大曾的作品，其《对影记》评价，“方多取材大众生活，热烈情绪跃然纸上。而技术则无所轩轾，俱臻上乘”。“方作以《吃黑面的人扛白面》一幅最动人，凝视影中码头苦力，若闻喘息声。”“方多时代思想，用字多深刻，《顶天立地男儿汉》《有武器的人》，皆明证。”

的确，《吃黑面的人扛白面》极具视觉冲击力。烈日当空下，码头搬运工艰难地扛起白面大包，两大袋一扛似乎压得喘不过气来。小方运用中午顶光拍摄，让黑白对比更加明显和强烈，揭示了“扛白面的人却吃不起白面”的时弊，

Some photos left behind by Fang Dazeng were taken when he visited coal mines in Hebei and Shanxi provinces, sometimes even deep in the mines. In these photos, miners who had never been paid attention to by the public became the main characters. Their poor fate and situations shocked this young man from a big city.

One early morning, Xiao Fang walked into the shaft of the Nangou Coal Mine. At the pithead, he saw a wounded worker being lifted from below by an elevator and supported to exit the shaft. This was Xiao Fang's first impression while conducting interviews in the coal mine area.

Many photos that Xiao Fang took were about the lives of the miners: Coalfaces deep in the shabby coal shaft, miners in rags, and miners picking firewood to prepare meals. These photographs were shocking and heart-breaking, moving readers to tears. If Xiao Fang had not ventured to the unseen corners of the miners' lives, we would never have seen these valuable photos. It was quite perilous to go to the coalface. Before he was well accepted, no one would be willing to lead Xiao Fang down the shaft.

Fang Dazeng sought out the optimal photography spots at the best times. He would get as close as possible to the target and try as many angles as possible before pressing the shutter at just the right moment. He established sincere trust and understanding with those he photographed. After observing various phenomena, Xiao Fang concluded in *Current Condition of the Coal Mining Industry in Northern Shanxi*: "Speaking of the coal mining industry in northern Shanxi, which is an exact reflection of the future of China, we must work hard to improve the lives of the masses and promote industrial development. Otherwise, we will just wait for our doom."

There is no record about when Fang Dazeng started using the pen name Xiao Fang. As indicated through his published reports and photos, this pen name was most frequently used during 1935-37. During this period, Xiao Fang's photos were often published in *Life Weekly*, *Young Companion*, *Modern Pictorial*, and *Voice of China* (weekly) in Shanghai; *Life* in the US; *Illustrated London News* in the UK; *Nouveau Observateur* in France, etc. Rare photos under the signature Xiao Fang are important visual material for people today to learn about the early stages of the Anti-Japanese War.

Qiu Chen, an art critic at the time, especially valued Fang Dazeng's works. In his book *Dui Ying Ji*, Qiu commented: "The subjects of Fang's works mainly relate to the common life of people, whose lively expressions are vividly presented in his photographs, using unparalleled techniques with superb quality....Fang's reports are full of modern thought and profound words. Such examples include *Indomitable Men* and *People with Arms*."

Indeed, *White Flour Carriers Feeding on Black Chaff* is very visually impressive. With the sun burning overhead, porters at the wharf

照片的表现，犹如一幅吸人眼球的版画。“方大曾的特点是贴得近些再近些，用他的心灵与劳苦大众贴近，使他的情感接地气。”范长江新闻奖获得者俞新宝在接受笔者采访时表示，“在深入现实生活中，他用敏锐的目光，熟练的技巧，真实地记录了最底层劳动人民的生活现状，展现了这位满腔热血的爱国青年时刻关注社会、体察民情的人文情怀，从而进一步表达了他与众不同的超越时代的博爱精神。在他的采访途中和旅行期间，他能够敏锐地体察当地百姓的真实状况，特别是通过一些细微的生活点滴，反映出表象背后的一些重大而意义深远的主题。”

1936 年的六、七月间，小方受邀担任邹韬奋先生主编的《生活星期刊》《生活日报》特约记者，负责写旅行通讯，将所见所闻以图文结合的方式介绍给读者，他选择了河北、山西和绥远实地探访。

旅途中，一路上的观感萦绕脑海，底层劳动者的苦难、统治者的腐化堕落，还有侵略者的虎视眈眈，他所看到的不仅是浮世的表象，还有关乎国家和民族命运的潜在危机。在发表于《生活星期刊》的通讯《从大同到绥远》中，他写道：“你若是在这样的环境里住上两三天，大概就不会再看得起那山青水秀的南国了。确乎是这样，时到如今，我们的民族再也不需要那温柔幽雅的陶醉，而该有魁伟豪迈的姿态了！江南的朋友们，你们都到这里来吧，不止是这里的风景好，而且是因为这里的疆土需要我们的保卫啊！”

在这次旅行途中，方大曾还留下了一组以黄河上的船夫为主人公的摄影作品。近 10 张景别不同、人物不同的照片中，船工们全身赤裸，或摇橹、或起帆、或拉纤，他们的各种不同表情，让阅读者强烈感受到他们劳作的艰辛、性格的坚韧、对待生活的达观。同时也能想见，方大曾是带着怎样的深厚情感，到黄河岸边去找寻他们的踪影，走进他们的生活，贴近他们的心灵，最后被他们所认可和接纳。如果不是这样，依照中国人的传统观念，船工们赤身裸体的形象是不会让外人拍摄并公之于众的。

小方在平绥路上进行了 5 个星期的旅行，沿途考察所得，尤以绥远的鸦片情形，使他既感到惊诧，同时也非常痛心。“鸦片在绥远可以称得起大众化了，

painstakingly carry packs of white flour. The two packs they carried at a time nearly made them suffocate. Xiao Fang used overhead sunlight to highlight the contrast of black and white in the photo, and reveal the social problem that the white flour carriers could not afford white flour. The photo is presented just like an appealing picture printed from an engraved plate. Fang Dazeng's works are typically characterized by a short distance between himself and his subject. He became close with the impoverished masses through his sincere heart so affection in his works could be well rooted.

When I interviewed Yu Xinbao, a Fan Changjiang Journalism Award winner, he said: "While going deep into real life, with acute eyes and skilled techniques, Xiao Fang faithfully records the life of bottom laborers. This showed the humane sentiments of this young, passionate, and patriotic man who always cared about society and the masses. Moreover, Xiao Fang's heart of universal love made him stand out from the crowd and transcend his era. While interviewing and traveling, he could keenly sense the real conditions of local commoners. He could reveal the significant, far-reaching themes behind the phenomena through subtle life details."

During June and July of 1936, Xiao Fang was invited to be a special correspondent for *Life Weekly* and *Life Daily*, with Zou Taofen as chief editor. He was responsible for writing travel reports to introduce what he learned during travel through photographs and reports. He chose to visit Hebei, Shanxi, and Suiyuan.

What Xiao Fang saw during this journey haunted him: Hardship of the bottom laborers, corruption of the rulers, and wild ambition of the invaders. What he saw was a potential threat to the fate of his country. In *From Datong to Suiyuan*, published in *Life Weekly*, Xiao Fang wrote: "If you live in such an environment for two or three days, you probably won't think highly of the beautiful scenery in southern China. This is indeed true. Today, our nation does not need that kind of intoxicating gentility and tranquility: It needs a kind of heroic bravery and boldness! My dear friends in the south, come here! Not because you can enjoy beautiful scenery here, but because the territory here needs our safeguarding!"

During this journey, Fang Dazeng also took a series of photographs with boatmen as the main characters. In the approximately 10 photos of different sceneries and figures, the boatmen were all naked, rowing, hoisting sails or towing boats. Their varied expressions make readers intensely feel the hardships of their work, tenacity in their personality, and optimism in their attitude toward life. Meanwhile, we can also infer how affectionate Fang Dazeng was to be able to find them by the Yellow River, get close to their lives and hearts, and ultimately be recognized and accepted by them. If this was not so, in traditional Chinese cultural context, boatmen would not allow their naked images to be seen by the public.

Xiao Fang traveled five weeks along the Beiping-Suiyuan Railway. What he learned from

小方（右）和友人在矿区采访
Xiao Fang (right) and his friend conducting interviews in the coal mine area.

富人家之吸食，自不用说，就连苦力们也有很多的瘾君子。我这次的旅途中，每在极穷陋的小店里，也可遇到那些连鞋都穿不起的同胞们，也二三其群地围着烟灯而为‘烟亩罚款’尽着义务。”“绥远的劳动本就很低贱，苦力劳动一日的工资只有两三角钱，幸而他们吃的莜面是很便宜，每天一角多钱的饭食，即已对付，所剩下的微数，则都溃耗在鸦片上。”

小方的报道总是和亲历的现场紧紧在一起，无疑已成为历史的“第一遍底稿”。范长江新闻奖获得者朱海燕认为，“流泪的山河，苦难的民生，是他报道的背景与深景，笔下涌出的东西，哪怕是苦难的，也有着排山倒海的力量，倒逼着中国人喊出：‘中国必须站起来！’对他的这些作品，我不是作为新闻作品来读的，而是在读中日开战之前一个承载战争的沙盘地形图。在一个鸦片泛滥、妓女猖獗、民不聊生、国难当头的时刻，即将爆发战争，会给中华民族带来怎样的艰难，便可想而知了。”

1936年6月到8月间，小方在《生活日报》及《生活星期刊》上连续发表了《张垣一瞥》《从张垣到大同》《晋北煤业现状》等通讯作品，将一路所见报告给读者。

“小方好像总是在走路，奔忙，不知疲倦。”在好友方殷印象里，他“人

this journey, especially regarding the rampant opium in Suiyuan, shocked and pained him: "Opium is indeed popular in Suiyuan, not to mention the rich people as opium consumers. Many poor laborers were also addicted to opium. During my trip, whenever I visited an extremely shabby store, I could see men who couldn't even afford shoes sitting around opium lamps in groups of two or three, making their contribution to the levying of the indiscriminate 'opium penalty' on those poor peasants....Laborers were paid merely two to three jiao (0.2 to 0.3 yuan) per day. Fortunately, the oat noodles they ate were quite cheap. After one jiao went to pay for their day's meals, the rest, even though there was almost none left, was all spent on opium."

Xiao Fang's reports were always closely linked to scenes he visited. These scenes had undoubtedly become the primary draft to record history. Zhu Haiyan, a Fan Changjiang Journalism Award winner, said: "The mountains and rivers in grief and the Chinese commoners in suffering constituted the deep background of his reports. What Xiao Fang wrote, even if full of pain, was overwhelmingly powerful, enough to make the Chinese shout 'China must stand up!' I read his reports not as news, but as a sand table of the war between China and Japan before it began. It was easy to imagine what calamity the upcoming war would bring to the Chinese nation when opium and prostitution were rampant, commoners were in misery, and the country was in crisis."

From June to August of 1936, Xiao Fang published in *Life Daily* and *Life Weekly* successive news reports, including *A Glance at Zhangyuan*, *From Zhangyuan to Datong*, and *Current Conditions of the Coal Mining Industry in Northern Shanxi* to introduce all he had seen along the journey.

"Xiao Fang always seemed to be on the move,

品纯正，热情，精力充沛”。两位志趣相投的战友最后一次合作是在1937年的4月前往门头沟煤矿采访，文章发表在上海杂志公司发行的《世界文化》半月刊第一卷第十一期上，题目是《门头沟——“黑”的世界》，文中所附的6幅照片都是小方拍摄的。

小方对艺术摄影的探索与追求不同于那些孤芳自赏的“唯美主义者”，他选景造型力求把变革中的社会内容尽可能完美地与艺术形式统一起来。《联合阵线》是他的代表作，被选印在《北平第一届摄影联合展览会特刊》的显著位置上。这幅作品取材于现实生活，画面简洁鲜明生动，构图用光恰到好处，它告诉人们坚持团结联合行动，组成强有力的统一阵线，才能同舟共济，战胜惊涛骇浪，争取最后胜利。它借景抒情，以形传神，把握住时代的脉搏，表现出了时代的最强音，因而被人们誉为抗战前夕最佳的摄影艺术作品之一。

本章照片选自方大曾摄影作品中内涵深邃、富有创建的经典部分，黑与白的交织中能够感受到他眼心合一按动快门时的怀想，以及跨越时空留给我们的遐想。拍摄时间约为1934年至1937年。

busy working, never tired." In the eyes of Fang Yin, one of his good friends, Xiao Fang was "righteous, passionate, and full of energy." The final collaboration between these two comrades-in-arms was the interview conducted at the Mentougou Coal Mine in April 1937. The report, entitled *Mentougou: "Black" World*, contained six photographs all by Xiao Fang, and was published in *World Culture* (No. 11, Vol. 1), semi-monthly issued by the Shanghai Magazine Company.

In exploring and pursuing the art of photography, unlike those indulging in self-admiration, Xiao Fang tried his best to represent the changing society in an artistic form when choosing scenes and designing compositions. The photo entitled *United Front* was a representative work of his that was later printed, conspicuously, in the *Special Issue for the 1st Beiping Open Photography Exhibition*. This concise, distinct, and vivid work was based on real life with perfect composition and lighting effects. It delivered the message that as long as people took united actions to forge a strong united front, they would be in the same boat, overcome violent waves, and eventually be victorious. This work effectively expressed the photographer's emotion and thought behind the picture and form, keenly sensed the pulse of the times, and gave voice to the most urgent appeal of the times: It is thus regarded as one of the finest artistic works of photography prior to the outbreak of the war against Japanese aggression.

The photos in this chapter are from those classic works by Fang Dazeng with profound content and ingenuity. In these black and white photos, you can feel his affection and thought at the very moment he spontaneously pressed the shutter, and fancy yourself having a time travel back to those days. These photos were taken between 1934 and 1937.

山西，矿区童工（1936 年）

A mine child laborer in Shanxi Province (1936).

河北，黑白交响制陶人（1936 年）

Pottery makers in light and shade (Hebei Province, 1936).

北平，妙高山上的独行客

A solitary traveler on Miaogao Mountain, Beiping.

岸边的小贩

A vendor on the bank.

长城脚下，拾荒的孩子

Small waste pickers below the Great Wall.

绥远，光明的保卫者（1937 年 6 月 24 日北平第一届摄影联合展览会，小方的参展作品）

A Guardian of Light in Suiyuan (a work of Xiao Fang at the 1st Beiping Open Photography Exhibition, June 24, 1937).

破冰

Ice breaking

绥远，迁徙
Migrating in Suiyuan

绥远的冬天

Winter in Suiyuan.

尚在天真期（1937 年 6 月 24 日北平第一届摄影联合展览会，小方的参展作品）

Still Innocent (a work of Xiao Fang at the 1st Beiping Open Photography Exhibition, June 24, 1937).

山西，黄河上的船夫（1936 年 6 月）

Boatmen on the Yellow River, Shanxi Province (June, 1936).

《生活星期刊》1 卷 19 号刊载组照《黄河上的船夫》

Photo series entitled *Boatmen on the Yellow River*, published in *Life Weekly* (No. 19, Vol. 1).

天津，装与卸（1935 年）
Loading and unloading (Tianjin, 1935).

天津，平常的一天（1935 年）
An ordinary day (Tianjin, 1935).

绥远一家人（1937 年 1 月）
A family in Suiyuan (January, 1937).

驼队远行（1937 年 1 月）
A camel team on a long journey (January, 1937).

前线指挥者（1936 年 12 月）
A commander in the front (December, 1936).

基础工作（1937 年 6 月 24 日北平第一届摄影联合展览会，小方的参展作品）
Preparation (a work of Xiao Fang at the 1st Beiping Open Photography Exhibition, June 24, 1937).

小方在展出作品《基础工作》前。这是目前已知他失踪前的最后一张照片（1937 年 6 月 24 日）

Xiao Fang before the exhibition of his work *Preparation*, currently the last photo before he disappeared (June 24, 1937).

山西，石刻佛像（1936 年）
Cliff inscriptions and a Buddha statue (Shanxi, 1936).

北平，青春的呼唤（1930 年）
Call of youth (Beiping, 1930).

绥远，拾粪人（1936 年 12 月）
A manure collector in Suiyuan (December, 1936).

小方代表作《联合阵线》不同角度样片（原图遗失，资料扫描）

Prints of a representative work of Xiao Fang entitled *United Front* from different perspectives (data scanning as the original photos are missing).

联合阵线（1937 年 6 月 24 日北平第一届摄影联合展览会，小方的参展作品）
United Front (a work of Xiao Fang at the 1st Beiping Open Photography Exhibition, June 24, 1937).

河北，农忙（1936 年）
Busy season in Hebei (1936).

河北，推碾（1936 年 7 月）
Grinding grains in Hebei (July, 1936)

河北，采石
Quarrying in Hebei.

山西，小河淌水（1936 年）
A flowing river in Shanxi (1936).

晾晒
Air-drying in sunlight.

河北，灌溉（1936 年）
Irrigating in Hebei (1936).

河北，排水（1936 年）
Draining in Hebei (1936).

河北，骡轿（1936 年）
A mule sedan in Hebei (1936).

绥远，大庙讲经（1936 年 12 月）
A sermon at the Xila Mulun Temple in Suiyuan (December, 1936).

唐山，华新纱厂（1936 年 6 月）
The Huaxin Cotton Textile Factory in Tangshan (June, 1936).

北平，天坛（1935 年）
The Temple of Heaven in Beiping (1935).

北平，颐和园（1936 年）
Summer Palace in Beiping (1936).

塔林
The Pagoda Forest.

绥远，大庙灵塔（1936 年 12 月）
The dagoba of Xila Mulun Temple in Suiyuan (December, 1936).

山西，穿行太行（1936 年）
Traveling in the Taihang Mountains (Shanxi Province, 1936).

北平，旅行归来的小方（1936 年 11 月）
Xiao Fang in Beiping, back from traveling (November, 1936).

第六章 **经历绥远**

Chapter Six: Experiencing Suiyuan

现在死于东山坡上的匪尸，大半已被野狗吃食，只留着几副可怕的头连着那架光杆的骨骼。有些完整的尸体，穷困的老百姓们，还正在剥他们身上的军衣，等衣服剥光了之后，就立刻跑来几只狗，它们又发现了新的美餐。战争是这样的残酷，然而疯狂的侵略者，则拼命在制造战争。

——方大曾《绥东前线视察记》

Most enemy bodies lying on the eastern slope had already been devoured by wild dogs, except for several horrible skulls joined to bare skeletons. There still remained some intact corpses, from whose bodies the impoverished commoners were peeling off military uniforms. Once undressed, several dogs immediately ran up, attracted to the new delicacies. This was the cruelty of war. Those maniac invaders were desperately provoking wars.

Inspection of the Front in Eastern Suiyuan, by Fang Dazeng

小方从战地寄给母亲的照片原图

Original photo of Xiao Fang sent from the battlefield to his mother

1936年11月，在绥远，傅作义率领的晋绥军和日本关东军配合下的李守信、蒙古德王旗下的大汉义军以及蒙古军发生激战，这场战争是抗日战争初期中日双方的一次重要冲突，其中有红格尔图战役、百灵庙战役和锡拉木楞庙战役三场主要战役，战争最后以晋绥军大获全胜而告终。

战事一开始，小方即到前线采访，这次长达43天的行程，使他全面报道了著名的“绥远抗战”。这是小方第二次到绥远，距上一次仅半年的时间，如果不是战事突变，估计他不会频密到此。上次的摄影报道《敌人觊觎下的绥远》刊登在1936年8月30日出版的《生活星期刊》第一卷第13号上。这一次，方大曾与先期到达集宁的范长江等人汇合，他的工作热情更加高涨，拍摄照片数百张，成果颇丰，并深入前线，写出了《绥远军事地理》等一些有影响的战地通讯。这次采访也是目前已知小方外出时间最长的一次，留下的照片和文字，成为今天的人们了解小方和他旅行经历的最好信息。

In November of 1936, in Suiyuan, the Shanxi-Suiyuan Army, led by Fu Zuoyi, fought fiercely against the Grand Han Righteous Army and Inner Mongolian Army under Li Shouxin and Prince Demchugdongrub, assisted by the Japanese Kwantung Army. This was a significant conflict between China and Japan, including three major battles: The Battle of Hongge'ertu, Battle of Bailing Temple, and Battle of Xila Mulun Temple, with the Shanxi-Suiyuan Army winning a complete victory.

Immediately after the war began, Xiao Fang went to the front to conduct interviews. Throughout this journey, which lasted 43 days, he comprehensively reported on the well-known Suiyuan Campaign. This was the second time Xiao Fang traveled to Suiyuan, the first time being six months before. But for the sudden change in the war situation, Xiao Fang would not have returned to Suiyuan so soon. *Suiyuan Coveted by the Enemy*, his last photographic report about Suiyuan, was published in *Life Weekly* (No. 13, Vol. 1, August 30, 1936). This time, Fang Dazeng joined Fan Changjiang and others who arrived at Jining in advance. He worked with greater enthusiasm and took hundreds of photographs, a great accomplishment. Also, he ventured deep into the front and wrote highly influential war reports, such as the *Military Geography of Suiyuan*. This was the longest known interviewing experience in Xiao Fang's career. The photos and words left by Xiao Fang are the best source for people today to learn about him and his travels.

On December 14, 1936, Fang Dazeng wrote, based on his interviews at the front in Suiyuan, a lengthy news report entitled *Inspection of the Front in Eastern Suiyuan*. This report included

1936 年 12 月 14 日，方大曾将他在绥远前线的采访内容，写成了长篇通讯《绥东前线视察记》，文章中有亲历，有观察，有评述，朴素简单，实话实说，体现出了一名优秀记者的职业素养。在文章的结尾处，小方的笔调是悲悯的，也是愤怒的，“现在死于东山坡上的匪尸，大半已被野狗吃食，只留可怕的头连着那架光杆的骨骼。有些完整的尸体，穷困的老百姓们，还正在剥他们身上的军衣。等衣服剥光了之后，就立刻跑来几只狗，它们又发现了新的美餐。战争是这样的残酷，然而疯狂的侵略者，则拼命在制造战争”。

战地采访之后，按照小方的计划是应该回北平的。由于新年之初，一则事情较少，二是检查所带来的照相材料中仍有不少未照的片子，他改变了行程，决定借此机会到绥北去一趟，并设想越过集宁与陶林间的大青山，经百灵庙等处，横穿一处所谓的“后草地”地带。这段路自绥远战争平定后，还没有记者走过。在暂时的平静中，他对民生投以极大关注，沿路上采访煤矿、访问牧人、拍摄喇嘛庙和天主堂、拜望友人，行程满满的。这次采访给我们留下了珍贵的图像，同样也留下了生动的文字。

1937 年 1 月 17 日，已经回到北平的方大曾，在协和胡同 10 号的家中，为绥远之行的通讯画上了最后一个句号：冲洗放大出来的照片，经仔细审视和挑选，写好说明，投寄中外新闻学社和《世界知识》等杂志。

绥远之行的照片和文字是小方留存下来作品的精彩部分，他把深情和厚意融入镜头和笔端的同时，一个直抒胸臆、关注民生、爱憎分明的小方也活脱脱地展现在我们面前。

为了使更多的青少年了解绥远的形势和战况，1937 年 2 月 2 日下午两点，方大曾应天津基督教青年会之约，做了“绥远近状”的专题演讲。他的绥远见闻和自己的分析判断，在那个微寒的午后，感动着全场的听众，时而平静时而激昂的语气，引领着大家仿佛看到冰封的荒原、可亲的将士、敌人的贪婪和危险的处境。在座的每个人都在想，山雨欲来，我们又该如何作为？

本章照片选自方大曾绥远之行留下的 400 多张底片，拍摄时间为 1936 年 12 月至 1937 年 1 月。

his experiences, observations, and commentary in simple, plain, and honest language, exhibiting the professionalism of an excellent journalist. At the end of this report, Xiao Fang's tone was sad, sympathetic, and indignant. "Most enemy bodies lying on the eastern slope had already been devoured by wild dogs, except for several horrible skulls joined to bare skeletons. There still remained some intact corpses, from whose bodies the impoverished commoners were peeling off military uniforms. Once undressed, several dogs immediately ran up, attracted to the new delicacies. This was the cruelty of war. Those maniac invaders were desperately provoking wars."

After conducting interviews on the battlefield, Xiao Fang originally planned to return to Beiping. As it was early in the new year, he did not have much work to do. and he realized he needed to take more photographs after examining the photographic materials he had brought. So, Xiao Fang changed his route and decided to go to northern Suiyuan. Along this journey, he planned to climb over Daqing Mountain between Jining and Taolin counties and traverse an area known as the Houcaodi Prairie, which had not been visited by a reporter since the victory in the Suiyuan Campaign. During this lull, he paid a great deal of attention to the plight of the common people. During the journey, Xiao Fang interviewed coal miners and herdsmen, photographed a lama temple and a Catholic church, and visited his friends on a tight schedule. This special journey by Fang Dazeng left us with his valuable photographs and vivid words.

On January 17, 1937, Fang Dazeng arrived back in Beiping to his house at No. 10 Xiehe Hutong. He noted the period of his travels in Suiyuan by developing and magnifying the photos. After careful review and selection, he combined the selected photos with notes and mailed them to the Chinese-Foreign Journalism Society, *World Knowledge*, and other magazines.

Xiao Fang's photographs and words during his journey to Suiyuan are among the best of his works. When Xiao Fang engraved his deep affection and sympathy into his lens and pen, a man who straight-forwardly expressed his thoughts, cared for people's livelihood, and took a clear stand on what to love and hate was vividly presented to us.

To enlighten young people about the trends and war situation in Suiyuan, at 2 p.m. on February 2, 1937, Fang Dazeng delivered a special lecture on the recent situation in Suiyuan, by invitation of the Chinese Young Men's Christian Association (YMCA) in Tianjin. What he had seen and heard in Suiyuan, along with his analysis and judgment, moved the audience that chilly afternoon. His voice was sometimes calm, sometimes emotional as he presented the frozen wasteland, lovable warriors, greedy enemies, and dangerous circumstances. Everyone in attendance wondered how to brave the upcoming tempest.

The photos in this chapter are selected from over 400 negatives left behind by Fang Dazeng which were taken during his trip to Suiyuan from December 1936 to January 1937.

绥远，方大曾翻越大青山时留影（1937 年 1 月）
Fang Dazeng riding over Daqing Mountain (January, 1937).

集宁，火车站上来自山西的慰劳团（1936 年 12 月）

Civilian representatives from Shanxi Province pay respect to the army while standing on the platform of a railway station in Jining (December, 1936).

红格尔图附近的部队换防（1936 年 12 月）

Rotation near Hongge'ertu (December, 1936).

冬天的集宁街头（1936 年 12 月）

A street in Jining during winter (December, 1936).

绥远的县城街道（1937 年 1 月）

A county street in Suiyuan (January, 1937).

范长江（左）与门炳岳师长，前往隆盛庄的路上

Fan Changjiang (left) and Division Commander Men Bingyue on their way to Longshengzhuang.

傅作义（左）与晋绥军骑兵司令赵承绶在集宁大礼堂前

Fu Zuoyi (left) and Zhao Chengshou, Calvary Commander of the Shanxi-Suiyuan Army, in front of the Grand Auditorium in Jining.

范长江等人在兴和前沿观察

Fan Changjiang and others inspect the front at Xinghe.

陶林，骑兵第二师孙长胜师长（1936 年 12 月）

Sun Changsheng, Commander of the 2nd Calvary Division, in Taolin (December, 1936).

红格尔图，前线指挥者

Commanders at the front in Hongge'ertu.

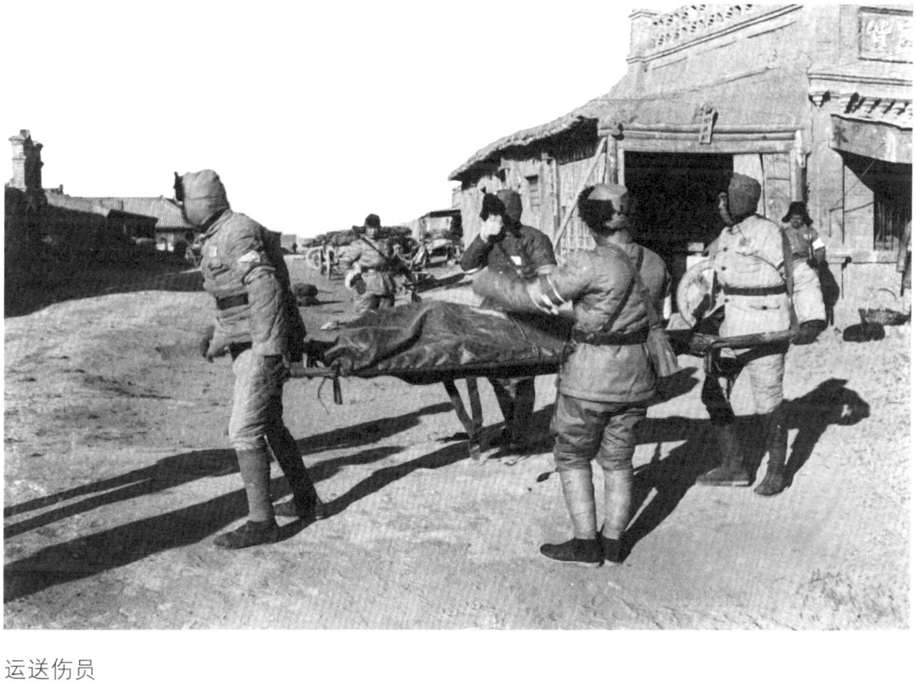

运送伤员

Carrying the wounded.

阵地加固

Fortifying the battlefield.

绥东四旗剿匪司令达密凌苏龙（中）

Dami Lingsulong, Commander of Enemy Suppression Headquarters in the Four Banners of Eastern Suiyuan (middle).

四子王旗，乌兰哈达，哈布其勒庙

Habu Qile Temple, Wulanhada, Siziwang Banner.

开掘工事

Digging trenches.

救火表演

Fire drill.

集合队伍

Assembly of troops.

消防演习

Fire drill.

前方补给

Supplies for the front.

兴和，街头抗日标语

Slogans against Japanese aggression on the street in Xinghe.

陶林县政府

Taolin County Government.

集宁，防空警戒
Air defense in Jining.

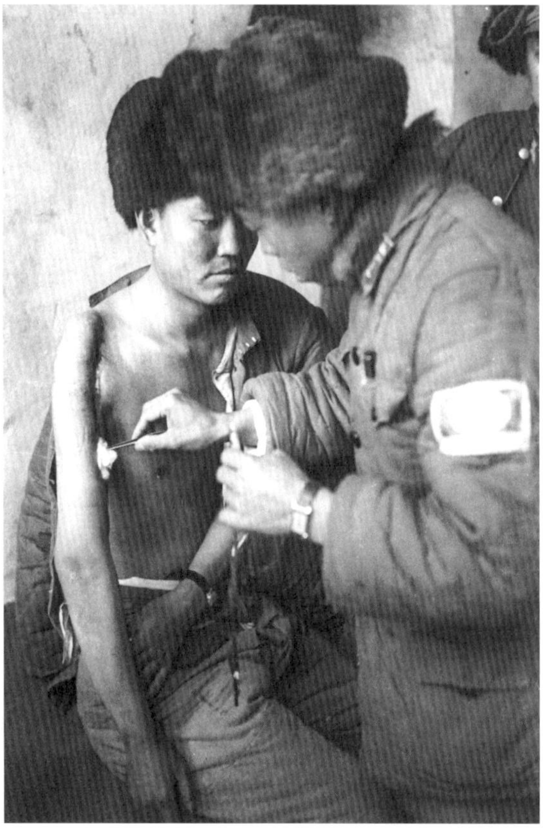

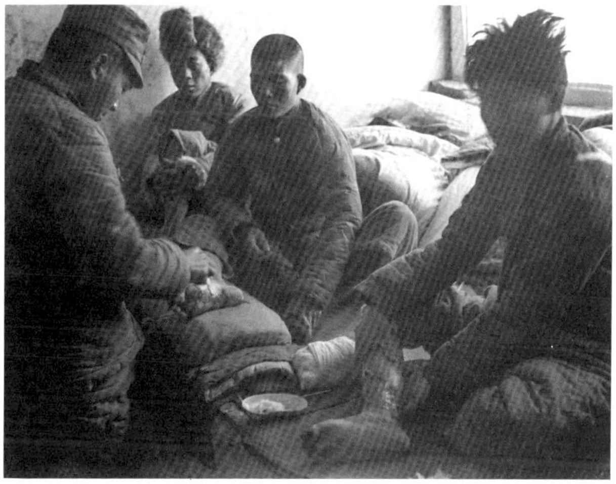

红格尔图、百灵庙等地的战地卫生院（1936 年 12 月）

Battlefield hospitals in Hongge'ertu, the Bailing Temple, and other places (December, 1936).

绥远战事后集宁、红格尔图等地步兵、炮队换防、集结（1936 年 12 月）

Rotation and assembly of infantrymen and artillerymen in Jining, Hongge'ertu, and other places after the Suiyuan Campaign (December, 1936).

兴和，义勇队（1936 年 12 月）

Volunteer squad in Xinghe (December, 1936).

兴和，保卫团指挥官与缴获的日本关东军陆军特务机关车辆

A security force commander and a captured secret service vehicle of the Japanese Kwantung Army, in Xinghe.

临战整备

Preparing before going into battlefield.

兵士道旁进食

Soldiers eating by the road.

前往高家地途中，四零一团步兵修筑工事（1936年12月）

The infantrymen of the 401st Regiment constructing defenses en route to Gaojiadi Village (December, 1936).

永宁煤矿，小方（左二）在绥远采访期间与记者同行合影
Xiao Fang (second left) and his peers during his interviewing travels in Suiyuan.

挖战壕的娃娃兵
A child soldier digging a trench.

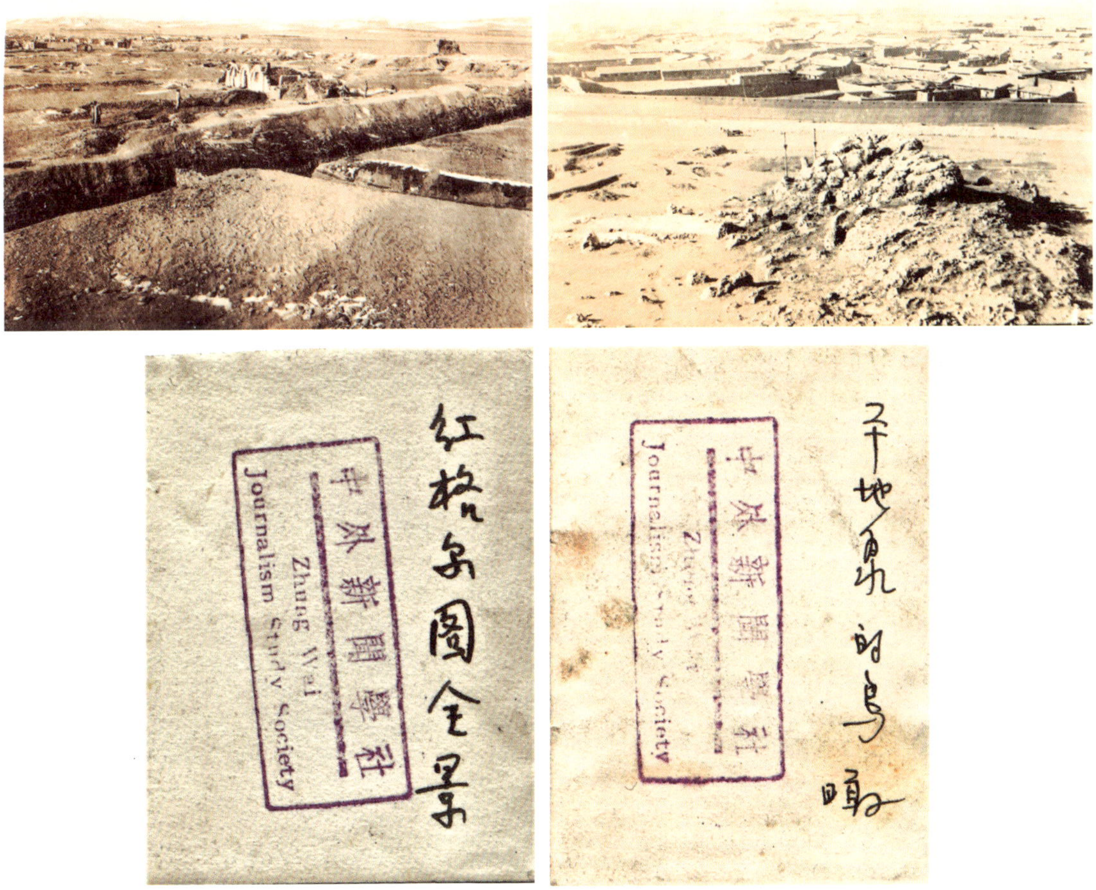

红格尔图全景和平地泉的鸟瞰原版图片，背面盖有中外新闻学社发稿印章（原件）

Original panoramic photos of Hongge'ertu and Pingdiquan, with the publishing seal of the Chinese-Foreign Journalism Society printed on the back.

集宁、红格尔图等地的防空、防化演习（1936 年 12 月）

Air and chemical defense drills in Jining, Hongge'ertu, and other places (December, 1936).

绥远，守疆卫土（1936 年 12 月至 1937 年 1 月）
Guarding borders in Suiyuan (December, 1936 – January, 1937).

绥远，守疆卫土（1936 年 12 月至 1937 年 1 月）
Guarding borders in Suiyuan (December, 1936 – January, 1937).

(652) 世界知識 第五卷

本刊特約通訊

從集寧到陶林

小方

集甯的朋友，再見

年末年初的這些日子，綏東平靜，大家閑得要命。我本來早預備着回北平去了，但又忽然想到：爲什麼不借着這機會到綏北去一趟呢？檢察一下箱子裏的照相材料，看看還剩着二三百張未照的片子，我決定把它消耗在蒙古去。

我計畫着越過集寧與陶林間的大青山，經烏藍花大廟百靈廟等處，橫穿一段所謂「後草地」地帶。這路程所經過的地方大部分是蒙漢雜處，同時又是王英僞匪曾經陷落過的地方，自戰爭平定後，還沒有新聞記者到那裏去視察過被匪蹂躪後的慘狀，其次，爲着多了解一點目前最值得我們注意的所謂蒙古民衆與綏遠大局的關係。以上面兩種意義而言，這也是很值得去冒一次辛苦的旅行。

湯恩伯軍長聽到我這個計畫，他要派汽車送我，但是他不知道這段原始狀態下的路程，是不適宜於現代化的交通工具的，我早已向王萬齡師長借好了兩匹駿馬，並蒙他派一個衛兵同行。

一月六日的中午，一位熱誠的青年朋友邱溪映君，幫助我安置了一切，目送我遠遠的走上征途，『再見吧，我一定給你們帶回來豐富的新聞！』我這樣望着邱君作默默的思想。

路過一個煤礦區

此行二十里至馬連灘，從老遠就已望見兩旁邊的山坡上現出一塊塊的黑點，這一帶地方出產煤炭，因爲炭質裏含有多量的硫磺，所以燒起來常發出一種強烈的氣味，本地人因此名之爲臭炭。開採臭炭全用土法，苦力們總是每三人湊成一個集團，到礦山主——亦即是地主那裏，交納三塊錢的稅金，就可以由他的礦面上得到一塊小小的地盤。他們三人開始工作是先從事掘井，繼之以採炭。礦井是垂直的，並且也有一二百尺深，但是並沒有機器絞車的設備。下井的苦工，只是憑着在井壁上鑿好了的梯槽，一蹬一蹬的往下走。井口的直徑很小，只能容一個人的身體爬上爬下，所以用這方法作爲「地獄」與「光明」間的交通媒介，還勉强可以辦得通，不過，在這梯槽上經過的人，萬一失足，亦是不堪設想的。

他們三人中，有兩個人帶着暗淡的油燈下到炭層上去工作，井口上面有一架「櫓櫓，」正和北方田莊裏的水井一樣。另一個留在上面的人，就掌管這架「櫓櫓」把底下那兩個人採下的炭照着汲水一樣地從井底用繩索絞上來，他們的工作決無時間的限制，他們有一輛「塞北式」的牛車，幾時把這一車裝載滿了，也就算今天的工作完畢，接着再把這用性命換來的臭炭，運到集寧陶林或其他的村鎭去求售。每車臭炭，地主還得以神聖的所有權資格抽收二角錢稅金。以集寧的市價而言，每車臭炭只能賣到一元有奇，那麼這三個礦工的純收入是可以估計得出了。他們的純收入，除了自己的用度之外，還得供養一個牛的生活；又，這車炭運到市上去賣，是否能立即遇到買主，也完全沒有把握；因之吃過了早飯，是不敢想到晚飯在哪裏的。

井底下的情形，因爲時間關係，未能親自下去看看，但是我在從前的旅行中，下過好多次煤礦，那些礦還都是有機器化的設備，工人的工作情形已是我們所想像不到的那樣苦了。自然，這種土窰裏的環境當是更加困難與危險。

作這種「採礦事業」的人，有一部分是亡命者，有一部分是除此以外再也找不到另外的生路之人。這個世界簡直不允許他們生存在光明中；我想，他們總會得到解放的吧。我這樣企望着，我確信這不是幻

刊登在《世界知识》1937 年第 12 期的通讯《从集宁到陶林》

From Jining to Taolin, a news report published in *World Knowledge* (No. 12, 1937).

永宁煤矿，绥远采访途中的小方（前）

Xiao Fang (front) during his journey to Suiyuan to conduct interviews (Yongning Coal Mine).

运石料，修掩体

Carrying stones to build cover.

绥远之行后小方发表在《美术生活》等杂志的报道

Reports by Xiao Fang published in *Fine Arts Life* and other magazines after his journey to Suiyuan.

绥远之行后小方发表在《美术生活》等杂志的报道

Reports by Xiao Fang published in *Fine Arts Life* and other magazines after his journey to Suiyuan.

Slogans 集羣街頭之防空宣傳標語

Policemen Wearing anti-gas Mask 佩帶防毒面具之街頭警士

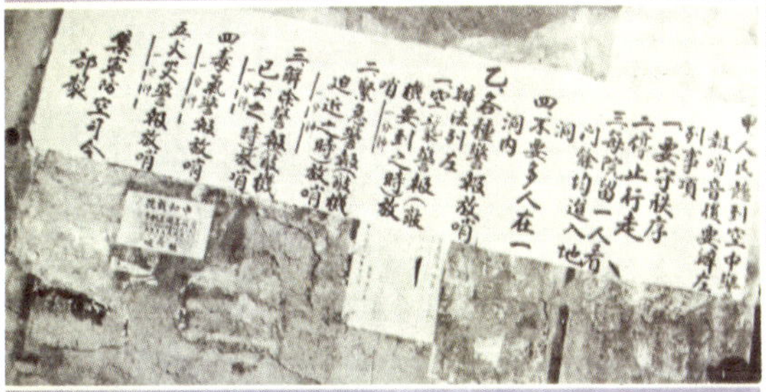

Anti-aircraft gun 偽網掩護濟小高射炮

Anti-aircraft gun under disguise 高射機關槍之陣地及偽裝(左圖)

Martial-law declared during practice 演習時之戒嚴情形

绥远之行后小方发表在《美术生活》等杂志的报道

Reports by Xiao Fang published in *Fine Arts Life* and other magazines after his journey to Suiyuan.

红格尔图，东山坡上的匪尸被当地百姓剥去衣裳，又被野狗撕食，小方在通讯《绥东前线视察记》中有详细介绍。20 世纪 90 年代，美国耶鲁大学教授曾商榷高价购买这组底片，被方澄敏婉拒

In Hongge'ertu, dead enemies on the eastern slope were being undressed by local commoners and devoured by wild dogs. Xiao Fang recorded this, in detail, in his report *Inspection of the Front in Eastern Suiyuan*. In the 1990s, a professor at Yale University tried to purchase this set of photos at a high price, but was declined by Fang Chengmin, Xiao Fang's sister.

陶林，牧羊人（1937 年 1 月）
A shepherd in Taolin (January, 1937).

绥远之行，小方经过乌兰花、大庙、百灵庙穿越后草地前往陶林的途中所见（1937 年 1 月）

What Xiao Fang saw along his journey to Suiyuan: From Wulanhua to the Xila Mulun Temple to Bailing Temple, across the Houcaodi Prairie and onto Taolin County (January, 1937).

四子王府，蒙古王公的结婚大典（1937 年 1 月）
A wedding ceremony of Mongolian nobles in Siziwang Banner (January, 1937).

迎親大隊的開路先鋒

新郎在馬上舉手向來賓答禮之姿勢

蒙古王公的結婚大典

Wedding Rites of Mongolian Nobles

（小方攝並記）

潘王從王府步入禮堂

來賓盛服參加結婚典禮

四子王府即是四子部落旗，在綏北烏蘭花的北面五十里，這次綏遠戰爭中，那地方亦恰當其衝。這部落的蒙古王公姓潘，所以人們都不稱他四子王，而稱之為潘王。潘王在綏北的勢力很大，除去現在身為漢奸的德王之外，就算潘王最有勢了，他是堅決擁護中央的，為了表示他的真誠起見，他的參謀長黃文錦君是常川駐在歸綏的。

今年一月十五日是他為他的公子「授室」之期，在典禮舉行的前幾天，四子王府的後面已經搭起許多蒙古包，這是為遠路來賓所預備的，賀喜的來賓多半帶着羊馬，這是蒙古人的最高貴的禮物。

新娘的家，離四子王府大約有二百里路，所以娶親的車，在前兩天就已經動身了。結婚這天，在四子王府的南面（迎親途中）臨時搭起一座帳篷，及兩座蒙古包，新娘用轎接到，即在此下車入包內休息，然後新郎即由王府出來，騎着馬，背着弓箭，帶領着百十個隨從，組織了一個「迎親大隊」，前面還有一個舉着黃旗的「開路先鋒」就馳騁到新娘休息的蒙古包來。在此經過了許多儀式之後，新郎與其「迎親大隊」原班先回，新娘則改換騎馬，緩着步由兩位武官護送到府，先在王府的四週圍繞一個大圈子，然後進入王府的側院休息。潘王與新郎即從王府裏來到另一座蒙古包來，這就是禮堂，新娘此時又用布把全身都包住，由一位女儐相扶持着，步入禮堂，然後全體再回到王府，由新郎用箭把新娘的蒙布挑開，結婚的典禮遂告完成。

在晚間，也舉行盛大的宴會，謳歌笙管，盛極一時！

《蒙古王公的结婚大典》原载《美术生活》第 37 期，1937 年 4 月出版

Wedding Rites of Mongolian Nobles, published in *Fine Arts Life,* No. 37, April, 1937.

小方在集宁，1936 年 12 月 4 日从北平出发，1937 年 1 月 17 日返回，共计 43 天

Xiao Fang in Jining. He left Beiping on December 4, 1936 and returned on January 17, 1937, away from home 43 days.

第七章 **卢沟桥抗战记**

Chapter Seven: Recording the Lugou Bridge Battle against Japanese Aggression

我站在卢沟桥上浏览过一幅开朗的美景，令人眷恋：北面正浮起一片辽阔的白云，衬托着永定河岸的原野；伟大的卢沟桥也许将成为伟大的民族解放战争的发祥地了！

——方大曾《卢沟桥抗战记》

Standing on the Lugou Bridge, I saw grand, beautiful, and fascinating scenery: Stretches of white clouds floating in the north, adding radiance to the open fields on the Yongding River's banks. The great Lugou Bridge may well be the birthplace of our great war for national liberation!

Lugou Bridge Battle against Japanese Aggression, by Fang Dazeng

1937 年 7 月 7 日，被历史学家们界定为中国抗日战争全面爆发的起点。从这一天起，日本军国主义撕下了伪善的面孔，从北京西边的卢沟桥挑起争端，给这个世界上人口最多的国家，带来了长达 8 年的灾难和无法弥补的创伤。

当时，正在北平家中休假的方大曾得知日军进攻的消息后，便决定前往卢沟桥。如果没有这场战争，他的命运很可能是另外一个样子。

7 月 10 日早晨，小方整理了相机和胶卷，带着简单的行李，与母亲和妹妹匆匆告别。当时的北平已处在一片恐慌当中，许多郊外的老百姓为了躲避炮火，源源不断地涌向城里。谁也不知道将来会发生什么，自己会遭受什么样的厄运，但是不祥的预感还是困扰着每一个人。从前方传来的信息得知，战争似乎已经离这座古老的城市越来越近了。

方大曾的战地笔记里写道：十日清晨，战争既停，记者骑自行车前往卢沟桥视察。在丰台岔道口，我被几名日军截住，我身边的相机引起了他们的注意，他们怀疑我是中国军队的高等侦探，理由是新闻记者没有勇气到日军方面来；我递上一张名片，加之态度自若，这个猜疑也就消除了。一小时后，我被放行，穿过涵洞，再行了一里多路，就到了宛平城下。这里正是战场地带，伤亡的兵士想必都已由双方运回了，只剩下一匹死去的骡子，肚肠流露在腹外。城角上飘着一面停战的白旗，城上有几个保安警察在放哨。城东门紧闭着，西门开了一半，我随一位姓于的警官各处拍照并了解战况。时已正午，忽然听到了两个消息，第一是大井村又被日军占领，第二是日军四五百人又从丰台出动，向卢沟桥进发。

方大曾是卢沟桥事变后最早抵临现场的记者。“战争空气由于这次的炮火变得突然紧张，大概全国的民众都确信一个全面抗战将要开始了吧”，从卢沟桥西头到东头 266.5 米，从宛平城西门到东门长 640 米，看到弹痕累累的城墙和城内残垣断壁，小方觉得形势比想象严峻得多。他各处拍摄战迹照片，卢沟桥石狮边，二十九军身背大刀巡逻的战士，透过镜头瞬间定格，成为永恒的历史。

上海《新闻报》记者陆诒 50 年后还清晰地记得方大曾那张年轻兴奋的脸庞，“他在第一时间赶到了宛平，最先报道了震惊中外的‘卢沟桥事变’。

July 7, 1937 has been decided by historians to be the beginning of the comprehensive outbreak of China's War of Resistance against Japanese Aggression. From this day forward, upon provoking a conflict at the Lugou Bridge to the west of Beijing, Japanese militarism tore off its mask of hypocrisy and brought to this country, with the largest population in the world, calamity lasting eight years and incurable trauma.

Upon learning of Japanese aggression, Fang Dazeng, vacationing at home, immediately decided to go to the Lugou Bridge. If not for this war, he would have had a different fate.

On the morning of July 10, Xiao Fang packed his camera and film, took simple luggage, and hurriedly said goodbye to his mother and younger sister. Beiping was overwhelmed by fear and panic. Many suburban commoners flooded into the city to flee gunfire. No one knew what would happen, but the ominous atmosphere bothered everyone. As learned from the front news, war was marching toward this ancient city.

In his battlefield notes, Fang Dazeng wrote: "On the morning of July 10th, the battle was over. I rode a bicycle to inspect the Lugou Bridge. At the crossing in Fengtai, I was stopped by several Japanese soldiers. My camera attracted their attention. They suspected I was a senior detective serving Chinese troops because they believed a journalist wouldn't dare come to the Japanese-occupied area. Then, calmly, I handed them my business card and their suspicion was alleviated.

One hour later, I was freed. After passing through the culvert and traveling over 500 meters, I arrived below the city of Wanping. This was the battlefield area. Wounded soldiers must have been carried back by the two sides because only a dead mule, whose intestines protruded from its belly, remained. On the corner of the city wall, there fluttered a white flag symbolizing a truce. On that same corner, there were several security policemen on duty as sentries. The eastern city gate was completely closed while the western gate was half closed. I followed an officer, surnamed Yu, to take photos and learn about the war situation. It was already noon and I suddenly heard two new messages. First, Dajing Village was occupied by Japanese troops again. Second, around 400-500 Japanese soldiers had marched out of Fengtai toward the Lugou Bridge."

Fang Dazeng was the first journalist to arrive at the site after the Lugou Bridge Incident. "After the battle, the air has become quite tense due to gunfire. Probably everyone in China will believe a comprehensive war to resist Japanese aggression is about to begin!" It was 266.5 meters from the western to eastern ends of the Lugou Bridge and 640 meters from the western to eastern gates of Wanping. Seeing the bullet-ridden city wall and debris inside the city, Xiao Fang realized the situation was much more serious than anticipated. He took photos of the traces of what was left behind. Scenery beside the Lugou Bridge's stone lions and the patrolling soldiers of the 29th Corps, carrying broadswords, was captured by his camera and became eternal frames for the ongoing history.

Fifty years later, Lu Yi, a journalist for the *Shanghai Press Journal*, still remembered the young, excited face of Fang Dazeng: "He immediately rushed to Wanping and was the first to report on the Lugou Bridge Incident that had attracted a lot of attention worldwide. In Xiao Fang's words, the battle was painfully miserable. Although decades have passed, his personal descriptions still make

在小方的笔下，战争的惨烈直刺心脾，虽然几十年过去，他留下的亲历描述，仍然让人心有余悸，仿佛战争就发生在眼前”。

1937 年 7 月 11 日至 22 日，方大曾在家中写出长篇通讯《卢沟桥抗战记》，洗印了卢沟桥、长辛店被日军轰炸后惨状的照片，紧张工作的同时，他在不平静中度过了自己 25 岁的生日。

23 日，他将文章和采访拍摄的照片从北平寄出，后刊登在 8 月 1 日出版的上海《世界知识》杂志第六卷第十号上，文章还加了编者按，“小方先生此稿于廿三日由平寄发，正在二十一日所得停战协定成立之后，末第二段所说和平解决，就是指当时的停战办法。但是日帝国主义显然没有和平的诚意，只有侵略的野心。在廿五晚廊坊事件，廿六日广安门冲突以后，日方对我已下最后通牒，中日大战已经迅速展开了”。

“我站在卢沟桥上，浏览过一幅开朗的美景，令人眷恋，”小方在通讯《卢沟桥抗战记》里写道，“北面正浮起一片辽阔的白云，衬托着永定河岸的原野，伟大的卢沟桥也许将成为伟大的民族解放战争的发祥地了！”

“美国几家著名电影公司的新闻摄影员，中央电影厂的技师以及国内的几位著名记者都纷纷赶到北方来，然而局势反趋沉寂下去。”再次来到卢沟桥畔，7 月 28 日，小方见到了《大公报》的范长江等人，绥远一别半载，本不知何年何月再聚，无奈战火逼人，这样的会面，还是令人喜忧参半。

据跟方大曾一起在前线采访过的陆诒回忆，小方给一个 16 岁小战士拍照片时，一颗炸弹在附近爆炸。别人招呼他赶紧躲避，他拍拍胸前的照相机，笑着说：“今天收获不小。”

1937 年 8 月 7 日，《伦敦新闻画报》刊登了小方拍摄卢沟桥事变的相关照片。来自现场的真相报道，撕下了日本在西方世界里伪善的面具。同时，《泰晤士报》报道称：“中国通常是不希望战争的，当前形势发展的结果取决于日方是否执意要挑起事端。”

据吴群先生考证，一段时间里，小方频繁往复平津之间，拍摄了《敌故意摧毁我文化机关——南开大学已成灰烬》《已沦敌手之天津市》等组照，以中外社的名义刊于第七期《良友战事画刊》。

平津陷落之后，范长江回到了上海，后来接到小方从北方来信说，“我的家在北平陷落了！我还有许多摄影材料工具不能带出来，我现在成为无家可归的人了！我想找一家报馆做战地记者，请你为我代找一岗位。”那时，上海《大

my heart tremble with fear as if the war were happening now."

During July 11-22, 1937, Fang Dazeng wrote, at home, the lengthy report *Lugou Bridge Battle against Japanese Aggression* and developed film regarding the misery at both Lugou Bridge and Changxindian when bombed by the Japanese invaders. While busily working, he spent his 25th birthday in turbulence.

On July 23, Fang Dazeng sent, from Beiping, his report and photos he had taken during interviews, which were published on August 1 in *World Knowledge* Magazine (Shanghai, No. 10, Vol. 6). In the article, the editor's note read: "Mr. Xiao Fang sent this report from Beiping on July 23, right after the truce agreement was signed on July 21. The so-called peaceful solution in the next to last paragraph refers to the truce at that time. However, the Japanese imperialists obviously have no genuine desire for peace, merely wild ambition for aggression. After the Langfang Incident on the night of the 25th, and the Guang'an Gate Conflict on the 26th, the Japanese have issued an ultimatum to us. The war between China and Japan is developing rapidly."

Xiao Fang wrote in the *Lugou Bridge Battle against Japanese Aggression*: "Standing on the Lugou Bridge, I saw grand, beautiful, and fascinating scenery: Stretches of white clouds floating in the north, adding radiance to the open fields on the Yongding River's banks. The great Lugou Bridge may well be the birthplace of our great war for national liberation!"

Xiao Fang continued: "Journalists from several American film companies, technicians from the Central Film Studio, and several well-known domestic journalists all came to the north, yet the situation became silent." Arriving at the Lugou Bridge again on July 28, Xiao Fang saw Fan Changjiang and other *Ta Kung Pao* journalists. It had already been half a year since they parted in Suiyuan. Originally, they had no idea when they would meet again. However, pressed by gunfire, they met again, filling them with both joy and sorrow.

As recalled by Lu Yi, who once went to the front with Xiao Fang to conduct interviews, when Xiao Fang took photographs of a 16-year-old soldier, a bomb exploded nearby. Some told him to flee, but he patted the camera in front of his chest and said with a smile: "A big harvest today!"

On August 7, 1937, *Illustrated London News* published photos, by Xiao Fang, about the Lugou Bridge Incident. This first-hand report from the original site ripped off Japan's mask of hypocrisy in the eyes of Westerners. Meanwhile, *The Times* stated that, normally China would not start a war and current developments depended on whether Japan would intentionally provoke a conflict.

Based on Mr. Wu Qun's textual research, we have learned that Xiao Fang traveled between Beiping and Tianjin making a photo series that included *Relics of Nankai University* and *Fallen Tianjin City*, published in the seventh issue of the *Young Companion* under the name of the Chinese-Foreign Journalism Society.

After Beiping and Tianjin were occupied by the enemy, Fan Changjiang returned to Shanghai. Later, he received a letter from Xiao Fang from the north, saying: "My home in Beiping was occupied by the enemy! Many of my photography materials and tools cannot be taken out from my home. Now, I am homeless! I want to work in a newspaper office as a war correspondent. Please help me find such a post." At that time, *Ta Kung Pao* (Shanghai) needed journalists. Fan Changjiang, who was mainly in charge of journalist deployment and liaison, invited Xiao Fang to report on the Beiping-Hankou Railway. Thus, Xiao Fang started writing reports for *Ta Kung Pao*.

At the end of August 1937, Fan Changjiang held a meeting of war correspondents in Datong. Participants included Fang Dazeng, Meng Qiujiang, and Qiu Xiying. "Then, Xiao Fang came to Datong, with Xiying. He

公报》正需要人，主要负责战地记者派遣和联络工作的范长江，就请小方负责平汉线工作，于是小方开始为《大公报》写通讯。

1937年8月底，范长江在大同召开了一次战地记者会，参加会的有方大曾、孟秋江和邱溪映。“小方至大同，同溪映同来，据云，系在保定闻八路军挺进热河，故赶去参加，到绥始知不确，并自承认单独行动之欠考虑。”范长江与小方等人交流了情况，主要研究了今后的工作布置，“溪映坚持绥远宁夏线，秋江支持同蒲线，而小方则仍挺进平汉线。”

9月初，大同已十分危急，日本飞机几乎每天来轰炸大同车站，前方运输只靠一条破败的平绥路。从现有的资料分析，在此期间，方大曾写过并寄出两篇文章，一篇是写于9月4日的《从娘子关到雁门关》，分两期刊登于9月17日和18日的《大公报》，一篇是写于9月7日的《血战居庸关》，刊登于9月25日的《大公报》。

不久，以天津中外新闻学社为基础，全民通讯社在太原成立。在穆欣先生的《抗日烽火中的中国报业》一书中特别提到全民社的成立，“全民社在着手筹办的时候，周恩来曾批示：‘定名为全民通讯社，李公朴任社长，实际工作由党负责，经费也由党负责。’通讯社成立时，青年摄影家沙飞（司徒传）、小方（方大曾）出任记者。”“建社初期，著名摄影记者小方所拍摄的战地照片，尤为各报刊欢迎。”

据陆诒回忆，担任《大公报》战地记者期间，小方独特的视角和作业方式引起广泛的关注，成为报道救亡爱国事迹的名记者。在同行眼中，诚挚、天真、勇敢、温和的方大曾对这场战争倾注了极大的精力，疯狂地奔逐于南口、保定、居庸关、太原、大同之间。

那时保定已万分吃紧，卫立煌将军所部三师增援南口落空，正与日军激战于永定河上游青白口一带。小方当时异常兴奋，他不只要到保定，更要到保定以北南口山脉中去。

“他的工作情绪愈来愈高涨，身体也愈来愈结实。北方的夏季，他穿着短裤衬衣，自己带着他的小箱子行李，在平汉路前线不断地突击。他那诚挚、天真、勇敢、温和的性格，博得各方面的好感。”范长江在《忆小方》里有这样一段珍贵的文字，让我们看见了战火中的小方。

他带上充分的蓝墨水、稿纸和照相器材，急急由石家庄登上北去的列车，临别时，范长江说：“希望你能写一篇‘永定河上游的战争’！”他平和坚

explained that while in Baoding, he heard the Eighth Route Army had marched into Rehe, so he decided to go there. However, after arriving in Suiyuan, he learned that this was false. He admitted that it was thoughtless of him to act alone." Fan Changjiang, Xiao Fang, and the rest exchanged ideas and decided their work plan: "We agreed that Xiying would report on the battles along the Suiyuan-Ningxia Railway, Qiujiang along the Datong-Puzhou Railway, and Xiao Fang along the Beiping-Hankou Railway."

Early in September, the situation in Datong was perilous. Japanese aircraft bombed the Datong Railway Station almost every day. Supplies could be transported to the front only via the broken Beiping-Suiyuan Railway. Based on current information, we know that during this period, Fang Dazeng wrote and sent two reports. One, written on September 4, was entitled *From Niangzi Pass to Yanmen Pass* and serialized in two issues of *Ta Kung Pao* on September 17 and 18. The other, written on September 7, was entitled *Heroic Battle at Juyong Pass* and was published in *Ta Kung Pao* on September 25.

Soon, the National News Agency was founded in Taiyuan, taking its roots from the Chinese-Foreign Journalism Society in Tianjin. In his book *Chinese Newspaper Industry during the Anti-Japanese War*, Mr. Mu Xin particularly mentioned the founding of the National News Agency: "When the National News Agency was founded, Zhou Enlai wrote an instruction to 'Name it National News Agency and appoint Li Gongpu President. The Party will administrate and fund its operation.' Upon founding, Sha Fei (also named Situ Chuan), a young photographer, and Xiao Fang (Fang Dazeng) were employed as journalists." "In the agency's early stages, war photos by famous photographer Xiao Fang were especially welcomed by all newspapers."

Lu Yi recalled that, while working as a war correspondent, Xiao Fang's unique perspective and work style attracted great attention, making him a well-known journalist who reported on patriotic stories about salvaging China from subjugation. In the eyes of his peers, as a sincere, innocent, brave, and amiable man, Fang Dazeng was highly devoted to reporting on the war and highly motivated, frequently traveling between Nankou, Baoding, the Juyong Pass, Taiyuan, and Datong.

At that time, the situation in Baoding was already extremely dangerous. The 3rd Division, under General Wei Lihuang, intended to reinforce troops in Nankou. However, it was too late. They were fighting the enemy fiercely in the Qingbaikou Village area at the upper reaches of the Yongding River. Xiao Fang was very excited. He not only wanted to go to Baoding, but also planned to travel to the mountains in Nankou, north of Baoding.

"...his body grew even stronger. In that summer in northern China, wearing shorts and a shirt, and carrying his luggage, he made constant breakthroughs on the Beiping-Hankou Railway front. His sincerity, innocence, bravery, and amiability won him popularity everywhere." These valuable words are taken from Fan Changjiang's article *In Memory of Xiao Fang*.

Xiao Fang took sufficient blue ink, paper, photography materials and tools, and hurriedly boarded a train going north from Shijiazhuang. Before they parted, Fan Changjiang said: "I hope you can write a report on the battle in the upper reaches of the Yongding River!" Plainly and sternly, Xiao Fang answered: "I'll surely submit a good one."

According to records in the book *Big Events of Baoding*, on September 14, 1937, the Zhuozhou-Baoding Campaign was formally launched, with around 120,000 Chinese soldiers battling 87,500 Japanese invaders. On September 16th, Zhou Enlai and Peng Dehuai, on behalf of the CPC Central Committee and 18th Group Army, respectively, arrived in Baoding and negotiated with

定地回答："我一定有很好的成绩答复你！"

据《保定大事记》记载，1937 年 9 月 14 日，涿保会战全面展开，日军投入兵力 87500 人，中国军队约 12 万人。16 日，周恩来以中共中央代表，彭德怀以第十八集团军代表身份抵保定，与当地驻军指挥官就坚持华北抗战、协同作战等问题进行了谈判。18 日，涿州沦陷，河北省政府、第一专署撤离保定南下。

当时保定吃紧，小方被迫退到保定东南的蠡县，就在涿州陷落的当日，他从这里向上海寄出了通讯《平汉线北段的变化》，并寄信给邯郸的亲属，表示要继续北上。

这篇"九一八"写于保定寄自蠡县的文章发表在 1937 年 9 月 30 日上海《大公报》的第二版，署名本报战地特派员小方。让人没有想到的是，从此以后，这个活力十足的生命，却神秘地消失了，没有任何征兆，也没有任何踪迹。此后，《大公报》就再也没有接收到他的任何报道，一个月，两个月，如同无线电静默，平汉线似乎一下子沉寂了。

《平汉线北段的变化》是小方为人所知的最后的文字，不知是有意还是巧合，文末"贡献"两个字既是文章的尾声，又是他在艰苦环境中为读者采访报道的写照，而他的消失，给人们留下的是至今未解的谜。

据周勉之、方仲伯等人在《周恩来同志亲切关怀和培育全民通讯社》一文中记载："原中外社的社员方大曾，当时在同蒲路沿线活动，就担任了全民社的战地摄影记者，拍摄了不少战地照片，所以全民社在武汉时，除发文字稿外，还发了照片稿。不幸的是，不久即和方失去联系，以后再也听不到关于他的情况，最有可能是在抗战前线牺牲了。"

本章照片的底片随着方大曾的失踪大部分遗失，读者所见系经过多年搜集的报刊的复制呈现，得之不易。这些散落的作品，是卢沟桥事变后向外界发出的第一批照片，极具新闻性和文献性，成为重大事件的代表性记录。拍摄时间为 1937 年 7 至 9 月。

commanders of the local garrisons on issues including the fight against Japanese aggression in northern China and cooperative combat. On September 18th, Zhuozhou was lost and the Hebei Provincial Government, along with its first prefectural commissioner's office, retreated southward, away from Baoding.

Due to the extreme danger in Baoding, Xiao Fang was forced to retreat to Li County, southeast of Baoding. On the day Zhuozhou was occupied, he sent a news report to Shanghai entitled *Changes in the Northern Section of the Beiping-Hankou Railway*, along with a letter to his relative in Handan saying he planned to continue northward.

This report, written in Baoding on September 18, and sent from Li County, was published on page two of the September 30, 1937 issue of *Ta Kung Pao* (Shanghai), under the signature "Xiao Fang, Special War Correspondent of *Ta Kung Pao*." To everyone's surprise, this energetic life disappeared after that report, without a trace before or after. *Ta Kung Pao* received no subsequent reports from Fang Dazeng. The Beiping-Hankou Railway seemed to become unexpectedly silent.

Changes in the Northern Section of the Beiping-Hankou Railway is the swan song of Xiao Fang as far as we know. I wonder whether it is a coincidence that the word "contribution" is both the last word in that report and the best description for his hard work during hard times. Fang Dazeng's disappearance remains a mystery to be unraveled.

An article written by Zhou Mianzhi, Fang Zhongbo, and others, entitled Comrade Zhou Enlai Concerned about and Nurturing the National News Agency, stated that: "Fang Dazeng, who used to work for the Chinese-Foreign Journalism Society, was a war correspondent for the National News Agency and was active along the Datong-Puzhou Railway. He took many war photographs. So, there were many textual and pictorial reports released by the National News Agency in Wuhan. Unfortunately, we were soon out of contact with Xiao Fang and received no news about him. Most likely, he lost his life at the front."

Most of the original negatives of the photos in this chapter were lost with the missing of Fang Dazeng. The photos presented to you are copies from newspapers and magazines collected for many years, very rare indeed. These works found from varied sources are the first batch of photos released to the public after the Lugou Bridge Incident. They are exemplary recorders of major events, serving as valuable news and documents. These photos were taken between July and September 1937.

卢沟桥事变前，小方和母亲方朱理、妹妹方澄敏在北平家中，这是目前发现的三人唯一的合影

Prior to the Lugou Bridge Incident, Xiao Fang, Fang Zhuli (his mother), and Fang Chengmin (his younger sister) at their home in Beiping. This is the only existing photo of these three together.

382　生活星期刊　第一卷

日軍秋操之後

——北平通訊——

小方

十月二十五日至十一月五日的日軍秋操，並不是無聲無息的就安穩度過了的。雖然在秋操的當時，並沒有掀起什麼大亂子，但由於這次『空前的壯舉』確給了北平民衆以一個新的刺激。北平的救亡運動與一般市民的抗敵情緒，不幸並沒有因爲『皇軍』的示威而感到氣餒或退縮，反之確更加熱烈了，更加進展了，這也眞是件怪難說的事。

俗語說：『耳聞不如目見，』這眞是很有道理的。當『友邦』的兵士在四郊演習的時候，當他們大隊的遊行全市的時候，民衆們都親眼瞻仰了『皇軍』的威武。從前還以爲『皇軍』眞是神兵天將一樣的吧？然而今朝一見，原來『不過爾爾，』這又有什麼可怕呢？爲什麼我們還不同他們幹一下子呢？在每個人的腦海裏都發生了這樣的疑問。

『皇軍』的趾高氣揚的態度，機械化的武裝……播散給民衆一個很深的印象，益發增加了民衆的憎恨情感，啟示了一種新的抗戰意識，使民衆在救亡鬥爭中增強了決心與勇敢。這，我們似乎應該對『秋操』這件事，表示感謝！

有的農民說：『××兵到我們村子只來了一百多個，若不是有中國警察來「維持，」我們早就把這羣東西都幹掉了！』有的市民說：『我當時手頭要有一個手溜彈，早就把它丟到坦克車底下了！』正因爲民衆的情緒是這樣，所以在此次秋操期中，北平的警察全體出動，加重『維持』，假以未生任何意外，亦屬萬幸了。

以上所說是指一般民衆的情形而言，其次我們再看着二十九軍的情形。

二十九軍不只是有過光榮的抗敵戰爭的歷史，並且就目前的地位來說，他是冀察平津四省市境內中國軍隊的主要部分，此外尚有五十三軍和三十二軍的一部，但人數都不多，因此二十九軍眞是我們民衆相依爲命的良友了，我們愛二十九軍，好像愛自己的手足一樣！

二十九軍態度的強硬化，自×軍秋操後表示得特別明顯，這是最令我們興奮的事。最近除了他們加勤打靶訓練之外，又針對着×軍秋操，而於十一月十日至十四日舉行了一次大演習；地點在平南固安縣一帶，參加者有兩師之衆，宋哲元軍長並親往指揮，各校學生亦發起了市民募捐，紛紛購買點心用品運往固安慰勞，並組織參觀團，更有以學生軍的資格參加在兵士中共同演習的。

兵士們的情緒是激昂極了，他們用以作爲靶梁的草人，故意弄得像某種人模樣，每當打靶時，必先鄭重宣讀下面的誓辭；『以老百姓的血汗換來的子彈打靶一定用心描準；……（中間還有幾句話記者想不起來了）……要準備戰死疆場，殺死我們的敵人××！』

雖然是豐台要隘已經沒有中國兵了，但是二十九軍的下級軍官們，都很自信地對參觀演習的學生們說：『豐台四面全是我們的人，一旦有事，立刻可把它佔領，我們二十九軍有十六萬弟兄，就連通縣附近也還有我們的隊伍駐紮呢。』當他們演習重機關槍等現代化的武器時，他們對參觀者說：『二十九軍並不都是大刀隊，我們有好些新式武器，我們有錢都製備了槍！』

有些人以爲中國還處於四面楚歌的地位，大勢已去，只等着死亡了。這實在是最不正確的觀念，因爲他們只看到侵略者那方面，而沒有見到主觀的抗敵力量的增強。這種人往往還自命爲很理智的，但實際上則是十足的神精衰弱者！

此外，作爲救亡運動的先鋒的學生大衆，自從本季開學之後，已經用了兩個月的工夫來整理自己的陣容，堅強團結的力量，恰巧趁着這次×軍秋操的激動，亦走向一個新的形態：從準備到行動！

在『秋操』期中，學生們就組織了許多宣傳隊，每天下午放學之後，即分散到各角落裏去宣傳，把敵人侵略的陰謀和目前急應抗戰等事，作爲宣傳的內容。

十一月八日這天，有三千個學生動員到四郊去作災區服務，並組織農民的工作，此後，差不多每天都有各校學生到郊外去作宣傳組織的職務，並且學生軍和民族解放先鋒隊的隊員們，都不斷的到四郊去舉行野戰演習的訓練。北平正處在一個民族抗戰狂熱的氛圍中。

十二日是中山先生誕辰紀念，在當年還有市黨部的時候，照例黨政要人舉行紀念儀式的。在去年因爲黨部沒有了，所以也根本無人想到這回事；然而今年的情形則不同了，各校學生多自動的召開熱烈的紀念會，並且學聯會在這天下午兩點，借基督教公理會的禮拜堂，號召了一個擴大的聯合紀念會，當天恰遇着大風天氣，然而到會者仍很踴躍。最滑稽的是在那將要宣佈開會的時候，來了大批的武裝警察，由大門口一直衝進會堂來，並且吶喊着『殺殺殺！』及衝鋒口令，看那神氣眞相如臨大敵一樣，然而不是的，這是向着紀念國民黨先總理孫中山先生誕辰的羣衆結果這個紀念儀式就在『大鬧公理會』這樣一幕『喜劇』下流產了。

在最近兩天，各校學生正爲了綏遠問題忙着，記者寫此通信時，學聯會正決定預備從十八號起，發動一個大規模的市民募捐運動，來援助綏遠的抗敵將士，並擬組織慰勞隊，隨軍隊到前綫去參加抗戰工作。

前些日子，北京大學和師範大學的學生，都爲了學生會的『組織法』問題，與學校當局鬧得意見很深；但是現在據當局方面都已無條件的表示了讓步，這也是與學生羣衆合作融洽的好現象。就某種意義說，這表示

卢沟桥事变前，小方经过细致采访和分析撰写的《日军秋操之后（北平通讯）》发表于《生活星期刊》1936 年第 26 期

Before the Lugou Bridge Incident, with Xiao Fang's detailed interview and analysis. *After Autumn Drill of Japanese Army: A Beiping News Report*, published in *Life Weekly* (No. 26, 1936).

卢沟桥事变后的卢沟晓月碑（1937 年 7 月 10 日上午）

"Lu Gou Xiao Yue" Stone Tablet on the Lugou Bridge after the incident (morning of July 10, 1937).

长辛店，前方慰劳队

Representatives paying respect to the front army in Changxindian.

小方作品《守卫卢沟桥军士之英姿》登上《申报》封面（1937 年 7 月 25 日出版）

Heroic Solider Guarding the Lugou Bridge, by Xiao Fang (cover photo for *Shun Pao* published on July 25, 1937).

守卫卢沟桥的二十九军战士

A solider of the 29th Corps guarding the Lugou Bridge.

宛平县长王冷斋（前右）和探访者（原图底片毁于战火，此图系刊物扫描件）

Wang Lengzhai (front, right), who was Head of Wanping County, with visitors (original copy destroyed by gunfire – this is a scanned copy from a magazine).

WANPING—UNDER JAPANESE BOMBARDMENT

The little district south of Peiping, being the starting point of the present crisis, becomes the center of the world's attention.

Interior view of the city government of Wanping, damaged by the bombardment.

Wang Lan-chai, magistrate of Wanping, and his staff.

Interior view of the police station of Wanping, after being disarmed by the Japanese troops.

A house near Lukouchiao, ruined by the Japanese guns.

After a truce agreement betwen the Chinese ane Japanese troops, the district was taken over by the peace preservation corps under Gen. Shi Yu-san.

Above, the white stone Lukouchiao (Marco polo Bridge) the very spot where the clashes began. Right, a monument at the bridge.

Chang Sin Dien Station, about 2 miles from Lukouchiao, now an important strategical point held by our troops.

Tai Ching Village an important to Peiping, now occupied by the Japanese

The Yung Ting River, across which the Lukouchiao spans

《美术生活》第 41 期刊登的部分小方作品

Works by Xiao Fang, published in the No. 41 of *Fine Arts Life*.

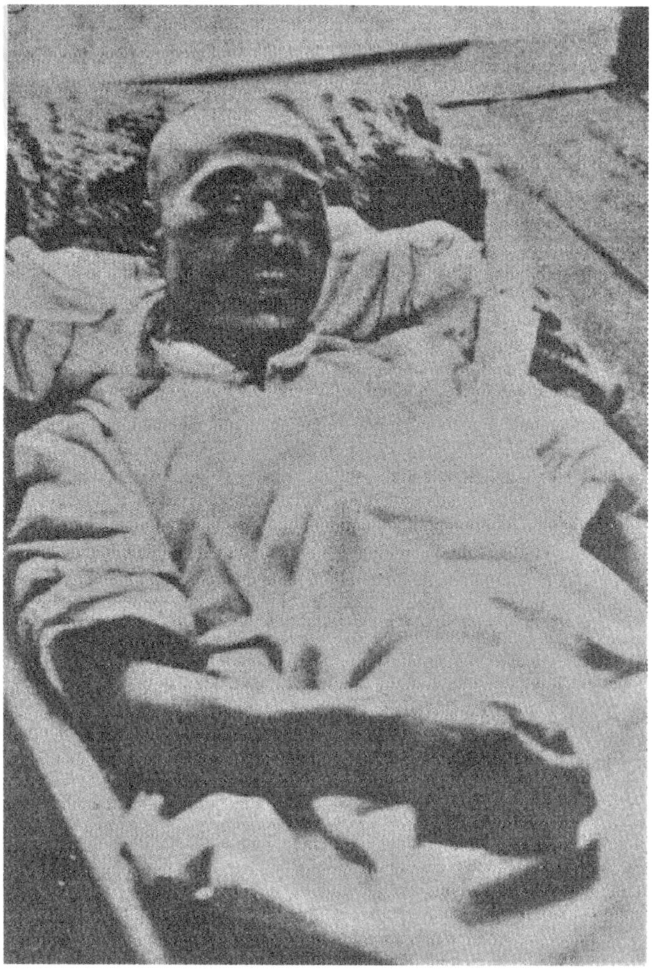

长辛店车站，二一九团三营营长金振中（1937 年 7 月）
Jin Zhenzhong, Commander of the 3rd Battalion of the 219th Regiment, at Changxindian Station (July, 1937).

受伤后即赴保定治疗的金振中和伤员们受到各方慰劳

People from all circles paid respect to Jin Zhenzhong and the wounded soldiers who received treatment in Baoding.

守桥卫士（1937 年 7 月 10 日）

A bridge guard (July 10, 1937).

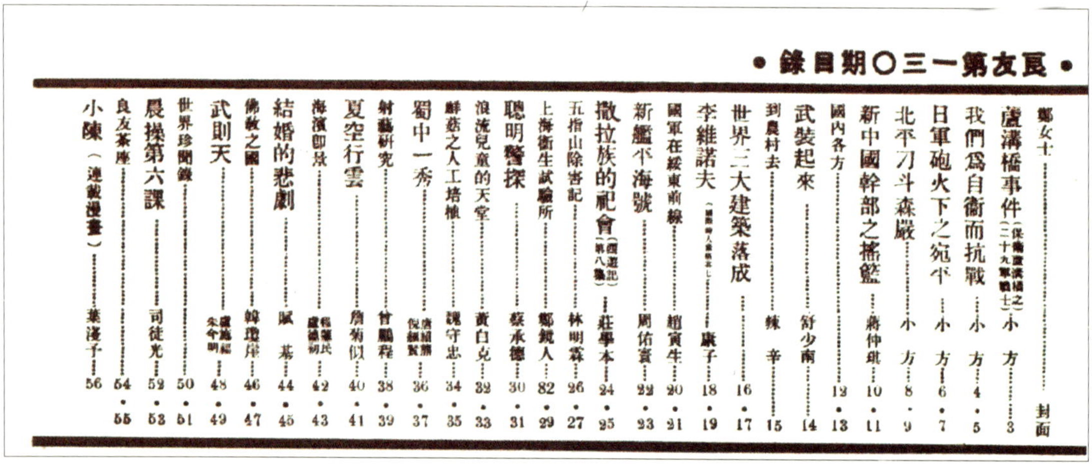

• 良友第一三〇期目錄 •

《良友》杂志第 130 期连续发表小方四组来自第一现场的摄影报道，照片 40 张

Four of Xiao Fang's reports, including 40 photos taken in primary scenes (published together in the No. 130 of *Young Companion* magazine).

③

蘆溝橋事件

保衛蘆溝橋之我廿九軍戰士・小方攝

CHINA AND JAPAN CLASH AT LUKOUCHIAO

At one o'clock in the morning of July 8 the Japanese troops at Lukouchiao (Marco Polo Bridge) about 12 miles south of Peiping, demanded a search of the walled city of Wanping, claiming that one of their soldiers was missing. Refused by the 37th Division of the 29th Army stationed in the district, they started to bombard the city. The Chinese troops returned fire and fighting has been continued ever since Peace negotiations are being carried out with seeming success, but both countries are prepared to fight if necessary. Peace or war, which will it be?

刊载于《良友》杂志第 130 期及《战事周刊》重要位置的《守卫卢沟桥 》等照片，影响广泛

Guarding the Lugou Bridge, published in the No. 130 of *Young Companion* magazine, and other photos prominently displayed in *War News Weekly*.

桥头守卫

A guard at the end of the Lugou Bridge.

守卫北平的二十九军高呼救国口号

29th Corps soldiers, in Beiping, shouting slogans for saving the country.

北平，戒备森严的市区（1937 年 7 月）
A heavily guarded urban area in Beiping (July, 1937).

北平市市长秦德纯（右一）与三十七师冯治安（右二）师长郊外视察部队
Qin Dechun (first right), Mayor of Beiping, and Feng Zhian (second right), Commander of the 37th Division, inspected troops in the suburbs.

蘆溝橋抗戰記

小方

蘆溝橋事件，很簡單的說，就是一個小規模的中日戰爭，這事件發生於一九三七年七月七日的夜午，截至記者寫稿時——七月二十三日，雙方已有「停戰」協定，但日軍仍由山海關繼續向平津增兵，進攻蘆溝橋的部隊，似乎也在擴大動。茲將此次事件之經過略記於後：

保衛北平的二十九軍

許多人對於華北的情形以及二十九軍發生猜疑，這不只是一個大大的錯誤，而且是神經過敏。兩年來二十九軍在艱難中支持了這危急的局面，不知費了多少苦心，這一點已經得到華北民衆的深切同情與了解。又有人說，冀察當局與中央有矛盾，這種說法正是日本當局的了解，而不是我們中國民族所當有的錯誤觀念。蘆溝橋事件發生的時候，謠言很大，但是事件的發展，就證實了冀察當局與中央之一致，總括的說，蘆溝橋戰役在軍事上，中國軍隊實保持了百分之百的勝利，雖然在後來的撤兵交涉條件上，這一切又當別論。然而，假使我們眞的就把這次事件「和平」解決了，而並未能借着這個機會發動了全部的抗戰，甚或容忍日本大量的增兵華北，這却又相反的會造成一個極大的危機。總之，大局尚在飄搖不定，現在的一切推測，都是沒有任何把握的。

蘆溝橋事件的發動，在日本方面早有詳密的計劃。自從六月下旬起，北平市內即已絡續發現許多「怪事」，於是駐在城外的二十九軍，就一點一點的往城裏開。這種軍事的調動，都在夜間，一般市民很少理會。

七月五日起，北平即已無形戒嚴，但人心則始終安定，市長秦德純早就對新聞記者表示說：北平將有擾亂，但平市治安則絕對無虞。的確，自一九三五年夏季，日本嗾使漢奸白堅武自豐台以鐵甲車砲擊北平的事變之後，北平市政當局即已重視城防問題，關於如何保衛北平，如何防備市內的擾亂，以及如何進行有計劃的巷戰，早在兩年前即已準備妥了。無論有什麽緊急事變，在十分鐘之內，全市警察均可佈置完畢。有了這樣的把握，所以在蘆溝橋事件發生後，北平的當局與市民均甚鎮定，這實在是一個最可貴的現象。

长篇通讯《卢沟桥抗战记》发表在《世界知识》1937 年第 6 卷

Lugou Bridge Battle against Japanese Aggression, a lengthy report published in *World Knowledge*, Vol. 6, 1937.

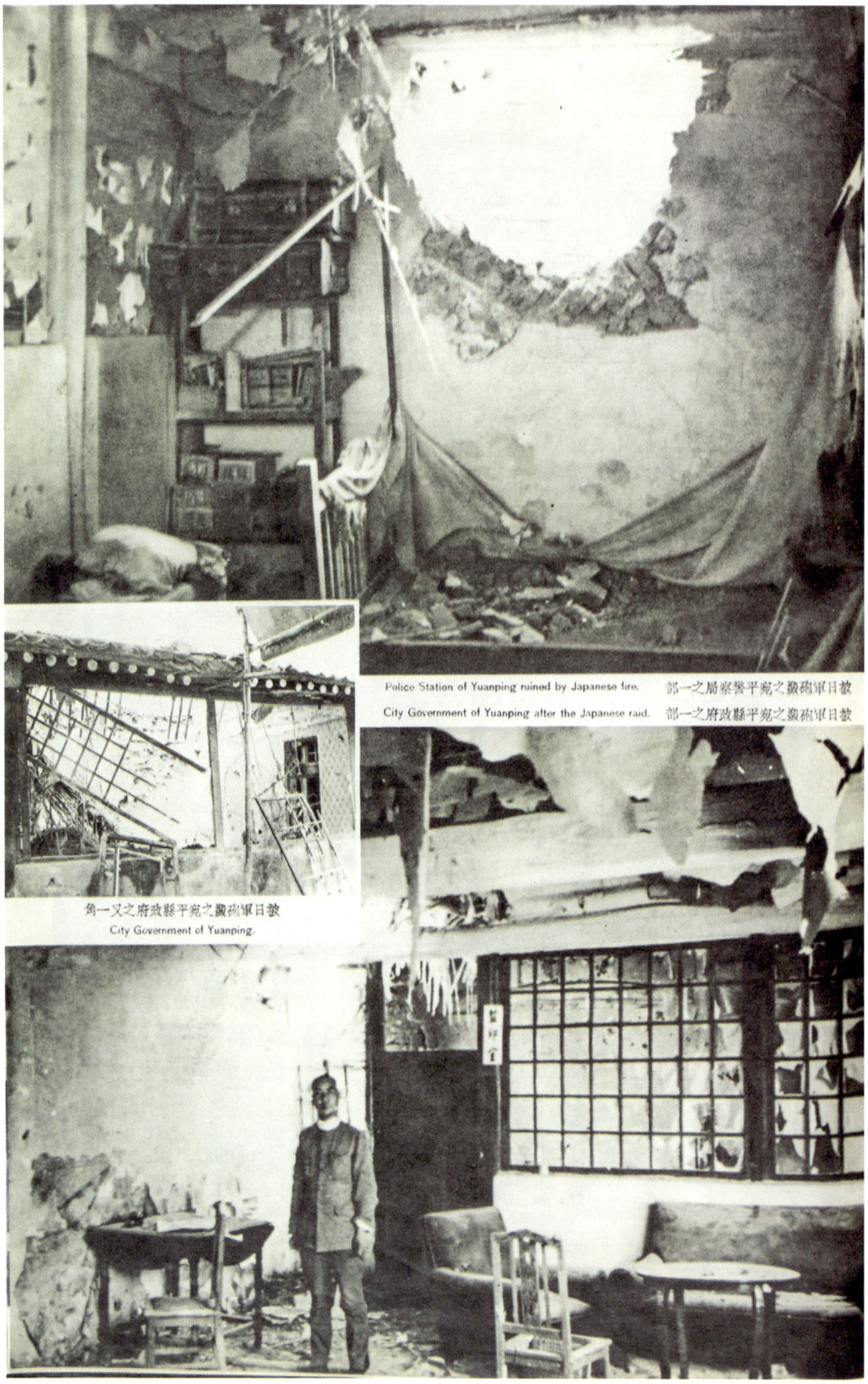

宛平，炮击后县政府惨状

Bombed county government in Wanping.

↓自平開往蘆溝橋的二十九軍士兵（張文元）

↓紅卍字會救護隊在北平街頭巡行（小方）

蘆溝橋事件發生後之北平

自蘆溝橋中日軍隊發生衝突以後，北平毗連戰區，爲防止日軍進襲及漢奸乘機蠢動起見，市當局遂頒佈戒嚴命令，將內外各城門全部關閉，城內衛要區域皆堆積沙袋等防禦物，以準備萬一。北平各界民衆，自蘆溝橋抗戰爆發，羣情甚爲振奮，募捐慰勞，不絕於途，圖示空氣最緊張時北平城中情況之一斑。

守衛北平之二十九軍高呼救國口號（小方）↓

→北平宣佈戒嚴時各城門皆關閉（小方）

東北婦女救國會慰勞團自平出發赴前線慰勞（小方）↑

↑北平衛要街頭之戒備情形（小方）

北平，卢沟桥事变后景象

Scenes after the Lugou Bridge Incident, in Beiping.

敵故意摧殘我文化機關

南開大學已成灰燼（中外社）

RELICS OF NANKAI UNIVERSITY

What Japan has done to one of our highest seats of learnings.

Japanese bombs wiped off most of the buildings of Nankai University, Tientsin. Among them, the library as shown in this picture.

天津南開大學，爲我國著名學府，敵人進攻天津時，故意派機前往轟炸，圖爲被敵機首次炸毀之該校圖書館。

南大科學館，亦爲敵機炸毀。
The Science Hall went the way of all crumbled buildirgs.

轟炸殆盡之南大宿舍。
What was spared of a dormitory.

被炸後之南開圖書館，內部已全爲炸毀。
The only things in the library that survived the fierce bombing were these pillars.

已淪敵手之天津市

THE FALLEN TIENTSIN

已成廢圩之天津東馬路，昔爲華界最熱鬧之地帶。

The once prosperous and crowded Tung Ma Lu (East Road) now quiet and desolate.

天津河北大經路口商店，被敵軍炸毀之慘狀。

Empty shells that once housed many a business firm along the Taiching Road.

The big Union Jack on the ground of a garden in the British Settlement, for an apparently known reason.

爲避免飛機之轟炸，天津英和界當局，特於民闊地上繪一大國旗，以爲標幟。

中外社小方报道《已沦敌手之天津市》《敌故意摧毁我文化机关》（《良友战事画刊》）

The Fallen Tianjin and *Relics of Nankai University*, by Xiao Fang of the Chinese-Foreign Journalism Society (published in *Young Companion War Pictorial*).

《东方画报》第 34 卷 15 号封面使用小方的作品《保卫我们的国土》

Safeguarding Our Territory, by Xiao Fang, on the cover of *Oriental Pictorial* (No. 15, Vol. 34).

刊载《国民（上海）》杂志的《奋勇杀敌的二十九军》组照

The photo series entitled *29th Corps Killing Enemy Bravely*, published in *Chinese People* (Shanghai) magazine.

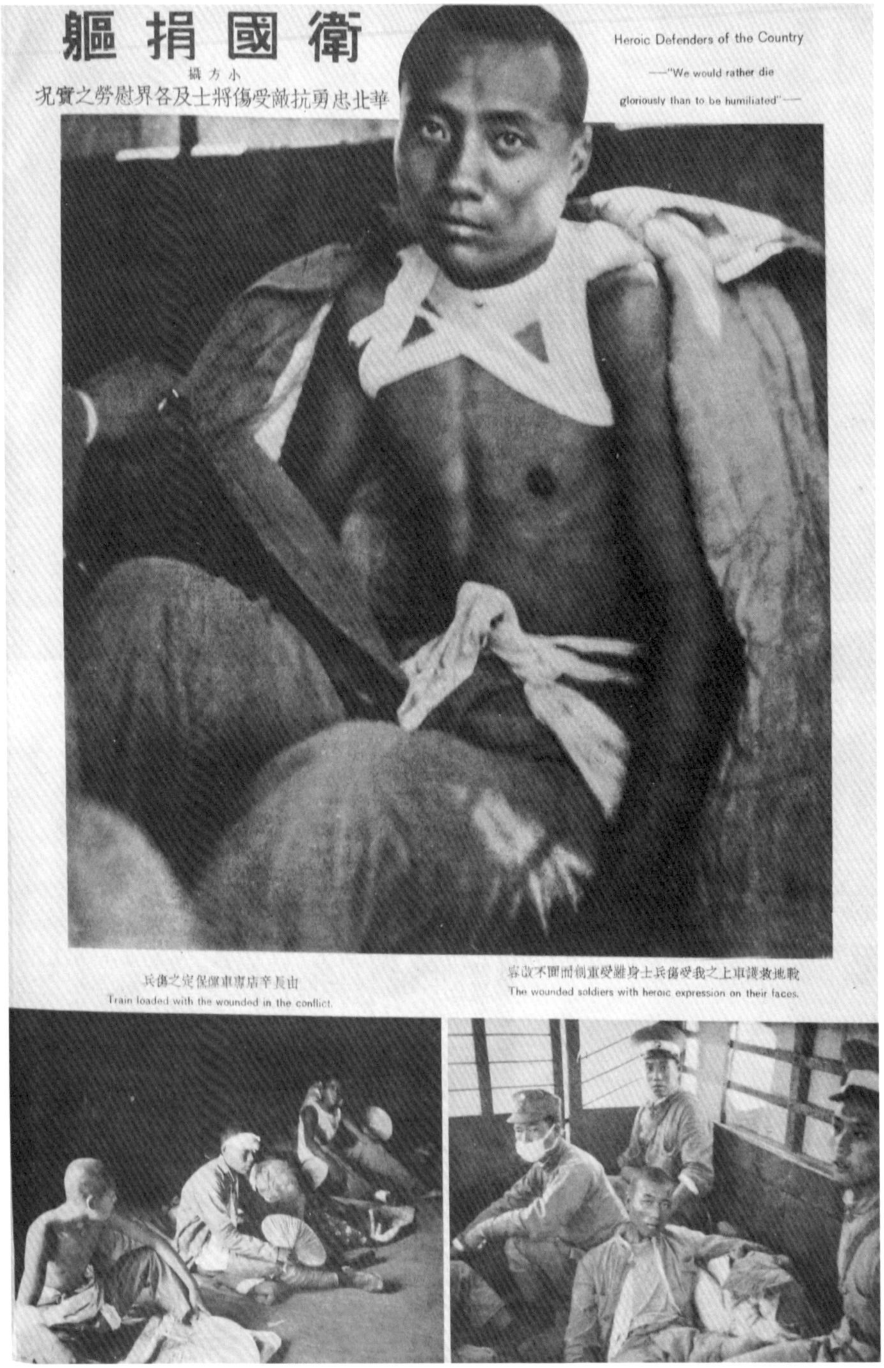
衛國捐軀

小方 攝

華北忠勇抗敵受傷將士及各界慰勞之實況

Heroic Defenders of the Country

——"We would rather die gloriously than to be humiliated"——

由長辛店專車運保定之傷兵

Train loaded with the wounded in the conflict.

戰地救護車上之我受傷兵士身雖受重創而面不改容

The wounded soldiers with heroic expression on their faces.

《为国捐躯》《抗战图存》载于《美术生活》（1937 年第 41 期），特加英文说明，是小方在卢沟桥事变后寄出的第一批照片

Sacrifice for Country, and Fight against Japanese Aggression to Salvage China from Subjugation, published in *Fine Arts Life* (No. 41, 1937), with English explanation added. These were the first batch of photos sent by Xiao Fang after the Lugou Bridge Incident.

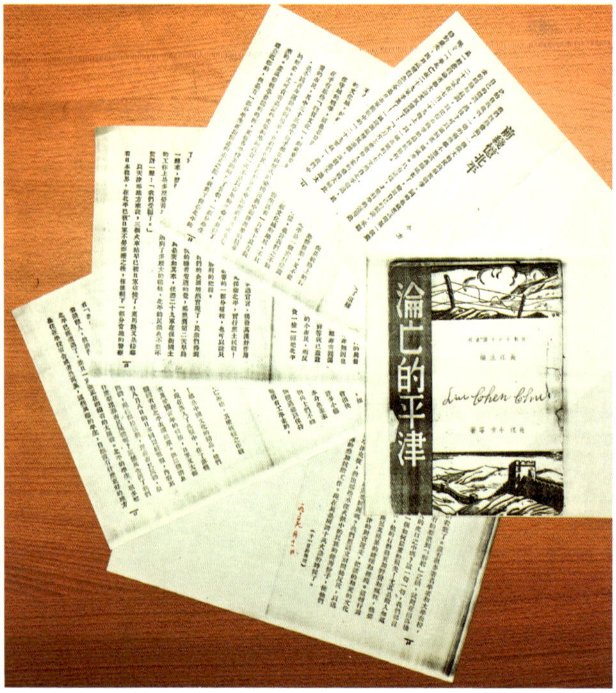

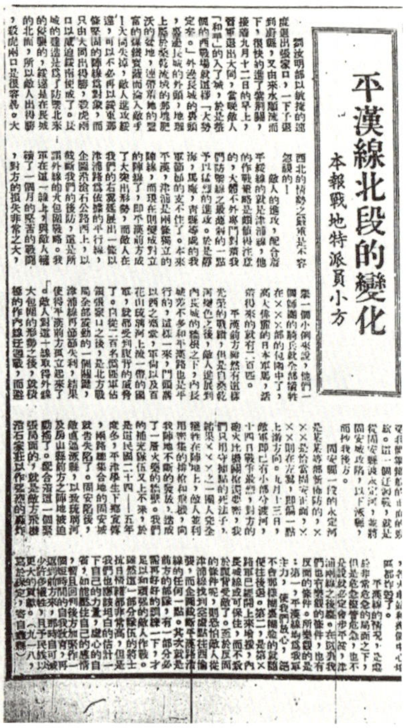
平漢線北段的變化
本報戰地特派員小方

1937 年 9 月 30 日，方大曾 9 月 18 日写于保定、寄自蠡县的战地通讯《平汉线北段的变化》在《大公报》发表，从此小方失踪

Changes in the Northern Section of the Beiping-Hankou Railway, a war report written by Fang Dazeng in Baoding on September 18, 1937 (sent from Li County and published in *Ta Kung Pao* on September 30, 1937). Xiao Fang was never heard from again.

北平沦陷后，有家难回的小方在保定撰写了《前线忆北平》一文

After Beiping was occupied, Xiao Fang could not return to his Beiping home and wrote the article *Recalling Beiping While in the Front*.

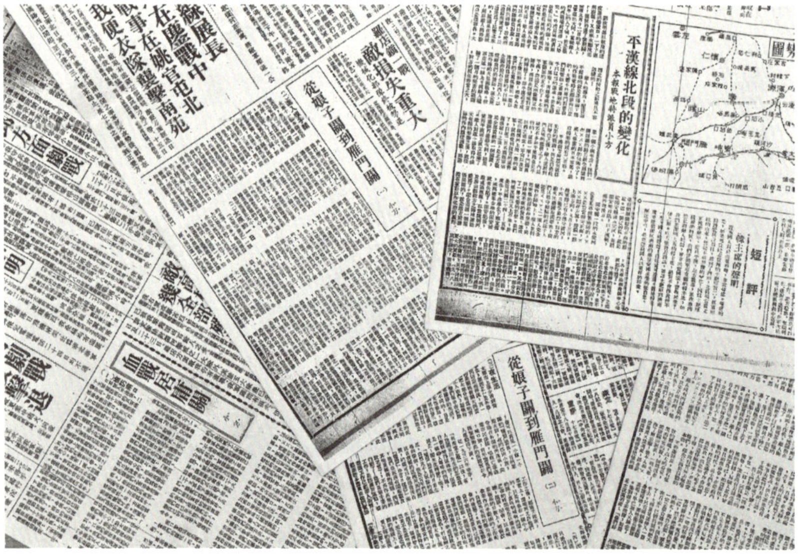

《血战居庸关》《从娘子关到雁门关》《平汉线北段的变化》是目前已知小方最后的 3 篇通讯。由于战事激烈，他已不具备拍摄和传递照片的条件，完全以文字记者的方式进行报道，并设法通过军线电话向上海《大公报》传递内容信息，这在王芸生回忆中有所提及

Heroic Battle at Juyong Pass, *From Niangzi Pass to Yanmen Pass*, and *Changes in the Northern Section of the Beiping-Hankou Railway* are the final three known news reports by Xiao Fang. Due to the fierce battle, he could not take and send photos. He reported in writing and managed to send the message via military phone line to *Ta Kung Pao* (Shanghai), which Wang Yunsheng recalled.

第八章 **消失与重现**

Chapter Eight: Disappearance and Reappearance

游览的兴趣随着我的年龄而渐增，这时那些旅行的杂志和航海书籍，已变成我心目中最爱的东西了。沉迷于书籍的诱惑，我真疏忽了学校里的正式的功课。在一个怪可爱的天气，漫游于神秘的码头的时候，多么令人沉思啊！我注视着将开往远方的帆船，很深切地望着它，直至它的船桅渐渐消失，而我的心灵这时随它飘荡于无涯的大洋了。

——方大曾译《一个作家的自述》

This propensity to ramble strengthened with my years. Books of voyages and travels became my passion, and in devouring their content, I neglected the regular exercises of school. How wistfully I wandered about the pier-heads in fine weather and watched the departing ships, bound to distant places. With longing eyes, I gazed at their slowly disappearing sails and waft myself in imagination to the ends of the earth!

The Account of Himself, by Washington Irving (Chinese version by Fang Dazeng)

据家人回忆，离家时，小方留下了1个背包，1只旅行箱，40个胶卷和两个放底片的小木盒，还有几件换洗的衣裳，没有发现他的文章底稿。方澄敏说："他也没什么东西，就是一个穷学生，他不抽烟，不喝酒，赚的稿费都买了照相器材和胶卷。"而在拍摄中我们唯一见到的就是他的旅行皮箱，其他物品，家人说，由于年代久远，加之数次搬迁，已经不知所终。

方大曾留下的1000多张底片，全部是卢沟桥抗战之前拍摄的，而离家之后的大量战地照片，随着他的失踪，也无从查询，有些散见于当时的报刊杂志，也有些毁于战火。

20世纪40年代，方大曾的父亲方振东病亡，家道中落，日渐冷清，靠"吃老底儿"度日。偶尔有人来，也都是小方从前的朋友，多半是来打听他的消息的，时间久了，来人就渐渐稀少了。唯有母亲方朱理守着儿子的底片盒，经常在院子里的国槐树下呆坐。每有院门的响动，她都会投去一缕希望的目光，一年又一年，人老了，眼睛花了，儿子回来的奇迹也没能出现。

"方澄敏为了保存哥哥的照片，付出了很多心血。"家里人把这些底片视作方大曾生命的延续，几十年来，无论社会环境如何动荡不安，命运如何起伏波动，始终把它珍藏在隐秘的地方和每一个人内心的柔软部分。他们固执地相信，只要底片在，小方就活着。

"文革"期间，方大曾底片中内容"敏感"的部分被烧掉了一些，方家因"社会关系复杂"而遭到抄家，好在方澄敏将哥哥的底片提前交给了单位的红卫兵，才幸免于难。

据吴群考证，小方交给天津中外新闻学社发稿的照片和底片，周勉之离津时，将它"全部装在一个衣箱内随身带走。经过采取一些必要的措施，未被侵略军及汉奸查觉，安全到达武汉。这部分照片和底片，连同后来全民通讯社在武汉、重庆时期所拍摄的时事照片底片，皆由吴寄寒在建国后备文送交中央档案馆保存"。

出版哥哥的画册，是方澄敏晚年唯一的愿望，她不认识出版界的人，也无法用文字将这些照片串联起来。

2006年3月16日，方大曾遗留的837幅珍贵原版底片，由其家人无偿捐

As recalled by his family, before he departed, Xiao Fang left at home a backpack, a travel suitcase, 40 rolls of film, two wooden boxes to hold negatives, and clothes to be washed, but no manuscripts. Fang Chengmin said: "He had no other property. He was just a poorly-paid graduate. He didn't smoke or drink. The money he earned through his works was all used to buy photography equipment and film." During our research and interview, the only personal belonging we saw was his travel suitcase. According to his family, other things left behind by Xiao Fang were lost because so many years had passed and his family moved several times.

Over 1,000 negatives that were left behind by Fang Dazeng were taken before the Lugou Bridge Battle. However, after he disappeared, the large number of war photos he took after leaving home were missing. Some were seen in various newspapers and magazines, others were destroyed by flames of war.

In the 1940s, Fang Dazeng's father died from an illness. His family began to decline and lived off past gains. Occasionally, there would be visitors, but they were just Xiao Fang's old friends who came to ask about him. As time passed, there were less and less visitors. Only Fang Zhuli, Xiao Fang's mother, kept safe her son's wooden box of negatives, often sitting alone below the locust tree in the yard. Whenever there was a sound from the yard's gate, she looked at it, full of hope. Year after year, she grew older and her vision degraded, but there was no miracle to bring her son home.

Fang Chengmin went to great lengths to keep her brother's photos.

Fang's family viewed these negatives as a continuation of his life. For decades, through changes in the social environment and various ups and downs in their lives, they always kept the photos in a secret place and in the tenderness of their hearts. They stubbornly believed that as long as the negatives were there, Xiao Fang was alive.

During the Cultural Revolution, some of Fang Dazeng's photos, containing "sensitive" content, were burned. Also, due to the "complex social relationship" of Fang's family, their house was ransacked. Fortunately, Fang Chengmin had turned-in her brother's negatives to the Red Guards in her work place, so they survived this calamity.

According to research by Wu Qun, regarding photos and negatives provided by Xiao Fang to the Chinese-Foreign Journalism Society in Tianjin for publication, before Zhou Mianzhi left Tianjin, he "placed all of them in a suitcase and left with it. He took the necessary precautions to avoid detection by the invaders and traitors, and safely arrived in Wuhan. These photos and negatives, as well as those about the latest news in Wuhan and Chongqing subsequently taken by the National News Agency, were all filed appropriately and submitted, by Wu Jihan, to the Central Archives for keeping after the People's Republic of China was founded in 1949."

Publishing an album of her brother's photos was the only wish of Fang Chengmin in her later years. She knew no one in the publishing circles.

赠给中国国家博物馆。而就在有关人士打电话联系捐赠事宜不久，保管了这些底片数十年的方澄敏悄悄地去世了。捐赠仪式上，纪录片《寻找方大曾》再度播放，方家三代人精心保管近 70 年，历经战火等多重磨难的珍贵影像，终于找到了安息的归宿，成为全社会公共的文化财富。

轻轻地从纸袋中取出黑白底片，仿佛怕惊动一个沉睡中的人。在阳光下，黑白色通透分明，影像瞬间呈现从前，隔世的人物、消失的景象、尘封的事件，我仿佛一瞬间与方大曾有了隐约的沟通。他曾用目光抚摸过的社会和指尖触碰过的时代，刹那间有了勃勃生机和无法拒绝的诱惑。

我“结识”方大曾，是他失踪 62 年后的秋天。当我第一次见到方大曾留下的盒子时，内心之中有一种朝圣的感觉。棕黑色的盒子不大，里面整整齐齐地码放着一些粉颜色的纸袋，所有纸袋上都印着德记商行的字号。这个位于王府井大街北口路西的店铺，现在已荡然无存，由地址看来离小方的家很近，想必是他洗印照片经常光顾的地方。

也就在那一时刻起，我决定用纪录片的方式寻找方大曾，尽管我知道影像表达不同于纸上描摹，需要一个一个坚实的画面去支撑，而除了几张个人照片外，小方没有留下一个活动影像，呈现的难度可以想见。但是我知道，从我偶然接到那份传真开始，就已经进入了一种新的工作状态，那种感觉前所未有。

我们的寻找是从寂静中开始的。时光倒流 70 年，照片中的影像流动，人们看到了已经消失了的码头和工厂，看到了生活在今天的老人们的青春时代，看到了 20 世纪 30 年代国际国内的社会风貌和生活景象，看到了一个叫方大曾的年轻人背着相机走过一个又一个历史的瞬间。

事隔 15 年，我再次走进了这条熟悉的胡同。虽处在闹市一隅，南北走向的协和胡同，却几乎没有太大变化，如同我们当年拍摄完成离开时一样。当我又一次用相机拍照时，10 号院已经更换了主人，他隐约从电视中看过，说什么人曾住过这里。年头久了，印象不深了，房屋已经翻盖，唯有小方家院子里的大槐树还在，摇摇曳曳了几十年，也不知道它都看见过什么。在它某一圈的年轮里，说不定就记录着小方的欢乐和气息。

我曾在当时的工作笔记里写道，“我们拍摄此片的目的不仅仅是去寻找一个人，是通过‘寻找’去还原一个真实的，热爱和平与自由的生命。他通过自己的目光，抚摸着 60 多年前国难当头的中国大地，他的镜头下描述的影像，是我们了解当时中国社会的生动图本。他以个体的高贵品质，为我们确立了

She did locate one of Xiao Fang's classmates, Li Xugang, at the Beiping No. 1 Middle School.

On March 16, 2006, Fang Dazeng's family donated the 837 precious negatives left by him to the National Museum of China. Sadly, soon after the museum contacted Fang's family to discuss the donation, Fang Chengmin, who kept these negatives for decades, silently passed away. At the donation ceremony, the documentary *In Search of Fang Dazeng* was re-played. These precious images, kept approximately 70 years by three generations of Fang's family and surviving various calamities, including gunfire, finally found a resting place and became a cultural fortune shared by the entire society.

When I gently removed a black and white negative from a paper envelope, I felt I was disturbing a sleeping creature. In the sunlight, the black and white negative looked crystal and translucent. Instantly, I was presented with figures from another world, disappeared scenery, and dust-laden events. I felt a momentary connection with Fang Dazeng. The society he once used his eyes to see and the time he once used his fingers to touch suddenly became vivid, vigorous, appealing, and absorbing.

I "met" Fang Dazeng in autumn, 62 years after he went missing. When I first saw the wooden box left by him, I felt like I was on a pilgrimage. That dark brown box was not large. It contained neatly organized pink paper envelopes with the name "De's Business House" printed on each. This shop, located west of the northern end of Wangfujing Street, had long since disappeared. As implied from its address, it was close to Xiao Fang's house and must have been a place he often visited to develop film.

At that moment, I decided to search for Fang Dazeng through a documentary. I was aware that video presentation differed from paper sketching and required many well-grounded pictures to support it. Except for several personal photos, Xiao Fang did not leave any motion pictures. It would be difficult to make a documentary, but ever since I accidentally found that fax, I had started working with unprecedented zest.

Our search began with silent contemplation. We went back 70 years and images in the photos started to flow. We saw the disappeared wharfs and factories, youth of elders living today, social landscape and life scenes at home and abroad during the 1930s, and a young man named Fang Dazeng walking in these historic moments, one by one, carrying his camera.

Fifteen years later, I walked again into this familiar hutong. Although it was located in a corner of the downtown area, the Xiehe Hutong, running north to south, seemed little changed, from the last time when we left after we finished filming the documentary. This time I learned that the No. 10 house had a new owner, who seemed to have seen on TV that somebody famous once lived here. After so many years had passed, I couldn't remember everything well. I found that the house had been completely rebuilt, except for the big locust tree that was in the yard of Xiao Fang's house. It withstood decades of vicissitudes and I wondered what it had witnessed. Probably within a certain ring of it, the joys and breaths of Xiao Fang were recorded.

I once wrote in my work notes: "We make this documentary not only to search for a man, but also to restore a real, peace-loving, and free life through our 'search' efforts. Over six decades ago,

一个物质之外的精神境界。”

从大学毕业到前线失踪，短短两年，小方留下的摄影和通讯作品是丰厚的。当历史的尘埃渐渐拂去，少年的笑容隐约浮现，我们似乎有必要随着他的成长，检视和珍藏时代留给今天的宝贵遗产。

本章照片多选取自方大曾及其家人的遗物、遗作，以及80年后的寻找之旅。

Xiao Fang stroked with his eyes a Chinese land in crisis. Images captured by his lens are vivid pictorials from which we learn about the Chinese society of that time. With his noble character, Xiao Fang created for us a spiritual realm beyond the physical."

From college graduation to his disappearance at the front, within two short years, Xiao Fang left a large number of photos and reports. When the dust of history is swept away, the smiles of this young man seem to appear. We feel obliged to follow his growth path – to study and cherish the valuable legacy Fang Dazeng passed down to us.

The photos in this chapter are mainly about things left behind by Fang Dazeng and his family and my journey in search of Fang 80 years later, together with some photos taken by him.

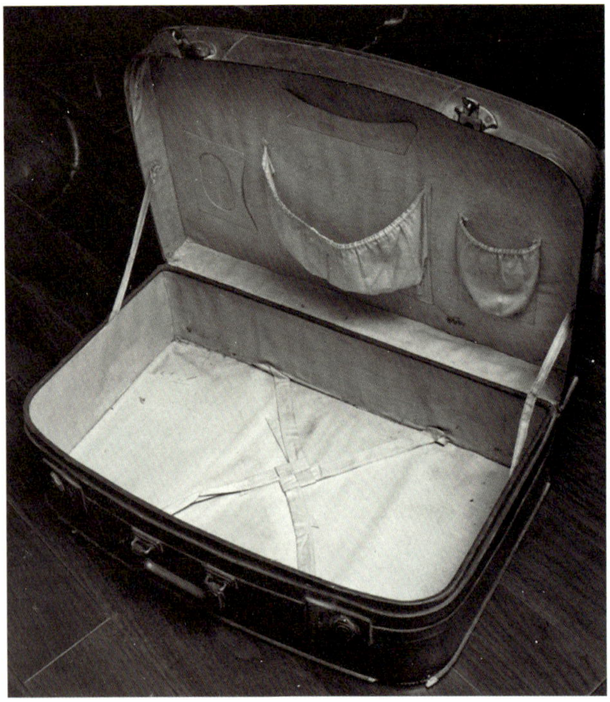

旅行皮箱，方大曾遗物，现存于保定方大曾纪念室（孙楠摄于 2015 年）

A leather travel suitcase, left by Fang Dazeng, and currently collected in the Fang Dazeng Memorial Hall in Baoding, Hebei Province (photo by Sun Nan, 2015).

小方留在家中的小木盒和部分底片（冯雪松摄于 2015 年）

The small wooden box and some of the negatives that Xiao Fang left at home (photo by Feng Xuesong, 2015).

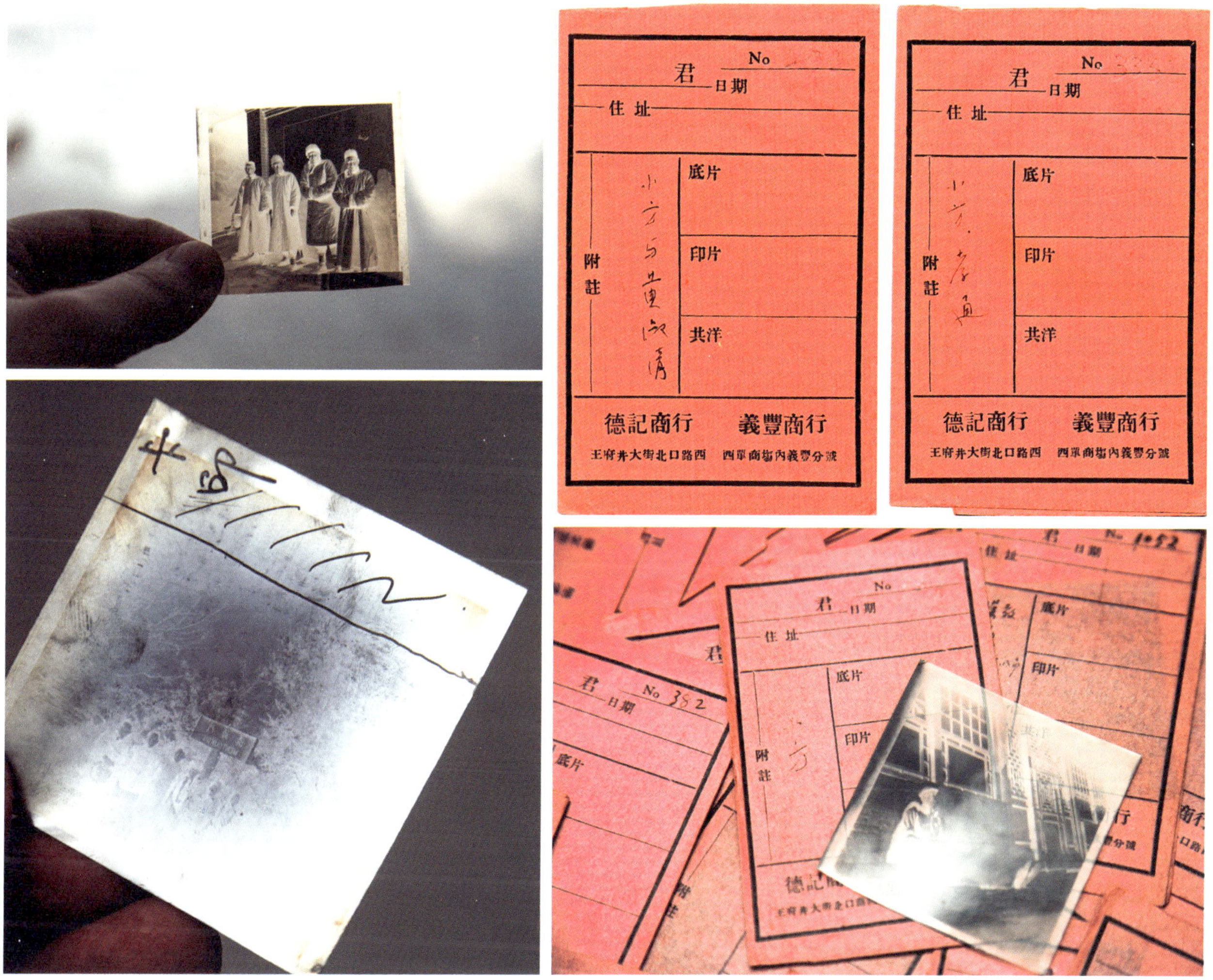

底片袋保存完好，虽经过了 80 年，小方画上去的剪裁线仍清晰可见（冯雪松摄于 2015 年）

Well-kept envelops to hold negatives. Although 80 years have passed, clip lines, drawn by Xiao Fang, remain clearly visible (photo by Feng Xuesong, 2015).

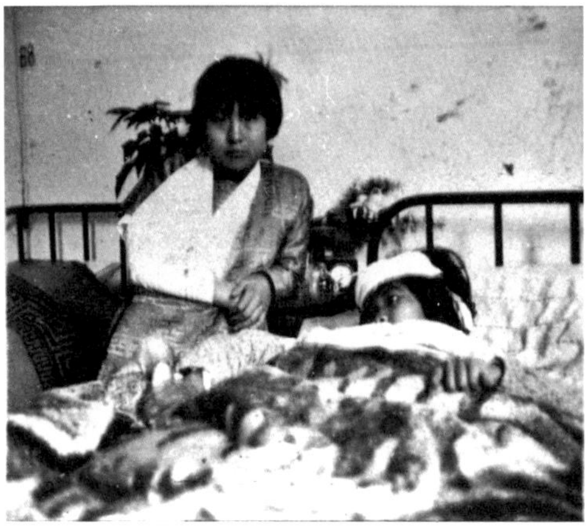

方澄敏保存的一二·九运动受伤学生照片小样

A print of a photo about students wounded in the December 9th Patriotic Parade, kept by Fang Chengmin.

一二·九运动被捕学生，此照曾出现在纪录片《斯诺》中（陈申提供）

A student who was arrested in the December 9th Patriotic Parade. This photo was shown in the documentary *Snow* (provided by Chen Shen).

一二·九运动游行照片小样（陈申提供）

Prints of photos about the December 9th Patriotic Parade (provided by Chen Shen).

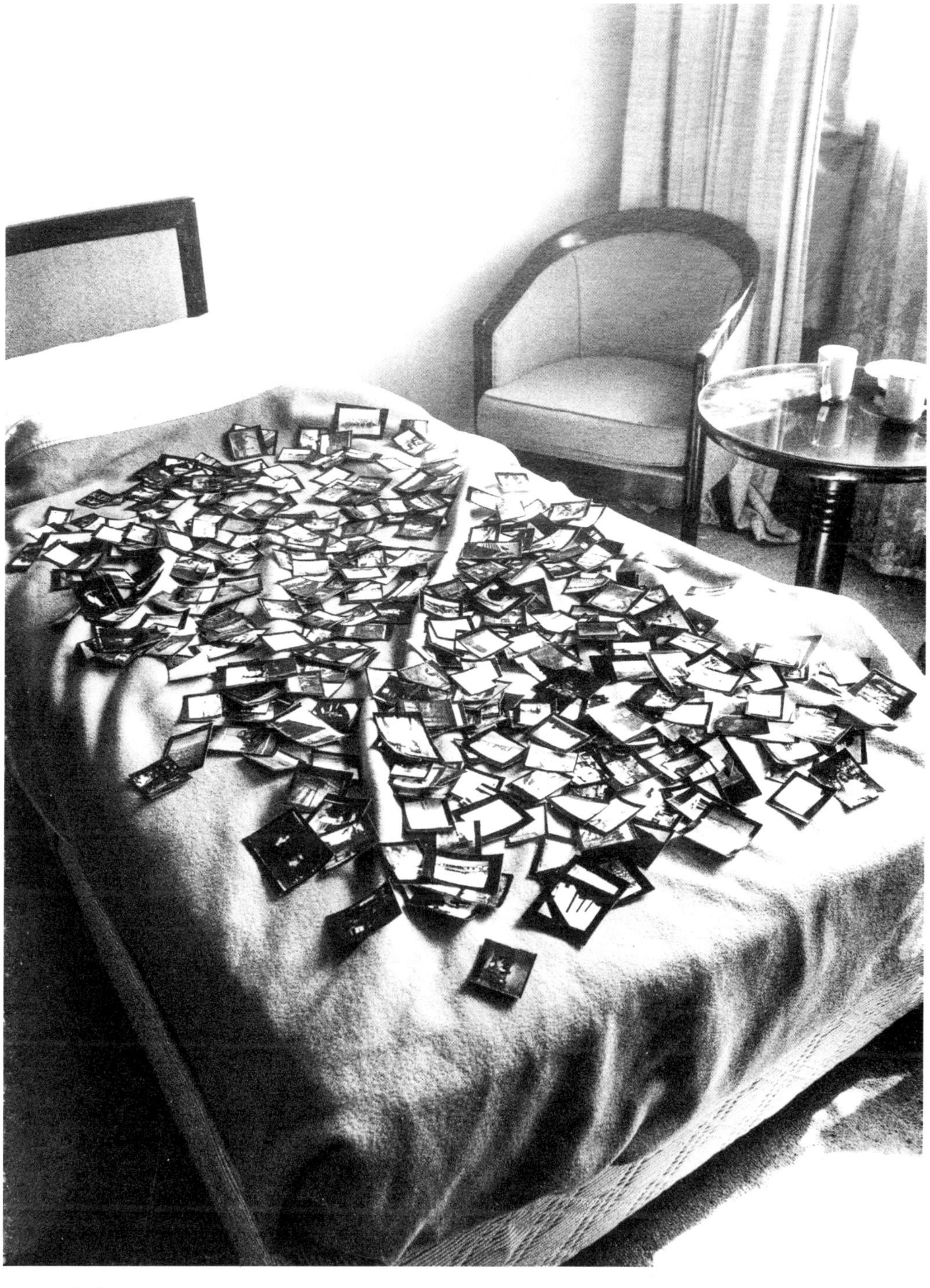

底片小样（阮义忠摄）
Prints of negatives (photo by Ruan Yizhong).

来自中外新闻学社的“七君子”之“六君子”狱中照（七君子之一的史良，关押在女子监狱，未在照片中出现）。范长江长子范苏苏、方大曾外甥张在璇确认该照为小方拍摄。沈钧儒（前排右二）在狱中时，小方的姐姐、姐夫因亲属关系才有探监的条件，曾两次前往苏州探监（范苏苏提供）

A photo of six out of the "Seven Gentlemen" of the Chinese-Foreign Journalism Society (the seventh, Shi Liang, was in women's prison and thus not in this photo). Fan Susu, the oldest son of Fan Changjiang, and Zhang Zaixuan, nephew of Fang Dazeng, confirmed that this photo was taken by Xiao Fang. When Shen Junru (second right) was imprisoned, Xiao Fang's sister and brother-in-law were allowed to visit him due to their kinship with him. They visited him twice, in Suzhou (provided by Fan Susu).

《良友》画报第 129 期刊登《狱中七君子》组照

Photo series entitled *The Case of the Seven Gentlemen*, published in *Young Companion Pictorial* (No. 129).

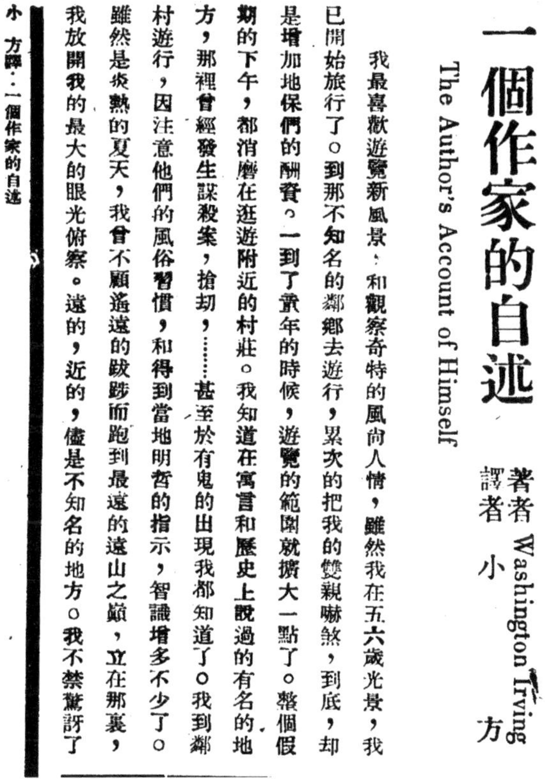

一個作家的自述

The Author's Account of Himself

著者 Washington Irving
譯者 小　方

我最喜歡遊覽新風景，和觀察奇特的風尙人情，雖然我在五六歲光景，我已開始旅行了。到那不知名的鄰鄉去遊行，累次的把我的雙親嚇煞，到底，却是增加地保們的酬資。一到了靑年的時候，遊覽的範圍就擴大一點了。整個假期的下午，都消磨在逛遊附近的村莊。我知道在寓言和歷史上說過的有名的地方，那裡曾經發生謀殺案，搶刼，……甚至於有鬼的出現我都知道了。我到鄰村遊行，因注意他們的風俗習慣，和得到當地明哲的指示，智識增多不少了。雖然是炎熱的夏天，我曾不顧遙遠的跋涉而跑到最遠的遠山之巔，立在那裏，我放開我的最大的眼光俯察。遠的，近的，儘是不知名的地方。我不禁驚訝了

小　方譯：一個作家的自述

新近发现的小方译文《一个作家的自述》，原作华盛顿·欧文（《市一中学生丛刊》1936 年第 4 期）

A recently discovered translation by Xiao Fang of *The Author's Account of Himself* by Washington Irving, published in the *No. 1 Middle School Students' Serial Magazine* (Beiping, No. 4, 1936).

方澄敏保存的《李大钊葬仪》照片小样，小方摄，原件遗失（1933 年 4 月）

A print of a photo about Li Dazhao's funeral, kept by Fang Chengmin. This photo was taken by Xiao Fang, but the original work was lost (April, 1933).

徐特立
Xu Teli.

史沫特莱
Agnes Smedley.

陈赓
Chen Geng.

小战士
A small soldier.

学文化

Learning.

抗大女学员

Female students of the Chinese People's Anti-Japanese Military and Political College.

小方遗物中翻拍自斯诺《延安之行》的一组底片，据方澄敏回忆，哥哥曾经与斯诺有过交往，还在青年会放过这些内容的幻灯片

A set of negatives copied from Snow during the "trip to Yan'an," left behind by Xiao Fang. As recalled by Fang Chengmin, her brother once had contact with Snow and played slides of these photos at the Chinese Young Men's Christian Association (YMCA).

在《抗战画报》（1937 年 4 期）《晋绥我军准备大战》组照中，首次发现小方在山西拍摄的朱德照片（左上）

From among photos in the series entitled *The Shanxi-Suiyuan Front*, published in *Anti-Japanese War Pictorial* (Vol. 4, 1937), a photo of Zhu De, taken by Xiao Fang in Shanxi, was discovered (upper left).

方大曾遗物中的少年时期在八达岭长城上的自拍像

A photo taken by young Fang Dazeng, of himself at the Badaling Great Wall.

小方失踪后，母亲方朱理等了他 32 年，1969 年去世

After Xiao Fang went missing, his mother, Fang Zhuli, waited for him for 32 years before passing away in 1969.

小方留下的底片是一家几辈人的“念想儿”，图为方大曾的妹妹方澄敏（冯雪松摄于 1999 年）

Negatives left behind by Fang Dazeng represent the longing that generations of his family had for him. This lady is Fang Chengmin, Fang Dazeng's younger sister (photo by Feng Xuesong, 1999).

·抗战摄影文史撷英·

抗战初期以身许国的新闻摄影记者小方传略

·方澄敏·

1936年，记者小方深入北平门头沟区中英煤矿、宏福煤矿采访，体察矿工生活，这是他下矿井前留影。

我的哥哥小方，姓方，名德曾，亦名大曾。小方是个英俊的青年，他身材高大，脸色红润，一双明亮的大眼睛透露出纯正无邪的光芒。他好像天天都是乐呵呵的。又好像从不知疲倦似的。他之所以称为"小方"，那是因为他童心未失，禀性活泼，喜欢同孩子们在一起的缘故。当朋辈们看到他这个大个子出现在欢蹦乱跳的小人群中时，就情不自禁地，亲昵地呼他为"小方"；他自己呢，也认为这个称呼并不孬。他说："方者：刚正不阿也，小则含有谦逊之意，正是为人处世之道，我就是要做一个正直的、于国于民有用的人。"因此他发表作品的时候，原用"小芳"后便改用"小方"为笔名了。

小方的一生是短促的，他祖籍江苏无锡，1912年生于北京。在北平市立第一中学毕业后，1930年他考入北平中法大学经济系。喜欢旅行、写稿和照像。"九·一八"以后从事抗日救亡活动。绥远抗战时他到前线采访，活跃于长城内外。1937年芦沟桥事变后任中外新闻学社（简称中外社）、全民通讯社（简称全民社）摄影记者及《大公报》战地特派员到前方采访，当年秋天就听不到关于他的情况，看不到他的战地报道，最大可能是在抗战前线以身许国光荣牺牲了。

小方的经历，他的走向革命，同三十年代那些忧国忧民的左倾青年学生所走过的道路大致一样：从不满现实，阅读进步书刊到参加党的外围组织的一些秘密活动。他从小就爱好摄影，第一次以照相机为武器进行战斗，是在他读中学的时候。他倡议组织少年摄影社"少年影社"，并举行过公开展览会。当时，他的一位同学李续刚（李对小方的影响很大，是小方的引路人，经常给他讲一些革命的道理。建国后李曾任北京市人民政府副秘书长，文革中受到四人帮的迫害，1969年含恨而逝。）因进行革命活动而被反动学校当局挂牌开除，小方为了抗议，为了留下历史见证，把那张布告拍下了。从那以后，小方逐渐懂事起来。"九·一八"时他正在中法大学读书，加入了"反帝大同盟"（简称"反帝"），也把我介绍了进去，并帮助我在我就读的北平市立女一中建立了支部。他编写过"反帝"的机关报《反帝新闻》。

1932年从天津南开中学来了另一名"反帝"的成员，名叫常钟元（笔名方殷，著名诗人，现已病故），他和小方共同主编了《少年先锋》。实际上，这个小小的周刊从写稿、编排到印刷、发行，都是这两个姓方的干的，有时候我也搞搞校对。

"九·一八"以后，小方真是席不暇暖，同时，我们家的"客人"也多了起来。大概由于我们有一位好母亲的缘故，小方的战友都喜欢把我们家作为接头晤面，讨论工作，或者赶写文章的地点，有时为了甩脱警特的盯梢，甚至也在我们家避住一两天。常来我们家的"客人"，除了李续刚和方殷以外，我现在能够记得的还有：李声簧（已故，生前为中国科学院科学出版社副主编）、夏尚志（曾在东北任厅长）、王兴让（原用名王

2

方澄敏发表的纪念文章

The article, by Fang Chengmin, in memory of Fang Dazeng.

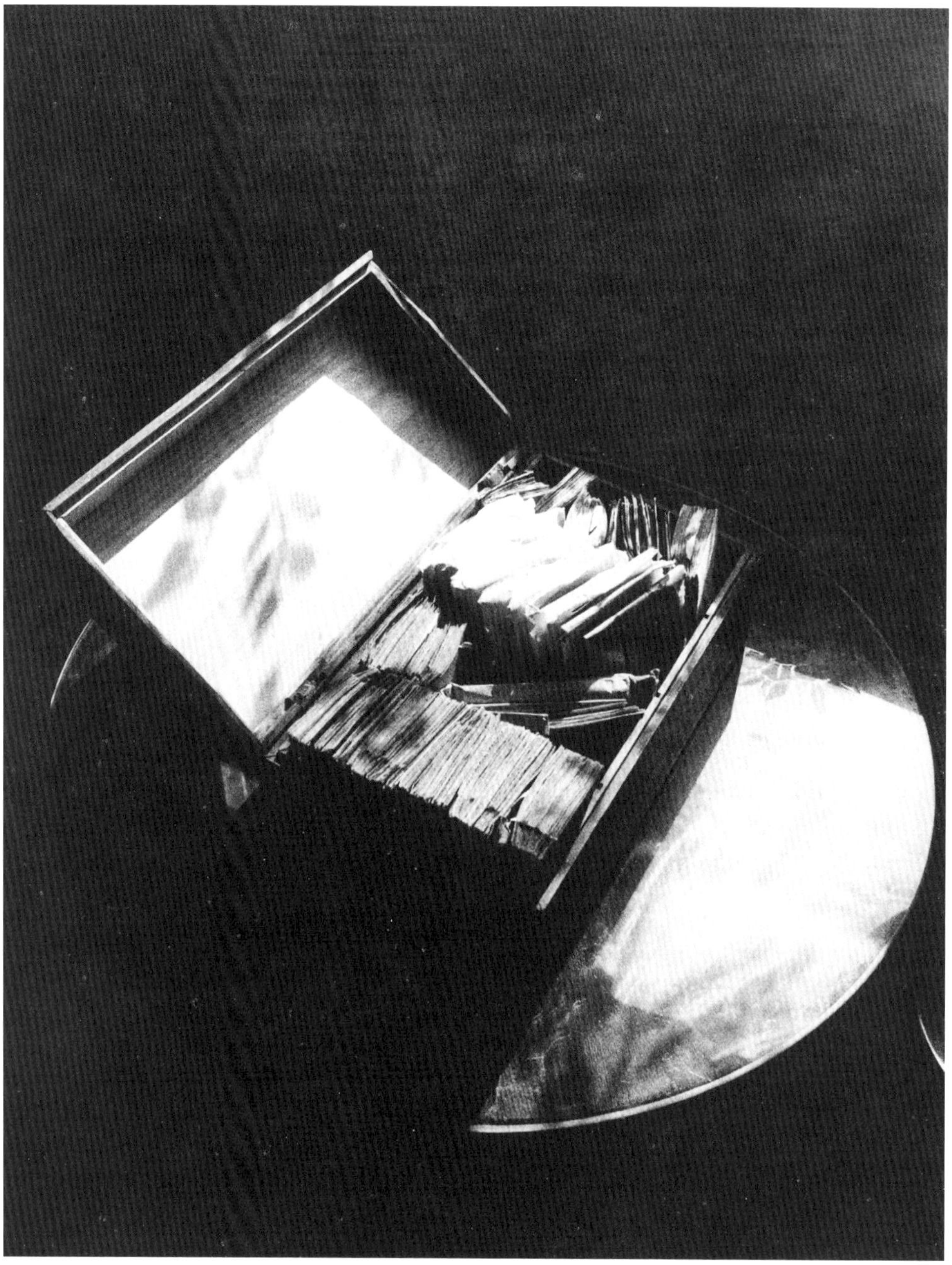

逃过难的底片箱（现存中国国家博物馆，阮义忠摄）

The box of negatives that survived various calamities (currently collected in the National Museum of China, photo by Ruan Yizhong).

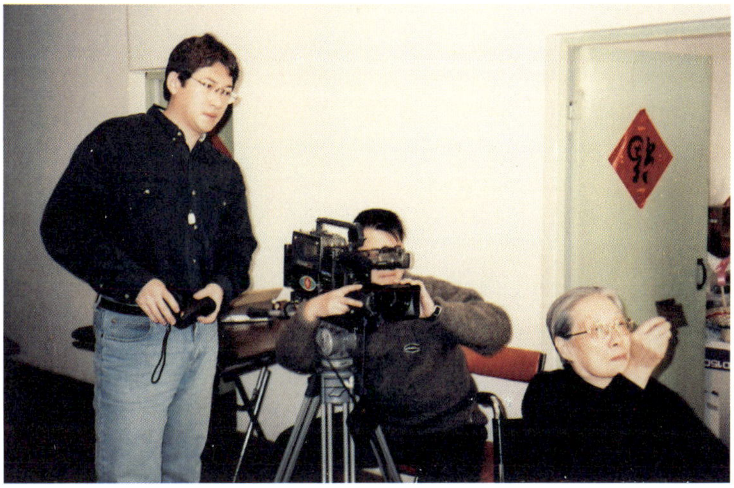

1999 年秋，纪录片《寻找方大曾》拍摄现场工作照（陈申 摄）

Autumn of 1999, at the production site for the documentary *In Search of Fang Dazeng* (photo by Chen Shen).

为纪念中华人民共和国首个记者节，2000 年 11 月，纪录片《寻找方大曾》作为特别节目在中国中央电视台播出

The documentary *In Search of Fang Dazeng* was aired on CCTV as a special broadcast in November 2000 to celebrate China's first Reporters' Day.

方大曾在山西大同云冈石窟（1936 年 7 月）
Fang Dazeng at the Yungang Grottos in Datong, Shanxi Province (July, 1936).

本书作者 2000 年 9 月拍摄纪录片《寻找方大曾》时在同一地点留影（马东戈摄）
Feng Xuesong at the same site while making *In Search of Fang Dazeng* (photo by Ma Dongge, September, 2000).

实地寻访——天津劝业场（孙楠摄于 2016 年 9 月）

Field research at the Quanye Mall in Tianjin (photo by Sun Nan, September, 2016).

实地寻访——北京卢沟桥（孙楠摄于 2016 年 11 月）
Field research at the Lugou Bridge in Beijing (photo by Sun Nan, November, 2016).

冯雪松出版的多种有关方大曾专著

Monographs about Fang Dazeng written by Feng Xuesong.

中国记协组织召开的冯雪松追踪采写方大曾事迹座谈会（孙楠摄于 2015 年 5 月 25 日）

The All-China Journalists' Association held a forum on Feng Xuesong's recording of Fang Dazeng's stories (photo by Sun Nan, May 25, 2015).

《为了正义与良知——战地记者方大曾摄影展》在澳门举行，张在璇（左）、冯雪松、陈申（右）应邀出席（《澳门日报》供图，2015 年 8 月 28 日）

"For Justice and Conscience – Exhibition for Fang Dazeng, the War Correspondent Who Reported on the Lugou Bridge Incident First" was held in Macao. Left to right: Zhang Zaixuan, Feng Xuesong, and Chen Shen (photo by *Macao Daily News*, August 28, 2015).

2016 年 7 月，冯雪松带领河北大学师生前往蠡县战地寻访，方大曾校园行活动迄今已经走进国内外 30 多所大学（孙楠摄）

In July 2016, Feng Xuesong led teachers and students of Hebei University to conduct field research at the Li County battlefield site. The campaign to introduce Fang Dazeng into universities has been carried out at over 30 universities at home and abroad (photo by Sun Nan).

方大曾像（李一夫作品，2015年，现存保定方大曾纪念室，冯雪松摄）

A bust of Fang Dazeng, a work by Li Yifu in 2015, currently collected in the Fang Dazeng Memorial Hall (photo by Feng Xuesong).

忆小方

范长江

一

“明天我要到百灵庙去，如果走得早，我就不来看你了！”二年前在塞外著名的高寒地方——绥东平地泉的冬夜，黑黑一屋子的塞外冬装青年人，屋内发黄的烛光，被屋外如万顷波涛呼啸而来的狂风震撼得发闪。这位硕壮身躯，面庞红润，头发带黄的斯拉夫型的青年方大曾先生走来和我握手。

“到百灵庙？”

“是的。”

“你怎样去法？”因为从平地泉到百灵庙，在塞上冬天如果不是走归绥经武川的汽车路，那么一定要斜穿阴山，出草原，那是雄壮而艰苦的旅程。这位平时没有被人重视的朋友，今天却来这样一个壮举，我有点不明白他如何去法。一则恐怕他太过于理想，一则恐怕他准备不够，途中容易发生困难。

“骑马去。”坦然的回答。

“几个人一路？”

“还有个马夫。”

“你带什么东西？”

“就是身上带的这一点。”

塞外的生活，我们多少经历过一些，总少像他这样冬季孤身翻阴山，而且正是百灵庙战争之后。

二

从此被人叫为“小方”的方大曾先生，在我们朋友心里占据了很重要的地位。因为联想起许多在绥远以前关于“方大曾”的印象。大概二十五年的夏天，我在天津《大公报》的编辑部桌上看到一张“方大曾”的名片，据同事告诉我，是一个来交涉投稿机会的人。因为这样的事情很多，当然没有什么特别注意。以后不久，在天津《益世报》的地方版上，看到有他的一篇长篇通信——“张垣至大同”，他把察晋间的社会黑暗情形暴露不少。不过，一则他名气还不大，再则初写通讯，还没有引起很多人注意。据绥远战争时同在绥远工作至中央社同业的王华灼先生谈及，他因为那时采用小方的通信，报馆当局认为对于社会黑暗之指摘为不妥，因而解除了他的职务。

在书刊上，我们常常看到“小方”的作品，他对于题材的选择和对于时间性的谨严，都是引起朋友们注意的地方。绥远战争以后，他更主要地以摄影记者姿态出现。

In Memory of Xiao Fang

By Fan Changjiang

One

"I'll go to the Bailing Temple tomorrow. If I leave early, I won't come to see you." Two years ago, on a winter night in Pingdiquan, eastern Suiyuan, a place in northern China known for high altitude and cold weather, a group of young people wearing typical thick clothing gathered in a dusty room. The fierce wind outside made the dim candlelight in the room flicker tempestuously. Then, a tall and strong man, with a healthy complexion and somewhat Slavic-like brown hair named Fang Dazeng, came to me and shook my hand.

"You're going to the Bailing Temple?"

"Yes."

"How?" From Pingdiquan to the Bailing Temple, if not traveling via the motor road from Guisui to Wuchuan, one had to climb the Yin Mountains and cross the prairie in extreme weather. That would be a magnificent and painstaking journey. This young friend, who had never attracted much attention, made such a magnificent move! I did not know how he could travel there. I was worried he was too idealistic and may not be prepared for such a difficult journey.

"Riding a horse," he answered.

"How many of you?"

"Me and a groom."

"What luggage do you take?"

"Just what I have with me."

We had more or less experienced life in northern China with extreme weather, but we had seldom climbed the Yin Mountains in winter, especially after the Battle of Bailing Temple.

Two

Since then, Mr. Fang Dazeng, known to others as Xiao Fang, has weighed so much in our hearts. I recall many things about my impression of Fang Dazeng when I was in Suiyuan. It was probably in the summer of 1936, at the desk of the editorial office of the *Ta Kung Pao* in Tianjin, that I saw a business card bearing the name Fang Dazeng. My colleagues told me this was a man who inquired about report submissions. Since this was common at the time, I paid little attention to him. However, before long, in Tianjin's local edition of *Yishi Daily*, I read a long, news report by him entitled *From Zhangyuan to Datong*, in which he revealed much of the social darkness he witnessed during his visit to Shanxi. However, because he was not famous and this was his first report, it failed to attract much attention. Mr. Wang Huazhuo, who worked with me in the same trade in Suiyuan during the Suiyuan Campaign and later worked for the Central News Agency, recalled that he was once dismissed from his post because he adopted Xiao Fang's reports, which were considered inappropriate by newspaper authorities as they referred to social darkness.

In books and periodicals, we often saw works by Xiao Fang. His choice of topic and serious attitude toward time were what attracted our attention. After the Battle of Suiyuan, he was known to us mainly as a photo journalist.

Three

After the Lugou Bridge Incident, we often met in the Lugou Bridge, Changxindian, and Baoding areas. He became increasingly devoted to work and his body grew

三

卢沟桥事变了，在卢沟桥长辛店保定一带，我们又常常碰头，他的工作情绪愈来愈高涨，身体也愈来愈结实。北方的夏季，他穿着短裤衬衣，自己带着他的小箱子行李，在平汉路前线不断地突击。他那诚挚、天真、勇敢、温和的性格，博得各方面的好感。

平津陷落之后，我回到了上海，后来接到他从北方来信说："我的家在北平陷落了！我还有许多摄影材料工具不能带出来，我现在成为无家可归的人了！我想找一家报馆做战地记者，请你为我代找一岗位。"

那时上海《大公报》正需要人，就请他担任平汉线工作，而以秋江任察哈尔，以溪映任绥东，他于是开始为上海《大公报》写通讯。

四

南口战争爆发之后，上海《大公报》令我赴察哈尔助秋江工作，以加强中央战场采访力量，与左翼之溪映，右翼之小方配合，总辖平绥平汉之战争消息。从察哈尔不守，我与秋江从察南退晋北，再转大同，仍冀主持中路战报。乃在大同突遇军邮友人陈虚舟先生，云小方已去绥东，使我大为惊异，盖不知其何故放弃右翼任务也。乃急电绥东请其返大同商工作。

小方至大同，同溪映同来，据云：系在保定闻八路军挺进热河，故赶去参加，到绥始知不确。并自承认单独行动之欠考虑。我们于是与秋江四人在轰炸中的大同城内商以后工作计划。战局紧急时，我们所住大同招待所在白日已无食物供给，我们经常在城墙边防空洞旁写文章。

大同吃紧时，我与小方先后到石家庄。当时协定溪映坚持绥远宁夏线，秋江支持同蒲线，而小方则仍挺进平汉线。

那时保定已万分吃紧，卫立煌将军所部三师增援南口落空，正与敌激战于永定河上游青白口一带。小方当时异常兴奋，他不只要到保定，而且更要到保定以北南口山脉中去。他带上充分的蓝墨水、稿纸和照相器材，急急由石家庄登上北去的列车，临别时，我说："希望你能写一篇'永定河上游的战争'！"他很平和坚定地对我说："我一定有很好的成绩答复你！"

五

以后我就回到上海，果然他来了两篇通信，那时他是平汉前方唯一的记者，所以通信很生色。

随着平汉战局恶化，保定失守，我们就不知道了他的消息。他身边带的旅费有限，汇款也不知从哪里汇起。写信到邯郸邮局去问他的亲戚，回信说，小方到保定时，正值保定失守，他被迫退到保定东南的蠡县，在蠡县曾发出一信，以后就没有了下文。不过，在他由蠡县给信与他邯郸的亲戚时，明白提到："我仍将由蠡县继续北上，达到长江原来给我的任务！"

以后石家庄陷落，太原失守，关于小方的踪迹，简直一点也打听不出来了。他的母亲，他的妹妹，他的女朋友，乃至关心他的朋友们都从

ever stronger. In that summer in northern China, wearing shorts and a shirt, and carrying his luggage, he made constant breakthroughs on the Beiping-Hankou Railway front. His sincerity, innocence, bravery, and amiability won him popularity everywhere.

After Beiping and Tianjin were occupied by the enemy, I returned to Shanghai. Later, I received a letter of Xiao Fang's from the north, in which he said: "My home in Beiping was occupied by the enemy! Many of my photography materials and tools cannot be taken out from my home. Now, I am homeless! I want to work in a newspaper office as a war correspondent. Please help me find such a post."

At that time, the *Ta Kung Pao* (Shanghai) needed journalists. Thus, the newspaper invited Xiao Fang to report on the Beiping-Hankou Railway, Qiujiang on Chahar, and Xiying on eastern Suiyuan. So, Xiao Fang began writing news reports for the *Ta Kung Pao*.

Four

After the outbreak of the Battle of Nankou, the *Ta Kung Pao* (Shanghai) dispatched me to Chahar, to help with Qiujiang's interview work in the central battlefield. I also worked with Xiying on the left wing and Xiao Fang on the right to manage all reports on the battles along the Beiping-Suiyuan and Beiping-Hankou railways. After Chahar was lost, Qiujiang and I retreated from southern Chahar to northern Shanxi, and later to Datong. However, I still wished to continue to report on the middle battlefield. Then, I encountered Chen Xuzhou, a friend working for the army post. He told me Xiao Fang had gone to eastern Suiyuan. I was very surprised and wondered why he abandoned the "right-wing mission." I sent an urgent telegraph to ask him to return to Datong to discuss this.

Then, Xiao Fang came to Datong, with Xiying. He explained that while in Baoding, he heard the Eighth Route Army had marched into Rehe, so he decided to go there. However, after arriving in Suiyuan, he learned that this was false. He admitted that it was thoughtless of him to act alone. Then, in Datong, a city suffering from bombing, the four of us discussed a work plan. When the war situation became urgent, we were living in a Datong guesthouse without food during the day. We often wrote reports beside the air-raid shelter at the corner of the city wall.

As the war situation in Datong became perilous, Xiao Fang and I, successively, went to Shijiazhuang. We agreed that Xiying would report on the battles along the Suiyuan-Ningxia Railway, Qiujiang along the Datong-Puzhou Railway, and Xiao Fang along the Beiping-Hankou Railway.

At that time, The situation in Baoding was already extremely dangerous. The 3rd Division, under General Wei Lihuang, intended to reinforce troops in Nankou. However, it was too late. They were fighting the enemy fiercely in the Qingbaikou Village area at the upper reaches of the Yongding River. Xiao Fang was very excited. He not only wanted to go to Baoding, but also planned to travel to the mountains in Nankou, north of Baoding. He took sufficient blue ink, paper, photography materials and tools, and hurriedly boarded a train going north from Shijiazhuang. Before we parted, I said: "I hope you can write a report on the battle in the upper reaches of the Yongding River!" Plainly and sternly, he answered: "I'll surely submit a good one."

Five

I returned to Shanghai, and, as promised, Xiao Fang sent back two news reports. He was the only journalist at the Beiping-Hankou Railway front at that time, so his reports were indeed precious and brilliant.

With the deteriorating war situation on the battlefield of the Beiping-Hankou Railway, Baoding was occupied by the enemy and we lost contact with Xiao Fang. He had a limited travel allowance and we did not know how to send him more money. I wrote a letter to the Handan Post Office to ask one of his relatives about

我这里来打听消息，甚至于始终在山西战地的溪映也写信来问小方，在上海和在汉口，我曾会到千百个关心小方的人！

“我相信他不会有问题，因为他的机智，足以应付非常事变，他的才能也应该为中国新闻事业，中国民族解放事业，多尽些力量。”我自己也如所想，也如此答复他人。

但是去年保定战争之后今天已经快一年了。我们还看不到我们这位硕壮身躯红润面庞头发带黄斯拉夫型的青年新闻战士！

9月13日汉口

摘自《范长江文集》

him. The relative replied in a letter that when Xiao Fang arrived in Baoding, the city had just been occupied, forcing Xiao Fang to retreat to Li County southeast of Baoding. That same relative received only this one letter from Xiao Fang, sent from Li County – never receiving any further news. However, in that letter, Xiao Fang said: "I'll continue northward from Li County to accomplish my mission as assigned by Changjiang."

Later, Shijiazhuang and Taiyuan were occupied by the enemy. We learned no news about Xiao Fang. His mother, younger sister, girlfriend, and all his friends asked me for news of him. Xiying, who regularly worked on the Shanxi battlefield, even wrote a letter asking about Xiao Fang. In Shanghai and Hankou, I met many people who cared about Xiao Fang!

"I believe he'll be fine because he is smart enough to handle all kinds of emergencies. With his talent, he should make more contributions to journalism and the national liberation of China."

This was what I thought, and what I told the others.

However, it has been around one year since the Battle of Baoding, and we still cannot find this tall, strong, and young journalistic fighter with a healthy complexion and somewhat Slavic-like brown hair!

Hankou, September 13

Excerpted from the *Anthology of Fan Changjiang*

我的舅舅方大曾

张在璇

灰色的小木屋

我没见过舅舅，听母亲说，在我还没出生之前，他就只身离家到烽火连天的抗日前线采访，从此再也没有回来。

我第一次听说家里还有个舅舅，是1950年5岁时随父母从上海回到北京协和胡同7号外婆的方家老宅。老宅很大，占地有一亩多，分前、后两个院落，布局呈“日”字形。北边一排房外婆住，南边一排房姨妈家住，中间一排是我们家。前院的西边有一条过道与后院相连，前院东南角坐落着一个碉堡样的灰色木质小屋，2米多高，4尺见方大。木屋做工十分精细，严丝合缝，拉开门的右手边1米多高的地方开了一个32开书本大的“窗”，上下安有木槽，可以插换定做的红、绿玻璃及木板，插上木板关上门黑得就什么都看不到了。这真是我和哥哥玩耍的绝好去处。一天，我们在“碉堡”里玩“打仗”游戏，动静很大，正玩在兴头，遭到外婆的一声厉喝：“你们别在那儿祸害，都给我滚出来，这是你大舅的东西，谁也不准进去！”我从此知道了母亲有个弟弟，我有个舅舅，外婆有个儿子，知道了舅舅在外婆心中的重要位置。后来我知道这个灰色的小木屋是舅舅冲洗胶卷制作照片的暗房，家里人谁都不愿去动它，直到1969年外婆去世，都原封原样地保留在前院的角落里，因为家里人都知道小木屋是外婆对儿子的念想。多年来，外婆一直不肯离开协和胡同老宅。外婆说，她和舅舅有个约定：“你无论走多远，走多久，回来就到协和胡同来找我，我永远不会搬家，一直等着你。”外婆到底没能等到舅舅归来。然而，忠孝不能两全，在国难当头时，舅舅所能做的首先是一名忠勇的爱国志士。

失踪的战地记者

舅舅方大曾，又名方德曾，笔名小方，1912年生于北平（北京），1931年毕业于北平市立一中。听母亲说，他在中学读书时就喜爱摄影，慈祥的外婆花了七块大洋给他买了一台蔡司折叠相机。从此，对摄影的酷爱使他一发不可收拾。姨妈方澄敏说，舅舅经常背着相机，一把雨伞，一个背包，徒步到处去拍照，1929年他在北平发起组织创立了“少年影社”，在社会上举办过公开影展。1930年考入中法大学经济系。1931年九·一八事变后以满腔热情投入抗日救亡运动，参加“反帝大同盟”，编写机关报《反帝新闻》，并与诗人方殷共同主编《少年先锋》。1935年一二·九运动后他加入“中华民族解放先锋队”，当年冬天就勇敢地背着相机到绥东抗日战场采访。1936年身为中外新闻社记者的他，又冒着生命危险深入绥远前线，进行了长达43天的抗战初期报道，采访了著名的绥远抗战，拍摄了数百张照片，发表了《绥

Fang Dazeng as My Uncle

by Zhang Zaixuan

A Grey Log Cabin

I have never seen Fang Dazeng, my uncle. I heard from my mother that he left home alone before I was born, never to return, to conduct interviews on the flaming anti-Japanese battlefield front.

I learned I had an uncle in 1950, at age five, when I returned with my parents from Shanghai to the old house of Fang's Family at No. 7 Xiehe Hutong in Beijing. The old house was quite large, over 600 square meters, and composed of two adjacent courtyards in the front and back. My grandmother lived in the rooms on the northern row, my auntie's family on the southern row, and my family on the middle row. In the western part of the front courtyard, there was a passageway leading to the back courtyard. In the southeastern corner of the front courtyard stood a fortress-like grey log cabin, standing over 2 meters high with an area of around 2 square meters. The log cabin was finely built and looked quite solid and steady. From inside the cabin, a "window" as large as an A5-paper-sized book was opened. On the top and bottom edges of this "window," two wooden grooves were installed. Red or green glass, or a wooden plate, could be inserted between the grooves. The cabin would go completely dark when the door was closed and the wooden plate was inserted.

This was a paradise for my older brother and me to have fun. One day, when we were playing a "battle" game in the "fortress," making a lot of noise, and having fun, we suddenly heard the stern voice of my grandmother: "Stop messing-up this place! Get out of there now! This place belongs to your uncle. No one can go in!" Since then, I learned that my mother had a younger brother, I had an uncle, and how important he was to my grandmother.

Later, I learned that this gray log cabin once was the darkroom where my uncle developed his film. No one in my family would disturb it. Until my grandmother passed away in 1969, the cabin was kept, untouched, in the corner of the front yard: The rest of my family knew that the cabin represented grandmother missing her son. For many years, grandma was not willing to leave the old house in the Xiehe Hutong. She said she made a pact with my uncle: "No matter where you go, how long you're away, when you return, come to Xiehe Hutong to find me. I'll never move away and will always wait for you." In the end, my grandmother never saw my uncle again. Since ancient times in China, there has been a great dilemma between loyalty to one's country and filial piety to one's parents. During the moment of national crisis, my uncle chose to be a loyal patriot first.

A Missing War Correspondent

My uncle is named Fang Dazeng. He has another name, Fang Dezeng, and the pen name Xiao Fang. He was born in 1912 in Beiping (currently Beijing). In 1931, he graduated from the Beiping No. 1 Middle School. I heard from my mother that my uncle was already a photography enthusiast in middle school. My loving grandmother spent seven silver coins buying him a *Zeiss* folding camera. Since then, he was obsessed with photography.

According to Fang Chengmin, who is Fang Dazeng's sister and my aunt, my uncle used to go outdoors and take photos, with a camera, an umbrella, and a backpack. In 1929, he set up the Youth Photography Club in Beiping and held a public photography exhibition. In 1930, my uncle

东前线视察记》等战地通讯。

1937 年，卢沟桥事变爆发。7 月 10 日，有着强烈新闻敏感和记者责任感的舅舅得到消息后，立即背着照相机骑着自行车第一时间赶到卢沟桥事变现场采访，向世界最先报道了震惊中外的卢沟桥事变，写出长篇报道《卢沟桥抗战记》，披露了事变的真相。据姨妈回忆，舅舅这次采访返回途中被日本兵拦阻盘查，因他个头很高，又长了满头斯拉夫型的栗色头发，加之遇事十分冷静，拿出了中英文的中外通讯社名片，也许是“外”字“唬”住了日本兵，居然得以脱身，平安回到家里。回来他匆匆发完稿后，7 月 23 日带上家中所有的 40 个胶卷、纸笔和墨水，最后告别了家人，又只身去了硝烟滚滚的抗日前线。他知道哪里能写出最好的抗战新闻和拍到最好的照片，他知道哪里是新闻记者最该去的地方。不久，《保卫卢沟桥之我二十九军英姿》《我们为自卫而抗战》《民众慰劳》《敌机轰炸我保定车站》等摄影报道相继被国内外报刊编发。多年以后，著名记者陆诒在《悼念抗战初期牺牲的小方》一文中写道：“我和小方相识，是在抗战初期的 1937 年 7 月 28 日，我们从保定去长辛店前线采访。范长江特赶到车站送别，并为我们做郑重介绍。当时小方已任《大公报》特派记者……，我们搭平汉路上的兵车到长辛店后，即直奔三十七师戴旅长部访问，戴旅长已到前沿阵地指挥去了。走回长辛店的路上，小方为一个年仅 16 岁的士兵照相，他身上背着自己的步枪和大刀，手执日本军官的指挥刀、望远镜之类的战利品，笑嘻嘻地凯旋。这时一颗炮弹正在附近爆炸，小方不屑一顾地对我说：‘今天收获不小！’当晚宛平县政府秘书长洪大中接待我们住在长辛店政府办事处，前线炮声彻夜不息。29 日上午，我们随军撤退。30 日早上回到保定，范长江为我们庆幸生还。当天下午，保定又遭敌机狂炸，孙连仲部队陆续开赴前线，接替二十九军防线。长江和我当晚即搭车回南方，留小方在保定，继续采访平汉路北段战讯。”这是范长江与陆诒最后和舅舅分手的情景。1937 年 8 月至 9 月《大公报》上舅舅的战地报道不断，真实地向国内外展现了中华民族不屈不挠奋勇抗敌的英勇场景。家里的亲人一直得不到舅舅的消息，只能通过《大公报》了解他的行踪，在上海的父亲每天回家都要买一份《大公报》，母亲说他们清楚记得 9 月 17 日和 25 日还看到舅舅的文章《从娘子关出雁门关》和《血战居庸关》，但自 9 月 30 日见到他的《平汉线北段的变化》这篇战地通讯后，就再也没有任何消息了。这篇署名本报战地特派员小方的战地通讯似乎成了他的“绝唱”，文尾注道：“九一八，写于保定，寄自蠡县”。

舅舅的底片

舅舅从此再也没有回来。他在北京协和胡同家中留下了两小木箱底片。外婆说，小木箱是舅舅在院子里盖灰色小木屋时请木匠一并做的，有 1 尺多长，半尺多宽，半尺来高，外面漆上土漆专门用来装底片用的。卢沟桥事变爆发不久平津沦陷，日伪统治下的京城一片恐怖，到处抓人，胆小的外公怕舅舅留下的那些记录抗日运动的底片惹事，先抱了一个木箱到厨房烧。因家对门的三层小楼上住着日本人，晚上烧怕有火光被发现引起怀疑，

was admitted to the Department of Economics at the Lyon Sino-French Institute. In 1931, after the September 18th Incident, he devoted himself to the campaign of resisting Japanese aggression and salvaging China from subjugation. He joined the China Anti-Imperialist League, worked as an editor at the official newspaper *Anti-Imperialist News*, and served as co-editor-in-chief of *Youth Pioneer* magazine with poet Fang Yin. In 1935, after the December 9th Patriotic Parade, my uncle, Fang Dazeng, joined the Chinese National Liberation Vanguard. That winter, he bravely carried his camera to conduct interviews on the anti-Japanese battlefield in eastern Suiyuan. In 1936, as a journalist with the Chinese-Foreign Journalism Society, he moved deep to the front in Suiyuan at his own peril. There, he reported on the preliminary stages of the anti-Japanese war for 43 days, recorded the well-known Suiyuan Campaign, took hundreds of photos, and published war news reports, such as the *Inspection of the Front in Eastern Suiyuan*.

In 1937, the July 7 Incident broke out. On July 10, learning the news, my uncle, as a journalist with an acute nose for news and strong sense of responsibility, immediately took his camera, rode his bicycle, and reached the site to conduct interviews. He was the first to report to the world this sensational incident known to the Chinese as the Lugou Bridge Incident. He wrote a long report entitled the *Lugou Bridge Battle against Japanese Aggression*, revealing the truth about this incident. As my aunt recalled, on his way back home, my uncle was stopped, interrogated, and examined by Japanese soldiers. Because he was tall with Slavic-style brown hair, and because he was calm enough to show his business card, printed in both Chinese and English, bearing the name Chinese-Foreign Journalism Society, and probably because the Japanese were spooked by the word "Foreign," he avoided trouble and returned home safely. After he returned home, he hurriedly published a report. On July 23, he gathered all his films, pens, paper, and ink, and said goodbye to his family to go alone to the flaming anti-Japanese battlefield front. He knew he could produce the best anti-Japanese news and photographs: He knew the place a journalist was most obliged to go.

Soon, news reports with photographs, including the *29th Corps: Heroic Guards of Lugou Bridge*; *We Fight against Japanese Aggression for Self-Defense*; *Civilian Representative Paying Respect to the Army*; and *Baoding Railway Station Bombed by Enemy Aircraft* were successively complied and distributed by newspapers at home and abroad. Years later, Lu Yi, a famous journalist, wrote the following in his article entitled *Mourning Xiao Fang, Who Sacrificed His Life in the Early Stages of the Anti-Japanese War*:

"I first met Xiao Fang on July 28, 1937. We traveled from Baoding to Changxindian to conduct interviews. Fan Changjiang saw us off at the station and introduced Xiao Fang to us. At that time, Xiao Fang was already a special correspondent for *Ta Kung Pao*. After we were given a lift in a military train on the Beiping-Hankou Railway to Changxindian, we went directly to visit Brigade Commander Dai of the 37th Division, but he had left to command at the front. On our way back to Changxindian, Xiao Fang took a photo of a 16-year-old soldier triumphantly returning with a rifle, a broadsword, and trophies such as a Japanese officer's sword and binoculars.

At this moment, a bomb exploded nearby. Notwithstanding the danger, Xiao Fang said: 'A big harvest today!' That night, Hong Dazhong, Secretary-General of the Wanping County Government, welcomed us and arranged for us to live in the government office in Changxindian, where we heard the thundering of guns all night. On the morning of July 29, we retreated with the troops. The next morning, we returned to Baoding. Fan Changjiang felt we were lucky to return alive. That afternoon, Baoding was savagely bombed by enemy aircraft. Sun Lianzhong's troops continued to march toward the front to take the place of the 29 Corps in defense. Changjiang and I went back to the south right that night, leaving Xiao Fang in Baoding to continue reporting on the war at the northern section of the Beiping-Hankou Railway." This was the scene where Fan Changjiang and Lu Yi saw my uncle for the last time.

In August and September of 1937, the *Ta Kung Pao* published a series of reports by my uncle, authentically presenting to people home and abroad scenes of the

白天笼火做饭时就烧一些，后来外婆发现就把另一箱底片藏在了她的大书箱里，这才使舅舅的一箱底片幸免于难。

日本投降后，外婆就把小木箱放在了她卧室的平柜上。这箱底片是家人对舅舅的一个念想，看见它就好像舅舅还在，觉得总有一天他会回家来拿他这箱底片。但没有想到 1966 年“文化大革命”中，家人差点失去它。

1966 年夏，“红卫兵运动”迅猛发展，最初是在社会上破除“四旧”（即所谓旧思想、旧文化、旧风俗、旧习惯），随后发展为抄家、打人、砸物。舅舅的那木箱底片让家里人很紧张，因为他拍摄的《绥远抗战》都是抗战初期布防在绥远前线的傅作义部队，官兵们服装、帽徽以及旗帜都有国民党青天白日的标识，在那个年代收藏这些是犯忌的；他在通讯《冀东一瞥》中，揭露冀东伪政府统治区十分猖獗的娼、赌、烟、毒、走私等社会丑恶现象的照片，那时也都是有口难辩的“四旧”。万一这些底片让红卫兵看到，不用说底片，家里的人将会遭受到灭顶之灾。在银行工作的姨妈就来和母亲商量怎么办，姨妈说她打算瞒着外婆把舅舅的那箱底片交到她工作单位的“红卫兵办公室”，告诉他们这是家里亲人留下的纪念物，看他们如何处置。母亲是一名家庭妇女也没有更好的办法，无奈地说，也只能这样了，但是你一定要注意自己的安全。姨妈在工作单位的人缘很好，说明情况后，“红卫兵办公室”负责人看她态度诚恳就没有为难她，只淡淡地说了一句：“那你就放这儿吧。”失落的姨妈回到家里，母亲告诉她外婆已经知道了送底片的事。母亲说，那天外婆问她小木箱怎么不见了，没想到告诉她真相后外婆表现异常平静，沉默了一会儿，像自言自语似的说了五个字：“听天由命吧。”

一周后的一天，我正在家休息，上午十点左右，突然听到擂鼓般的打门声并夹杂着喊开门的吼声，我刚打开院门，一群带着“红卫兵”袖标的男女们冲进来直奔后院姨妈家，进屋就乱翻乱砸。他们说是姨父工作单位的红卫兵，莫名其妙地说姨父私藏有手枪。因为是亲戚，我们家也没能幸免，连地板都撬了。抄家一直持续到午后，结果什么有价值的东西都没找到，只好扫兴而去。下午，姨父下班回家，见到疮痍满目的劫后院落，满腹冤屈的他气得以头撞门，姨妈含泪安慰他说：“人能平安回来就已经是万幸了。”家人都很庆幸舅舅的底片没有在家里，否则后果是可想而知的。

1968 年初，我离开北京到四川工作，行前去看外婆。83 岁的她精神已经不是很好了，在卧室里正斜靠在床上闭着眼睛养神，床边平柜上原放置小木箱的地方已改放了一张舅舅在中学读书时的自拍照。那时我也已经非常喜爱摄影，自然就和外婆聊起舅舅，她可能已经意识到舅舅回不来了，很伤感地对我说：“你照相时可别像你大舅，他太爱冒险了。”她也知道自己身体已大不如从前，又说：“你们记着，等我死了用小木屋给我做个棺材。”我非常难受，心中在流泪，明知道这是一个不可能实现的愿望，但当时还是点头应下了这个不能兑现的承诺。我知道，外婆至死都想和儿子在一起。一年后，外婆去世，她到底没能等到舅舅的归来。

“文化大革命”结束后的 1979 年，退休后的姨妈有一天到原工作单位去玩，在工会办公室

unrelenting, heroic Chinese nation fighting foreign aggression. My family received no news directly from Xiao Fang, but could learn about his whereabouts through the *Ta Kung Pao*. My father was in Shanghai at the time. Every day, he would buy a *Ta Kung Pao* before returning home. My mother told me they remembered reading *From Niangzi Pass to Yanmen Pass* and *Heroic Battle at Juyong Pass*, written by my uncle, on September 17 and 25, respectively. However, after reading his report entitled *Changes in the Northern Section of the Beiping-Hankou Railway* on September 30, they heard no further news. This war report, filed under the pen name "Xiao Fang, Special War Correspondent of *Ta Kung Pao*," seemed to be his swan song. At the end of the report was a note reading "September 18, written in Baoding, sent from Li County."

My Uncle's Negatives

My uncle never returned. He left behind two small wooden boxes of negatives at his home in Xiehe Hutong, Beijing. According to my grandmother, the wooden boxes were made by a carpenter when helping my uncle build the courtyard's grey log cabin. Each box was about one-third of a meter long, one-sixth of a meter wide, and one-sixth of a meter deep. The exterior was painted using raw lacquer, and inside, both boxes contained negatives. Soon after the Lugou Bridge Incident, Beiping and Tianjin were occupied by the enemy. Under the Japanese puppet regime, Beiping was rife with horrors, with people being arrested everywhere. My grandfather was so intimidated and worried about the trouble that could result if my uncle's negatives, recording anti-Japanese campaigns, were discovered, that he took one box to the kitchen to burn the negatives. Since there were Japanese living in the three-story building facing my grandfather's house, he worried the flames at night would generate enemy suspicion. So, he chose to burn some of the negatives in the stove's fire while cooking during the day. My grandmother found out about this and hid the other box of negatives in her big bookcase, thus rescuing them.

After the Japanese invaders surrendered, my grandmother placed the small box on the flat cabinet in her bedroom. This box of negatives represented the family missing my uncle. Looking at it, they felt like my uncle was still alive and would return to pick up the negatives someday. However, in 1966, during the Cultural Revolution, they nearly lost these negatives.

In the summer of 1966, the "Red Guards Campaign" was so intense and ferocious that it morphed from a campaign of destroying the "Four Olds" (old customs, old culture, old habits, and old ideas) into one of confiscating private property, battering innocent people, and destroying personal belongings. My uncle's wooden box made the family very nervous because his photo of the *Suiyuan Campaign* showed Fu Zuoyi's troops at the front in Suiyuan during the early stages of the anti-Japanese war with the KMT's "Blue Sky with a White Sun" symbol on the suits, cap emblems, and flags of those troops, a very serious taboo at that time. In addition, my uncle's report *A Glance at Eastern Hebei*, contained photos revealing social evils such as prostitution, gambling, opium smoking, drug trafficking, and smuggling, all rampant in eastern Hebei under the puppet government regime and typical of the Four Olds. If the Red Guards saw these negatives, let alone all the other negatives, the entire family would face great calamity.

My aunt, who worked in a bank, came to my mother to discuss what they should do. My aunt said she planned to give, without my grandmother knowing, the box of negatives to the Red Guards' Office in her bank and tell them this was merely a memento left behind by a relative and at their disposal. My mother was a housewife and had no better option, so she helplessly said: "OK, but please be safe." After my aunt explained the situation, the person in charge of the Red Guards' Office just said "Leave it here, then." My aunt felt so sad and returned home, where my mother told her that grandma knew she had submitted those negatives. My mother said grandma asked her that day why the small wooden box was gone. She was surprised that after hearing what happened, grandma was exceptionally calm, remained silent awhile, then said five words as if talking to herself: "It is in God's hands."

A week later, while resting at home around 10 a.m., I suddenly heard drum-like knocking at the door and people

的角落里几张废报纸包着一叠叠粉红色的袋子散落在地上，姨妈一眼就认出这是她哥哥的底片。这些底片每一张都是装入一个半透明纸做的内袋，然后再放入一个粉红外袋里，外袋上印有“德记商行”“王府井大街北口路西”的字样。兴奋的姨妈立即找到工会负责人，负责人说：“‘红卫兵办公室’早就不在了，这些东西没人管，是你的你就拿回去吧。”欣喜若狂的姨妈迅速把底片小心拾回，仔细包好带回了家。又过了些日子，姨妈又去工会参加退休职工活动，聚餐时看见食堂大师傅用装底片的小木箱在卖饭票，她就跑到街上买了一个白铁皮做的箱子，找到大师傅商量换回小木箱。说明情况后大师傅很爽快地答应了。失而复得，舅舅的小木箱和底片离开家13年后又奇迹般地回到家中，这是它躲过的第二次劫难。

舅舅的底片回来了，姨妈开始悉心整理，她希望能出版点什么来纪念她的哥哥，一个退休的老人凭着妹妹对哥哥的崇敬和思念，苦苦地不断寻找着各种机会。1989年，姨妈通过上海一个熟人的关系终于结识了在中国摄影出版社工作的摄影史学家陈申先生，之后就把舅舅的底片交给了他进行系统整理和研究。1993年在陈申先生的推介下，台湾摄影家阮义忠先生看到了这些底片。阮先生对舅舅的摄影才华，对中国30年代有如此杰出的摄影师感到惊叹，决定在他办的《摄影家》杂志上出一期专辑，为了保证质量要把选出的底片带到台湾，因为只有他亲自放大，才能把作品做最好理解和呈现。姨妈非常乐意舅舅的作品出版，但得知阮先生要把选好的50张底片漂洋过海带去台湾就十分犹豫，最后阮先生的诚意打动了姨妈，同意了他的要求。我记得后来姨妈还曾写信到四川，嘱咐我写信给阮义忠先生询问，生怕底片邮寄回来时丢失，我很理解她的担心。其实，阮义忠先生对舅舅底片的珍爱并不亚于姨妈，就在他怀揣着50张底片乘飞机回台湾在香港着陆时遇到台风，阮先生在《摄影家》杂志“方大曾专辑”中有如下一段让我很感动的惊心动魄的描述：“一想到那一天，那种紧张恐怖，死里逃生的感觉就明显地回来了。第一次觉得如此接近死亡。我的右手和太太的左手紧紧地握在一起，不用看脸色也知道，两人都已经吓得半死了。我们和东方航空公司飞机上的100多位乘客一样，在一片惊吓的惨叫声中意识到，自己可能就这样没有了。飞机是从上海飞来的，在香港启德机场的跑道上，轮子已经快要触地，可感觉上好像坐在摇篮里，或是断了线的大风筝上。机外正刮着强烈的台风，我们那位十分可能是战斗机驾驶员转行的机长，在飞机被强风迎面刮上来之后，还不死心地想做第二次降落，飞机一往下冲就被风吹上来，一往下冲就被风吹上来。这个时候，惨叫声已经变成了无助的哀号，所有的人都把命交出去了，只能任机长和死神拔河……”后来飞机返航平安降落广州，“久久之后才有办法平息下来的我跟太太，彼此相询，快要完蛋的那一刻在想什么，太太说，她的脑子里翻来覆去就是一件事——才12岁的儿子该怎么办？我老实告诉她，我一心只挂着左胸口袋里的50张底片，觉得我对不起它们的作者小方，这位可能是当时中国最优秀的摄影家，将随着我的死去而使他最好的作品永不为世人所知。他已经够倒霉地失踪，且被遗忘了50多年，这下子，岂不如同他又死一次。”这是舅舅的底片第三次遇险。

yelling to be let in. When I opened the door, a group of men and women wearing Red Guard armbands rushed in and went directly to my aunt's home in the back yard. They ransacked the rooms. They said they were Red Guards from the workplace of my aunt's husband, and claimed he had hidden a pistol. Because we were relatives, they even ripped up the floor in our rooms. This continued until the afternoon, when, after finding nothing valuable, they finally left disappointed. When my aunt's husband returned home from work, he felt so wronged and angry that he beat his head against the door. Crying, my aunt consoled him, saying: "We are so lucky to be home and safe." The family felt very lucky that my uncle's negatives were not there at that time. Otherwise, they would have faced severe consequences.

Early in 1968, I left Beijing to work in Sichuan. Before I left, I went to see my grandmother. She was 83 and not well. She was in her bed, resting, with her eyes closed. On the flat cabinet beside her bed, where the small wooden box used to be, was a photograph of my uncle when he was a middle-school student. At that time, I was into photography as well. So, I naturally talked about my uncle with my grandmother. She realized my uncle probably wouldn't return, so she said, sadly: "When you take photos, don't be like your uncle. He loved adventure too much."

She was aware that her body had become much worse, and said: "Remember this. After I die, make me a coffin using the wood from that log cabin." I felt so sad and wept inside. I knew this was a wish that could never be realized, but I nodded and made a promise that could never be fulfilled. I knew grandma wanted to be with her son all her life and in death. One year later, my grandmother passed away. In the end, she never enjoyed the return of my uncle.

One day in 1979, after the Cultural Revolution had ended, my retired aunt went to visit her previous work place. In the corner of the Labor Union Office, there were piles of pink envelopes wrapped in old newspapers. My aunt immediately recognized that these were the negatives of her elder brother. Each negative was inside a transparent inner envelope contained within a pink outer envelope with the words "De's Business House" and "west of the northern end of Wangfujing Street" printed on it. My aunt was so excited. She found the person in charge and was told: "The Red Guards are long gone. No one takes care of these things. If they're yours, take them."

My aunt immediately picked up the negatives with great care, packaged them well, and took them home. Days later, she attended an activity organized by the labor union for retired staff. As they dined, she saw the canteen cook selling meal vouchers contained in my uncle's small wooden box. She ran to the street, bought a box made of tin, returned, and asked to exchange it for the wooden box. Hearing her explanation, the cook agreed. After 13 years, the small wooden box and negatives of my uncle miraculously returned home. This was the second time they escaped doom.

After re-acquiring the negatives, my aunt began to carefully file them. She hoped to publish them in memory of her elder brother. Out of a younger sister's respect, and out of missing her elder brother, this retired woman painstakingly sought all sorts of opportunities. Finally, in 1989, introduced by an old friend in Shanghai, my aunt met Mr. Chen Shen, a photography historian working for the China Photographic Publishing House. She later gave him those negatives for systematic filing and study.

In 1993, on the recommendation and introduction of Chen Shen, Mr. Ruan Yizhong, a photographer from Taiwan, saw these negatives and was astonished by my uncle's talent and the fact that there existed such a talented photographer in China during the 1930s. Mr. Ruan decided to issue a volume of his *Photographers* magazine dedicated to my uncle. However, he needed to take selected negatives to Taiwan to ensure the quality of the publication since he had to magnify them himself to best interpret and present them. My aunt was willing to publish my uncle's works, but was very hesitant about the 50 selected negatives being taken across the strait to Taiwan. Finally, she was persuaded by Mr. Ruan's sincerity and agreed. As I recall, she later wrote me, while I was in Sichuan, asking me to write Mr. Ruan and inquire about the negatives. Understandably, she worried they would be lost when mailed back home.

In fact, Ruan Yizhong cherished these negatives as much as my aunt did. When about to land in Hong

回归

然而，舅舅又是幸运的。1993 年《摄影家》杂志“方大曾专辑”在台湾出版，这是舅舅作品的第一本影集。当时海峡两岸文化交流的大门刚刚打开了一条缝，少量进入大陆的这期“方大曾专辑”在大陆摄影界产生了很大反响，舅舅的作品引起了人们的关注。

1999 年，中央电视台高级编辑、著名纪录片导演冯雪松先生，为纪念中华人民共和国第一个记者节，带着摄制组沿着舅舅从采访到失踪的路线艰难寻访，先后两次前往保定、石家庄、大同、太原、蠡县，往复行程达 4000 公里，并用四个半月的时间，翻阅了大量的史料，从历史的碎片中拼接出了一个鲜活的方大曾，使他的生命轮廓逐渐清晰，重新回归了当代人的视野。他拍摄的纪录片《寻找方大曾》在中央电视台播出后，反响强烈，并荣获第十五届全国电视文艺星光奖。

同年年底，陈申、冯雪松等人策划的《寻找方大曾》一书由中国摄影出版社出版。

2006 年，国家博物馆得知方大曾底片已由姨妈转交我保管的信息，派专人到成都找到我，后来经与家人协商同意，由我代表全家把舅舅留下的几经磨难的底片共计 837 张，无偿捐赠给了国家博物馆。

2014 年 11 月，又经过 15 年锲而不舍地艰难寻访，冯雪松先生的《方大曾：消失与重现》一书出版。该书出版后即引起社会广泛关注，中国新闻史学界泰斗、中国新闻史学会创会会长、中国人民大学一级教授方汉奇先生见到这本书格外激动。他表示，在几十年的教学和研究当中，真不知道有方大曾这么一个人，相信绝大多数专业和非专业的人士都不知道，封笔多年后，他写下了阅读感言：“冯雪松的这部专著《方大曾：消失与重现》，把湮没了 80 多年的一位杰出的新闻工作者和摄影记者方大曾推到了历史的前台，让他的名字开始为公众所知晓，这是对中国新闻事业史人物研究和中国战地新闻摄影史研究的一大贡献。方大曾有关卢沟桥事变和抗战前线的一大批新闻照片，是对伟大的全民抗战的忠实纪录。它体现了抗日军民抵御外侮敌忾同仇的民族精神，鼓舞了士气和斗志，也保存了许多拍自第一现场的珍贵画面，具有重要的历史文献价值。我们为历史上有过如此杰出的新闻摄影记者感到骄傲。他将永远活在我们的心里。”

2015 年两会期间，全国人大代表、澳门日报社社长陆波先生，在阅读《方大曾：消失与重现》后，建议中宣部、中国记协以官方的名义纪念这位新闻先驱，使他的精神得以弘扬，这样有利于两岸同胞的亲情融合。

2015 年 5 月 25 日，中华全国新闻工作者协会（简称中国记协）组织召开冯雪松追踪采写方大曾事迹座谈会，中国记协党组书记翟惠生指出，中国记协举办这次活动是在纪念抗战胜利 70 周年之际讲两个人的故事——方大曾和冯雪松。以历史为镜，两代记者的故事讲的是同一个主题：面向现实，深入实际，不畏艰难困苦，忠实记录时代，为民族为国家为人民鼓与呼。这种精神在每个时代都是必要的，今天更应在中国记者中进行弘扬。

Kong, en route to Taiwan with the 50 negatives, he had an experience that greatly moved me. He described this in the *Photographers* magazine's Special Volume for Fang Dazeng:

"When I recall that day, I clearly remember the horror, fear, and feeling of narrow escape from death. I was so close to death for the first time in my life. My right hand tightly held my wife's left hand. One need not look at our expression to know we were deadly frightened. Like the other 100 or so passengers on that China Eastern flight, we knew from the desperate cries and screams that we were probably gone.

"The flight was from Shanghai. On the runway of Hong Kong's Kai Tak Airport, the wheels were nearly touching the ground, but we felt like we were sitting in a rocking cradle or on a large lost kite. Outside was a fierce typhoon. Our captain, probably a former fighter pilot, refused to abort a second attempt to land, even faced with gusty winds. Right after the plane shot downward, it was blown back up by winds. Desperate cries became helpless wailing. Everyone's fate awaited the result of the tug-of-war between the captain and death..."

Ultimately, the captain chose to return and landed safely in Guangzhou. "Calming down after a long while, my wife and I asked each other what we were thinking at the moment of impending death. My wife said she only thought of our son's future, he was just 12 years old. I honestly told my wife I only thought of the 50 negatives in my left shirt pocket. At that moment, I felt so guilty toward their creator, Xiao Fang, probably the best photographer in China in those days, because with my death, his best works would never be known to the world. He had been missing and forgotten for over half a century. He would, in essence, die a second time." This was the third time my uncle's negatives cheated death.

Returning Home

Actually, my uncle was quite lucky. In 1993, the Special Volume for Fang Dazeng of the *Photographers* magazine was released in Taiwan. This was the first photo album of my uncle's photographs. Through a cross-strait cultural exchange, a small number of these photos were introduced to, and greatly welcomed by photography circles on the mainland. People were attracted to my uncle's works.

In 1999, Mr. Feng Xuesong, a CCTV senior editor and well-known documentary director, in memory of the first Reporters' Day after the founding of the PRC, took his film crew on a painstaking journey to follow the entire interview route of my uncle. They visited Baoding, Shijiazhuang, Datong, Taiyuan, and Li County twice, covering 4,000 kilometers. They spent four-and-a-half months studying voluminous historical material and created a fresh image of Fang Dazeng from the fragments of history: Thus, helping to clarify the outline of his life to contemporary people. His documentary *In Search of Fang Dazeng* was aired on CCTV and greatly received, winning the 15th National TV and Art Starlight Award. At the end of that same year, the book *In Search of Fang Dazeng*, planned mainly by Chen Shen and Feng Xuesong, was published by the China Photographic Publishing House.

In 2006, hearing that my uncle's negatives had been given to me by my aunt for preservation, the National Museum of China sought me out. Following discussion, and agreement, with my family, I donated the 837 negatives left by my uncle to the National Museum. I donated these negatives, which endured so many vicissitudes, on behalf of my family.

In November of 2014, after another 15 years of perseverance and painstaking investigation, Feng Xuesong published *Fang Dazeng: Disappearance and Reappearance*, which attracted much attention in society. After reading it, Fang Hanqi, a titan in the field of Chinese journalism history, the first President of the Chinese Association of History of Journalism and Mass Communication (CAHJMC), and a top-grade professor at the Renmin University of China, was thrilled, saying that although he had taught and researched for decades, he was unaware of the existence of Fang Dazeng. He believed most professionals, and non-professionals, did not know of Fang Dazeng. After not writing for years, Fang Hanqi wrote the following about this book:

"*Fang Dazeng: Disappearance and Reappearance*, by Feng Xuesong, put Fang Dazeng, an excellent journalist and press photographer, onto the stage of history and made his

是冯雪松先生一一拾回了舅舅丢失在战地破碎的灵魂，重现了一个有血有肉、生动鲜活的方大曾。我仿佛感觉到舅舅回家了。

2015 年 7 月 7 日，在舅舅最后失联的战地保定，方大曾纪念室在冯雪松的倡议推动下落成，舅舅的灵魂终于有了归宿。

中国人民抗日战争暨世界反西斯战争胜利 70 周年纪念日前，在香港《大公报》隆重举行的“一份报纸的抗战”活动上，冯雪松先生发表了主旨演讲《伟哉大公报　壮哉方大曾》，我则把舅舅 464 张底片的电子文件捐赠给了《大公报》，舅舅的作品回到了他最后供职的报社。

8 月 28 日，澳门新闻工作者协会联合澳门中华教育会隆重举办了《为了正义与良知——七七卢沟桥事变战地记者方大曾遗作展》。同时冯雪松先生的《方大曾：消失与重现》一书的繁体字版也在澳门出版发行。澳门特别行政区行政长官崔世安和时任中央人民政府驻澳门特别行政区联络办公室主任出席活动，海内外的中国人民没有忘记过为抗战做出过贡献的人们，这真让人高兴！

记得 2012 年夏，我在北京遇见陈申先生，他交给了我一张舅舅拍摄的外婆的底片，是他以前写书时从姨妈手中借用的，现在转交给我留作纪念。这是现在我手中仅有的一张舅舅拍摄的外婆的底片。我又把底片找了出来，看着外婆慈祥的面容，感慨万千，外婆、姨妈和母亲若在天有知，定会感到欣慰的。我小心地把外婆的底片夹在了《方大曾：消失与重现》一书中舅舅的照片旁，以了却我曾答应过的承诺——让她和她的儿子在一起。

2015 年 9 月 6 日写于成都家中

name known to the public; a major contribution to the study of Chinese journalistic and photographic history regarding Chinese war news. The large batch of news photographs by Fang Dazeng regarding the Lugou Bridge Incident and anti-Japanese front faithfully record the great nationwide anti-Japanese war. They exhibit the Chinese national spirit of safeguarding national dignity against Japanese aggression, and preserve a record of the many valuable scenes at their original sites, serving as important historical documents. We feel proud of such an eminent journalist who lived in history and who will live forever in our hearts."

During the 2015 sessions of the National People's Congress (NPC) and the National Committee of the Chinese People's Political Consultative Conference (CPPCC), Mr. Lu Bo, President of the *Macao Daily News*, after reading *Fang Dazeng: Disappearance and Reappearance*, suggested that the Publicity Department of the CPC Central Committee and the Chinese Journalists' Association officially commemorate this pioneer of journalism and promote his spirit to strengthen relations across the Taiwan Strait.

On May 25, 2015, the Chinese Journalists' Association held a forum on Feng Xuesong's recording of Fang Dazeng's stories. Mr. Zhai Huisheng, Party Secretary of the Association, pointed out that this event was held to discuss stories between Fang Dazeng and Feng Xuesong, under the auspices of celebrating the 70th anniversary of victory in the Chinese people's War of Resistance against Japanese Aggression. The stories of these two journalists, of different ages, were about the same theme: To face reality, relate to practicality, brave difficulty, record the times loyally, and inspire the Chinese nation and its people. Such spirit was a necessity at each age, and should be particularly promoted among Chinese journalists today.

It was Feng Xuesong who brought back and helped mend the broken soul of my uncle lost in the battlefields; who put forth a vivid, fresh Fang Dazeng with flesh and blood. I felt as if my uncle had returned. On July 7, 2015, in Baoding, the battlefield where my uncle sent his last report, the Fang Dazeng Memorial Hall was built following proposal and promotion by Feng Xuesong. This is a place where my uncle's soul can rest.

Prior to the 70th anniversary of victory in the Chinese People's War of Resistance against Japanese Aggression and the World Anti-Fascist War, at the "A Newspaper Fighting Japanese Aggression" forum organized by *Ta Kung Pao* (Hong Kong), Feng Xuesong delivered a keynote address entitled *Great Ta Kung Pao, Great Fang Dazeng*. To have my uncle's works finally returned to the newspaper agency for which he worked, I also donated the electronic versions of 464 negatives of my uncle to *Ta Kung Pao*.

On August 28, the Journalists' Association of Macao and the Chinese Educators' Association of Macao jointly held "For Justice and Conscience – Exhibition for Fang Dazeng: the War Correspondent Who Reported on the Lugou Bridge Incident First." Meanwhile, the traditional Chinese version of Feng Xuesong's *Fang Dazeng: Disappearance and Reappearance* was released in Macao SAR. Fernando Chui Sai On, Chief Executive of Macao, and Director of the Liaison Office of the Central People's Government in Macao SAR, were present. It was so exciting to see that the Chinese people never forgot those who contributed to victory in China's War of Resistance against Japanese Aggression.

In the summer of 2012, I met Chen Shen in Beijing. He gave me a negative of my grandmother taken by my uncle, which he borrowed from my aunt in writing his book and returned to me out of remembrance for the deceased. This is the only negative I have of my grandmother that was taken by my uncle. Looking at my grandma's gentle expression, I feel overwhelmed with so many feelings. If my grandmother, aunt, and mother knew what I had done, they would surely feel comforted. I have carefully placed this negative next to the photo of my uncle in the book *Fang Dazeng: Disappearance and Reappearance*, to honor the promise I once made to my grandmother to let her stay with her son.

At home in Chengdu, September 6, 2015

方大曾生平及研究年表

—1912 年　7 月 13 日，生于北京。

—1929 年　8 月，发起组织青少年摄影社团，创立“少年影社”，参加过公开展览。

—1930 年　考入中法大学经济系。

—1932 年　因参加进步学生游行被捕，遂由校方降级一年。

—1935 年　大学毕业。

在天津基督教青年会任职员。

与吴寄寒、周勉之等人成立中外新闻学社。

一二·九运动后，参加中华民族解放先锋队（简称“民先”）。

—1936 年　夏天，到北平基督教青年会工作，任少年部干事，邀高尚仁（北平基督教青年会少年部负责人）看斯诺访问陕北延安革命根据地拍摄的照片。

6、7 月间，方大曾经山西前往绥远旅行采访，后完成了《从大同到绥远》等文。

11 月初，方大曾与许智方在天津青年会举办联合摄影展。

11 月 8 日，在北平写成《宛平之行》采访记。

11 月 23—28 日，到河北唐山、昌黎等地采访冀东伪政府辖区，写成《冀东一瞥》。

12 月初，离开北平到绥远前线进行了长达 43 天的抗战初期著名的“绥远抗战”采访，拍摄了数百张照片，写成《绥东前线视察记》等战地通讯，期间，与著名记者范长江相遇。

—1937 年　7 月 10 日，离家前往卢沟桥采访卢沟桥事变。

7 月 23 日，由北平寄出《卢沟桥抗战记》。《良友》第 130 期同时刊载方大曾有关卢沟桥事变的 4 组摄影报道。

7 月 28 日，与范长江再次相遇，并结识陆诒、宋致泉。

8 月，经范长江介绍，开始担任上海《大公报》战地特派员。

8 月中旬，由平汉线转至山西，在同浦铁路沿线进行采访。

9 月 18 日，从河北蠡县寄出《平汉线北段的变化》一文，为方大曾最后的消息。

Timetable of Fang Dazeng's Life and Research on Fang Dazeng

— On July 13, 1912, Fang was born in Beijing.

— In August of 1929, Fang proposed to establish a youth photography organization, created the Youth Photography Club, and participated in an open exhibition.

— In 1930, Fang was admitted, by the Department of Economics, to the Lyon Sino-French Institute.

— In 1932, Fang participated in a parade of progressive students and was arrested. Because of this, the school made him repeat a year.

— In 1935, Fang graduated-worked for the Chinese Young Men's Christian Association (YMCA) in Tianjin.

— Fang founded the Chinese-Foreign Journalism Society with Wu Jihan, Zhou Mianzhi, and others.

— Following the December 9th Patriotic Parade, Fang joined the Chinese National Liberation Vanguard (CNLV).

— In the summer of 1936, Fang went to Beiping, where he worked for the YMCA as Secretary of the Youth Department. Fang invited Gao Shangren (in charge of the Youth Department) to view photos taken by Edgar Snow during his visit to the Yan'an Revolutionary Base in Northern Shaanxi.

— During June and July, Fang traveled to Suiyuan via Shanxi to conduct interviews, and later completed reports, including *From Datong to Suiyuan*.

— In early November, Fang Dazeng and Xu Zhifang held a joint photography exhibition at the YMCA in Tianjin.

— On November 8, Fang completed, in Beiping, the interview-based report *Travel in Wanping*.

— From November 23-28, Fang traveled to Tangshan, Changli, and other places in Hebei Province to conduct interviews in the areas under control of the eastern Hebei puppet government and wrote *A Glance at Eastern Hebei*.

— Early in December, Fang left Beiping for the front at Suiyuan to conduct a 43-day interview on the well-known Suiyuan Campaign during the early stages of the Chinese People's War of Resistance against Japanese Aggression. He took hundreds of photos and wrote war reports, including *Inspection of the Front in Eastern Suiyuan*. During this period, he met Fan Changjiang, a famous journalist.

— On July 10, 1937, Fang left home for the Lugou Bridge to conduct interviews about the Lugou Bridge Incident.

— On July 23, *Lugou Bridge Battle against Japanese Aggression*, by Fang, was sent from Beiping. The No. 130 of the *Young Companion* published four sets of photographic reports by Fang Dazeng about the Lugou Bridge Incident.

— On July 28, Fang met Fan Changjiang again and got to know Lu Yi and Song Zhiquan.

— In August, introduced by Fan Changjiang, Fang began working as a war correspondent for the *Ta Kung Pao* (Shanghai).

— In mid-August, Fang moved from the Beiping-Hankou Railway to Shanxi to conduct interviews along the Datong-Puzhou Railway.

— On September 18, Fang sent the report *Changes in the Northern Section of the Beiping-Hankou Railway* from Li County, Hebei Province. This marks the last known news of Xiao Fang.

— On September 30, *Changes in the Northern Section of the Beiping-Hankou Railway* was published in the *Ta Kung Pao*.

— In December 1994, the 17th volume of the *Photographers* magazine in Taiwan was released, focusing on Fang Dazeng's

9 月 30 日，《平汉线北段的变化》在《大公报》发表。

—1994 年　12 月，台湾《摄影家》杂志第 17 期推出方大曾专集。

—2000 年　11 月 8 日，中央电视台播出纪录片《寻找方大曾》（导演、撰稿冯雪松），同名书籍由中国摄影出版社出版。

—2002 年　7 月 1 日至 9 日，“追溯——方大曾摄影作品展”在成都举行，106 幅照片与公众见面。

—2006 年　3 月 16 日，方大曾的亲属将其 837 张底片捐赠给中国国家博物馆。

—2012 年　7 月 13 日，央视网举办方大曾诞辰一百周年纪念活动。

—2014 年　10 月，《方大曾：消失与重现》一书由上海锦绣文章出版社出版。

—2015 年　5 月 25 日，中国新闻工作者协会组织召开冯雪松追踪采写方大曾事迹座谈会。

6 月 29 日，香港大公报“一份报纸的抗战”论坛，冯雪松应邀发表主旨演讲《伟哉大公报　壮哉方大曾》，方大曾的外甥张在璇先生一同出席。

7 月 7 日，方大曾纪念室在保定光园落成，方汉奇先生题匾。

8 月 28 日，“为了正义与良知——七七卢沟桥事变战地记者方大曾遗作展”在澳门综艺馆举行，《方大曾：消失与重现》繁体字版同时首发，澳门特别行政区行政长官崔世安、中联办主要官员及方大曾亲属出席剪彩仪式。

9 月 23 日，“方大曾校园行”公益计划在清华大学启动。

12 月 5 日，北京大学举办“方大曾及抗战报人学术研讨会”。

—2017 年　5 月，“寻找方大曾”特别讲座应邀走进美国纽约州立大学。

6 月，《解读方大曾——方大曾作品及范长江新闻奖获得者的阅读笔记》由中国社会科学出版社出版。“方大曾校园行”公益计划在范长江新闻学院圆满收官。

7 月，《方大曾：消失与重现》由新世界出版社修订出版。

8 月，“小方眼中的抗日战争”图片展在中国人民抗日战争纪念馆展出。

12 月，《方大曾：遗落与重拾》由新世界出版社出版。

12 月 24 日，方大曾纪念室改陈布展开幕。

—2018 年　3 月，“寻找方大曾”特别讲座在澳门大学、澳门科技大学举办。

4 月，《方大曾：遗落与重拾》新书发布座谈会在中国外文局举办。

7 月 7 日，方大曾研究中心在保定成立，方汉奇先生题匾。

works.

On November 8, 2000, CCTV aired the documentary *In Search of Fang Dazeng* (written and directed by Feng Xuesong). A book with the same name was published by China Photographic Publishing House.

— On July 1-9, 2002, the "Remembering – Fang Dazeng's Photographic Works Exhibition" was held in Chengdu, with 106 pictures exhibited.

— On March 16, 2006, relatives of Fang Dazeng donated 837 negatives of his to the National Museum of China.

— On July 13, 2012, cctv.com held a celebration for the 100th anniversary of the birth of Fang Dazeng.

— In October of 2014, *Fang Dazeng: Disappearance and Reappearance* was published by Shanghai Embroidered Literature Publishing House.

— On May 25, 2015, the Chinese Journalists' Association held a forum on Feng Xuesong's recording of Fang Dazeng's stories.

— On June 29, at the "A Newspaper Fighting against Japanese Aggression" forum organized by *Ta Kung Pao* (Hong Kong), Feng Xuesong delivered a keynote speech entitled *Great Ta Kung Pao, Great Fang Dazeng*. Mr. Zhang Zaixuan, nephew of Fang Dazeng, was also present.

— On July 7, the Fang Dazeng Memorial Hall was completed in Guang Garden, Baoding. Fang Hanqi wrote the inscription for the hall.

— On August 28, "For Justice and Conscience – An Exhibition for Fang Dazeng, the War Correspondent Who Reported on the Lugou Bridge Incident First" was held at the Macao Forum. Meanwhile, the traditional Chinese version of Feng Xuesong's *Fang Dazeng: Disappearance and Reappearance* was released in Macao. Fernando Chui Sai On (Chief Executive of Macao SAR), other major officials, and Fang Dazeng's relatives were present at the ribbon-cutting ceremony.

— On September 23, the Fang Dazeng in Schools Public Welfare Plan was initiated at Tsinghua University.

— On December 5, Peking University held the "Symposium on Fang Dazeng and Other Journalists against Japanese Aggression."

— In May 2017, by invitation, the special lecture "In Search of Fang Dazeng" was given at the State University of New York, USA.

— In June, *Interpreting Fang Dazeng – Fang Dazeng's Works and the Reading Notes of Fan Changjiang Press Award Winner*s was published by China Social Sciences Press. The "Fang Dazeng in Schools" public welfare scheme concluded successfully at the Fan Changjiang College of Journalism.

— In July, *Fang Dazeng: Disappearance and Reappearance* was revised and published by New World Press.

— In August, the exhibition themed "Chinese People's War of Resistance against Japanese Aggression in Xiao Fang's Eyes" was held in the Museum of the War of Chinese People's Resistance Against Japanese Aggression.

— In December, *Fang Dazeng: Lost and Found* was published by New World Press.

— On December 24, the Fang Dazeng Memorial Hall was renovated and opened.

— In March of 2018, an "In Search of Fang Dazeng" special lecture was presented at the University of Macao and at the Macao University of Science and Technology.

— In April, a book release forum entitled *Fang Dazeng: Lost and Found* was held by China International Publishing Group.

— On July 7, the Fang Dazeng Research Center was built in Baoding. Mr. Fang Hanqi wrote a plaque for it.

方大曾通讯作品目录

1 《矿区杂记》原载《大众知识》1936 年第 5 期

2 《北平学生的灾区服务》原载《生活星期刊》 1936 年第 25 期

3 《日军秋操之后》原载《生活星期刊》 1936 年第 26 期

4 《绥远的鸦片问题》原载《申报》（每周增刊） 1936 年第 41 期

5 《冀东视察记》原载《申报》（每周增刊） 1936 年第 49 期

6 《张垣一瞥》原载《生活日报》 1936 年 6 月 26、27 日连载

7 《从张垣到大同》原载《生活日报》 1936 年 6 月 28、29、30 日，7 月 1、2 日连载

8 《晋北煤业现状》原载《生活日报》 1936 年 7 月 12、13 日连载

9 《从大同到绥远》原载《生活星期刊》 1936 年第 13 期

10 《宛平之行》原载《世界知识》1936 年 5 卷 5 号

11 《走私在海滨》原载《国民》 1937 年第 2 期

12 《绥远的军事地理》原载《世界知识》 1937 年第 6 期

13 《冀东一瞥》原载《世界知识》 1937 年第 7 期

14 《绥东前线视察记》原载《世界知识》 1937 年第 8 期

15 《兴和之行》原载《世界知识》 1937 年第 9 期

16 《集宁见闻记》原载《申报》（每周增刊） 1937 年第 20 期

17 《四子王府见闻记》原载《申报》（每周增刊） 1937 年第 20 期

18 《从集宁到陶林》原载《世界知识》 1937 年第 12 期

19 《北平学生联合大露营》原载《国民》 1937 年第 11 期

20 《卢沟桥抗战记》原载《世界知识》 1937 年 6 卷

21 《前线忆北平》原载《沦亡的平津》

22 《保定以南》原载《从卢沟桥到漳河》

23 《保定以北》原载《从卢沟桥到漳河》

List of News Reports by Fang Dazeng

1. *Anecdotes in Coal Mining Area*, originally published in *Popular Knowledge* (No. 5, 1936)
2. *Beiping Students Serving Disaster-hit Area*, originally published in *Life Weekly* (No. 25, 1936)
3. *After Autumn Drill of Japanese Army*, originally published in *Life Weekly* (No. 26, 1936)
4. *Opium Problem in Suiyuan*, originally published in *Shun Pao* (weekly supplement, No. 41, 1936)
5. *Inspection of Eastern Hebei*, originally published in *Shun Pao* (weekly supplement, No. 49, 1936)
6. *A Glance at Zhangyuan*, originally published in *Life Daily* (serialized, June 26-27, 1936)
7. *From Zhangyuan to Datong*, originally published in *Life Daily* (serialized, June 28 - July 2, 1936)
8. *Current Conditions of the Coal Mining Industry in Northern Shanxi*, originally published in *Life Daily* (serialized, July 12-13, 1936)
9. *From Datong to Suiyuan*, originally published in *Life Weekly* (No. 13, 1936)
10. *Travel in Wanping*, originally published in *World Knowledge* (No. 5, Vol. 5, 1936)
11. *Smuggling on the Beach*, originally published in *Chinese People* (No. 2, 1937)
12. *Military Geography of Suiyuan*, originally published in *World Knowledge* (No. 6, 1937)
13. *A Glance at Eastern Hebei*, originally published in *World Knowledge* (No. 7, 1937)
14. *Inspection of the Front in Eastern Suiyuan*, originally published in *World Knowledge* (No. 8, 1937)
15. *Travel in Xinghe*, originally published in *World Knowledge* (No. 9, 1937)
16. *Sketch of Jining*, originally published in *Shun Pao* (weekly supplement, No. 20, 1937)
17. *Sketch of Siziwang Banner*, originally published in *Shun Pao* (weekly supplement, No. 20, 1937)
18. *From Jining to Taolin*, originally published in *World Knowledge* (No. 12, 1937)
19. *Beiping Students Camping*, originally published in *Chinese People* (No. 11, 1937)
20. *Lugou Bridge Battle against Japanese Aggression*, originally published in *World Knowledge* (Vol. 6, 1937)
21. *Recalling Beiping when in Front*, originally published in *Occupied Beiping and Tianjin* (January, 1938, Life Bookstore)
22. *South to Baoding*, originally published in *From the Lugou Bridge to the Zhang River* (September, 1938, Life Bookstore)
23. *North to Baoding*, originally published in *From the Lugou Bridge to the Zhang River* (September, 1938, Life Bookstore)

24 《由保定向北去》原载《广西日报》 1937 年 8 月 15 日

25 《从娘子关到雁门关》原载《大公报》 1937 年 9 月 17 日

26 《血战居庸关》原载《大公报》1937 年 9 月 25 日

27 《平汉线北段的变化》原载《大公报》 1937 年 9 月 30 日

译文：

28 《一个作家的自述》原载《市一中学生丛刊》（北平）第四期

24. *Going Northward from Baoding*, originally published in *Guangxi Daily* (August 15, 1937)

25. *From Niangzi Pass to Yanmen Pass*, originally published in *Ta Kung Pao* (September 17, 1937)

26. *Heroic Battle at Juyong Pass*, originally published in *Ta Kung Pao* (September 25, 1937)

27. *Changes in the Northern Section of the Beiping-Hankou Railway*, originally published in *Ta Kung Pao* (September 30, 1937)

Translated Work:

28. *A Writer's Autobiography*, originally published in *No. 1 Middle School Students' Serial Magazine* (Beiping, No. 4)

后记

《珍藏方大曾》不是一本严格意义上，以唯美方式编辑的画册，私人照片、作品和文献交织，构成了少年方德曾、大学、天津时光、行走与记录、黑与白、经历绥远、卢沟桥抗战记、消失与重现这八个彼此关联又相互独立的生命篇章，若称之为画传或图传也许更为贴切。

我没有研究过任何一种编写方式，关于这本书，任何讨巧的技术都多余，因为把小方的故事稍加规整就足够精彩。他不需要人为的光，他会在暗夜里发光，我则是尊崇于内心的唤引，做些搬运工人该做的事情罢了。

虽然方大曾的摄影作品完全可以作为欣赏的读本，但我更希望读者看到它们背后的价值，也许这正是作者要传达的思和想。相信我，你尽可以从新闻学、社会学、人类学、历史学、文艺学等多个角度，或是你认为的适合角度去读解；图片本身内涵多元、蕴藏丰厚，这也是我寻找方大曾近二十年来的体会和被他吸引的魅力所在。

北京、天津、河北、山西、内蒙古，我曾跟随着方大曾的足迹一路寻行，乡村、僻壤、荒原，人迹罕至处尚在，单凭现代交通仍有险难，那么八十年前呢？小方说：“凡事不到当头不知难，然而不到当头也不会发现它的容易，这是双关的问题。”我在途中寻路不着，抱怨喝不到一杯热咖啡的时候，这个二十多岁年轻人的言行令我惭愧，在他留下的十余万文字里，没有畏惧，没有怨言，没有逃避。

这本书涵盖了《方大曾：消失与重现》和《方大曾：遗落与重拾》两本书的大部分图片，并有小方家人新近提供的未曾面世的部分补充进来，也有诸多新发现，是新知非旧识，可以说是多年来寻找方大曾的新成果。

Postscript

Strictly speaking, *Treasuring Fang Dazeng* is not a photo album edited according to the principles of aestheticism. Private photos, personal works, and documents depict the eight interrelated, yet mutually-independent, lively chapters: "Fang Dazeng's Youth," "College Days," "Life in Tianjin," "Traveling and Recording," "Black and White," "Experiencing Suiyuan," "Recording the Lugou Bridge Battle against Japanese Aggression," and "Disappearance and Reappearance." Thus, it may be more suitable to categorize it as a pictorial, or illustrated, biography.

I have not researched compilation methods. Writing techniques are not necessities for this book because a plain collection of Xiao Fang's stories is already brilliant. He does not need additional light to be seen because he shines even in the dark night. I am just a porter at his service due to my inner respect for him and sense of responsibility.

Although Fang Dazeng's photographic works can be taken as subjects of appreciation themselves, I'd prefer my readers learn the value behind them, the ideas and thoughts Fang intended to express. You can feel free to interpret them from the perspective of journalism, sociology, anthropology, history, literary theory, or your own perspective. The pictures are diverse and rich in content – my conclusion after a two-decade-long journey in search of Fang Dazeng and his charms.

From Beijing to Tianjin, to Hebei, Shanxi, and Inner Mongolia, I followed the steps of Fang Dazeng. Along the journey, villages, remote areas, wastelands, and unfrequented places remained: Hard, perilous places to reach via modern transportation, never mind 80 years ago! Xiao Fang said: "You won't know how difficult it is until it confronts you, and you won't know how easy it is until you stick it out. This is a twofold truth." When I could find no way forward during my journey and complained about the lack of a cup of hot coffee, I recalled what was said by this young man, only in his 20s, and felt ashamed. Amidst the over 100,000 words left behind by Xiao Fang, there is no fear, no complaint, no retreat.

This book collects most of the photographs included in the books *Fang Dazeng: Disappearance and Reappearance* and *Fang Dazeng: Lost and Found*. Some new pictures have recently been provided by Xiao Fang's family that were never before revealed to the public. This book also contains new findings of mine based on my years of hard work constantly in search of Fang Dazeng.

经过八十年时光打磨的黑白片，因变故、因保存、因遗失、因战火、因潮湿或因其他，从品质上已经有了缺憾和遗憾，脱粉、残缺、失焦或许能够模糊影像，却并不能够掩盖碎裂下真实的品格。年深月久，归集艰难，我愿把一路用心的捡拾全息给你。

感谢中国外文局！感谢新世界出版社！对于《珍藏方大曾》选题的确立，我感慨于你们的魄力，更感动于你们的情怀，我知道，这两者的交集是责任——对于国家，对于民族！

相信这本书会给你带来一个生命样貌鲜活的方大曾，一种不用保鲜剂的鲜活，一种自身光辉的鲜活。他用行动告诉我们，在八十年前的那一头，正义与良知是可以穿越时空影响当下的，只要你珍藏了这种品质，在任何时代都会无坚不摧。

冯雪松

2018 年 6 月 10 日　北京雪窗山馆

Regretfully, eight decades of vicissitudes, including accidents, improper preservation, war, humidity, and other factors, have degraded the quality of some black-and-white photos, with some being lost forever. The photos themselves may have been worn, broken, or blurred, but the true virtues behind the broken bodies shall never be buried. I hereby present what I have carefully and painstakingly collected along my long journey.

I extend my sincere thanks to the China International Publishing Group and New World Press for selecting the theme of "Treasuring Fang Dazeng." I am impressed by your resolute support and moved by your deep attachment to history. I am aware that what underpins these two virtues is a sense of responsibility for our China and our Chinese nation!

I believe this book will bring you a vivid, fresh image of Fang Dazeng. It is vivid and fresh not because of intentional decoration, but simply due to his own brilliance. From his great deeds, we have learned that regardless of the time and space gap, the sense of justice and conscience of a man who lived 80 years ago can impact people today. If you cherish such a great virtue, you will be indestructible and invincible whatever your age.

Feng Xuesong

June 10, 2018, Xuechuangshan Pavilion, Beijing

图书在版编目（C I P）数据

珍藏方大曾：战地记者的光影故事：汉英对照 / 冯雪松著；么文浩译．-- 北京：新世界出版社，2018.8

ISBN 978-7-5104-6590-1

Ⅰ．①珍… Ⅱ．①冯… ②么… Ⅲ．①方大曾—传记—画册 Ⅳ．① K825.72-64

中国版本图书馆 CIP 数据核字 (2018) 第 198931 号

珍藏方大曾：战地记者的光影故事

Treasuring Fang Dazeng: A War Correspondent's Stories

作　　者：冯雪松
翻　　译：么文浩
英文审定：韩清月　Eric Allen Cooper
责任编辑：李莎莎
装帧设计：贺玉婷
责任印制：王宝根　苏爱玲
出版发行：新世界出版社
社　　址：北京市西城区百万庄大街 24 号（100037）
发 行 部：（010）6899 5968　（010）6899 8705（传真）
总 编 室：（010）6899 5424　（010）6832 6679（传真）
网　　址：http://www.nwp.cn
　　　　　http://www.nwp.com.cn
版 权 部：+8610 6899 6306
版权电邮：nwpcd@sina.com
印　　刷：小森印刷（北京）有限公司
经　　销：新华书店
开　　本：787mm × 1092mm　1/16
字　　数：368 千字　印张：20.5
版　　次：2018 年 8 月第 1 版　2018 年 8 月第 1 次印刷
书　　号：ISBN 978-7-5104-6590-1
定　　价：198.00 元